HOPES AND ASHES

Hopes and Ashes

THE BIRTH
OF MODERN TIMES
1929-1939

ALICE G. MARQUIS

The Free Press
A Division of Macmillan, Inc.
NEW YORK

Collier Macmillan Publishers
LONDON

The Free Press
A Division of Macmillan, Inc.
866 Third Avenue, New York, N.Y. 10022

Collier Macmillan Canada, Inc.

Printed in the United States of America

printing number
1   2   3   4   5   6   7   8   9   10

Library of Congress Cataloging-in-Publication Data

Marquis, Alice Goldfarb.
  Hopes and ashes.

  Bibliography: p.
  Includes index.
  Contents: Written on the wind, the impact of
radio—Sound and fury, Hollywood and the writers—
Men to match my media, the print empires—[etc.]
  1. United States—Civilization—1918-1945. 2. United
States—Popular culture—History—20th century.
3. Mass media—United States—History—20th century.
I. Title.
E169.1.M274   1986   973.91'6   86-25626
 ISBN 0-02-920250-7

The publisher gratefully acknowledges permission to reproduce the following photos:

WORLD'S FAIR RAMP. Alfred Eisenstaedt, Life Magazine © 1939 Time Inc.

OPENING DAY AT THE FAIR. David E. Scherman, Life Magazine © 1939 Time Inc.

GENERAL ELECTRIC PAVILION. David E. Scherman, Life Magazine © 1939 Time Inc.

NATIONAL CASH REGISTER EXHIBIT. David E. Scherman, Life Magazine © 1939 Time Inc.

"AMERICAN BEAUTIES," Cover, *Life Magazine.* Alfred Eisenstaedt, Life Magazine © 1939 Time Inc.

SCENE FROM THE WORLD'S FAIR. Alfred Eisenstaedt, Life Magazine © 1939 Time Inc.

DEMOLITION OF THE AMERICAN TOBACCO COMPANY'S LUCKY STRIKE BUILDING, 1940. AP/Wide World Photos.

To my parents
who survived it all

Contents

ACKNOWLEDGMENTS

No one needs friends more than the solitary historian sculpting masses of research notes into a convincing, three-dimensional memorial to a particular time and place. Many generous people helped me with this work. Reva Greenburg and Ariss Treat critically read the entire manuscript; they fully played their roles as surrogate audience, asking important questions and kindly, insistently making me answer them.

The impact of radio on Thirties culture was clarified for me by Carroll Carroll and Bob Horwitz, who were part of it. Members of San Diego Independent Scholars patiently listened to my tentative notions about radio and made many helpful—and tactful—suggestions. Richard Snow arranged for a deft trimming of the essay on radio for publication in *American Heritage* in August 1983 and gathered a host of telling illustrations for it. I wish to thank *American Heritage* for permission to publish certain portions of this chapter. Another version of the essay was published in *The Journal of Contemporary History* in July 1984.

For a close-up of the writers who went to Hollywood, I enjoyed the excellent library of the Academy of Motion Picture Arts and Sciences in Los Angeles.

I could not have studied the periodical publishing revolution of the Thirties without help from two key private archives. At J. Walter Thompson, the archivist Cynthia Swank and her assistants, Annamarie Sandecki and Farris Buck, showered me with source material no less valuable than the suggestions they offered. At Time Inc., Otto Friedrich pointed me in the right direction and the archivist Elaine Felsher came through with immense stacks of fascinating, meticulously kept materials. Also helpful was the fine periodical collection of the University of California at San Diego. It was while woolgathering in the library stacks there that I was suddenly struck by the great number of magazines that died during the Thirties and began to wonder why.

The library of New York's Museum of Modern Art provided a fine archive and a handsome reading room in which to consult original sources on how modern art spread across America during the Thirties. The special collections librarian, Janis Ekdahl, had relevant material at her fingertips and the librarians Paula Baxter and Daniel Pearl were also helpful. Barbara Rolfes at the Archives of American Art encouraged my research at the Huntington Library branch in San Marino, while Marlene Park and Gerald Markowitz generously shared their expertise on WPA art.

Research about the New York World's Fair of 1939 would have been impossible without the rich resources of the New York Public Library and its expert staff. In particular Susan Davis and her resourceful people in the Manuscript Room produced drawer after drawer of original materials accurately and quickly.

More than its research facilities and the stunning views from its windows, the Central University Library at UCSD has provided me with a warm and helpful research base. In particular, the history librarian Sue Galloway and the art librarian Karen Richardson anticipated what I wanted and unfailingly provided. Others whose helpful suggestions, ideas, and gentle critiques I appreciate are: H. Stuart Hughes, John O'Connor, Freda Kramer, Frances Butler, Gerry Horwitz, Tom Trunnell, my editor Edward Rothstein, and my agent, Bill Gladstone.

ALICE G. MARQUIS

August 1986
La Jolla, California

HOPES AND ASHES

Introduction

A LIGHT SHOW of popping flashbulbs on the site of the 1939 World's Fair, on September 23, 1938, attended the burial of an 800-pound cylinder. Squat and snub-nosed as the Fat Boy atomic bomb, it was made of Cupaloy, a futuristically named new copper alloy. The mimeographed press release accompanying the photo said it was "capable of resisting the effects of time for 5,000 years." Inside the cylinder was a 6-foot glass tube filled with nitrogen and sealed, containing 100 objects of daily use, more than 10 million words and 1,000 illustrations on four reels of microfilm, and three spools of newsreels. Thus would the earthlings of the year 6939 learn what the world was like five millennia ago.

It was a time capsule. We can see it being lowered into 50 feet of muck at Flushing Meadows, New York, by way of a glossy black-and-white press photo. To accompany the capsule on its long and perilous journey into the future, the industrious publicizers of the World's Fair printed directions for finding the capsule and an inventory of its contents on paper they said would last for at least 5,000 years. Some 3,650 copies of this *Book of Record* were sent to libraries in the hope, said the press release, that they would cherish it until the date for the capsule's exhumation arrived.

Understandably, the actual objects laid away inside the capsule had to be compact. Among the hundred items were a can opener, a lady's hat, a toothbrush, a safety pin, a pipe and cigarettes, and a fountain pen; bits of wool, silk, plastic, coal, asbestos, and cement; a selection of seeds; and a Bible printed on the same imperishable paper as the *Book of Record.*

The microfilm offered a rich, though idiosyncratic, cross-section of contemporary culture: Margaret Mitchell's *Gone with the Wind* and Sinclair Lewis's *Arrowsmith;* Van Loon's *The Arts* and Orrin Dunlap's *The Story of Radio;* the Rand McNally Atlas and the Lord's Prayer in 300 languages; a biography of George Westinghouse (president of the corporation that sponsored the capsule) and the 1937 *Yearbook of Dentistry;* histories of philosophy, printing, science, and the oil industry; a 760-page chunk of the *Encyclopaedia Britannica* and 600 pages of patents; the 39th Annual Report of the New York Superintendent of Schools and an address on "Management's Responsibility to the Public" by Westinghouse board chairman A. W. Robertson; dictionaries of English and of slang; and, of course, a Sears, Roebuck catalog.

Under "Our Arts and Entertainment" appeared rules for bridge, poker, golf, football, and baseball; reproductions of paintings by Clemente Orozco, John Marin, Charles Sheeler, Charles Burchfield, Salvador Dali, Grant Wood, Piet Mondriaan, and Otto Dix, and Pablo Picasso's *Guernica;* the music for Jan Sibelius's *Finlandia,* John Philip Sousa's *Stars and Stripes Forever,* and a hit song, *Flat Foot Floogie,* plus photos of Arturo Toscanini, a string quartet, and a night club. Under "How Information Is Disseminated Among Us," the microfilm showed issues of all New York newspapers; magazines like *Harper's, Weird Stories, Saturday Evening Post, Collier's, Detective Story, True Confessions, The Ladies Home Journal,* and *Amazing Stories;* and comics including *Terry and the Pirates, Moon Mullins,* and *Mickey Mouse.* In the "Where We Live and Work" section were photos of houses, apartments, and industrial plants; a book about Rockefeller Center; and a trailer catalog.

The newsreels displayed the same lively mixture of substance and trivia. There was Theodore Roosevelt's speech at Gettysburg on the fiftieth anniversary of the battle in 1915; Howard Hughes leaving and arriving back in New York on his "epochal" three-day, nineteen-and-a-half-hour flight around the world in April 1937 (which he had dedicated to the World's Fair); the 1936 Harvard–Yale Game; Moscow's 1938 May Day parade; maneuvers by the American Pacific Fleet and U.S. Army tanks, and the 1938 bombing of Canton by the Japanese.[1]

Clearly, the culture embalmed with such meticulous care barely touches the rarified world of the concert hall, the serious stage, the literary elite, or even, in any intimate way, the world of the painter or sculptor—the high arts usually implied by the word "culture." Rather, the glass inside the Cupaloy casket entombed the ephemera of mass culture, strongly tinged with the promise of technology and science. It was a typically American vision, as pluralistic and, at least officially, as tolerant and open as the sunny American ideal. The cultural smorgasbord so graphically offered in the time capsule is commonplace today, but in the Thirties this copious mingling of high and low, of gold and dross, was newly hatched and by no means unopposed. This book will exhume that time capsule and the world it enclosed—after half a century instead of fifty centuries. It contains a similar mixture of small objects and large projects, minutiae and grand gestures. And it will attempt to document—like the capsule itself—the restless interface between high culture and mass culture, a battleground where during the Thirties the last aristocracy—the peerage of art, music, literature—gave way to the democratic impulse.

For along with the deep economic crisis of which the 1929 stock market crash was only a symptom, the Western world's cultural universe was also in crisis. Long dominated by a small European intellectual aristocracy, the cultural world was beset by a multitude of populist challenges. Fascists in Italy, Spain, Britain, and France detested "high" culture as exclusive, degenerate, obscure, and "difficult." The ugliest, most blatant expression of popular hatred for high culture was the Nazi revolution in Germany, with its burnings of books, banning of paintings, and persecution of artists, writers, and intellectuals.

Frightening and unconscionable as those attacks were, they expressed a popular dismay at being decisively shut out from "the finer things in life." Viewed from below, European high culture was indeed the monopoly of a tiny elite, especially when it embraced complex modernist works that baffled virtually everyone. Even well-educated people disagreed violently over the meaning and merits of Cubism, atonal music, and free verse, all of which jolted the cultural scene during the first two decades of the twentieth century. Indeed, the avant-garde seemed to regard the shock of novelty as the whole point of its work; no musical or theatrical performance, no art opening seemed successful unless it provoked a scandal or, better yet, a riot.

While even the cultivated middle class was struggling to grasp the meaning of avant-garde works, their shocking complexity, their frank sexuality, and their overt mockery of accepted values effectively alienated those lower on the educational and social ladder. For many bourgeois art lovers, enthusiasm for modernism in the arts was a means of separating themselves from the masses. They feared that the political democracy and mass education that had been the hallmarks of nineteenth-century social progress now also implied some kind of cultural egalitarianism. Yet few arbiters of taste truly believed that the masses were to be welcomed into the concert hall, the art museum, or the literary circle. By embracing a high culture whose cutting edge was increasingly cryptic, the European cultural elite could draw a sharp line between its own elevated sensibilities and the hopelessly crude mass below. The Spanish philosopher José Ortega y Gasset could write in 1930: "It has been impossible to do more than instruct the masses in the technique of modern life; it has been found impossible to educate them."[2]

Few Americans were so dogmatic. In their distant outpost of Western culture (as it was viewed from Europe) the promise of equality was taken seriously, and no public figure would have dared to express such blatant elitism. During the Twenties, H. L. Mencken flayed the "booboisie" and Sinclair Lewis excoriated "babbittry," but both critics of American culture ascribed American provincialism to simple ignorance. Far from believing, as Ortega y Gasset did, that the masses were hopelessly dense and crude, American social critics deemed all their fellow citizens capable of salvation in the cultural realm. As the Twenties were ending, the prospect for American culture brightened further. With mass immigration shut off and mass education in full swing, social mobility and geographic mobility, the twin motors of American society, lent weight to the optimistic American prognosis for the common man: not just that anyone could become a millionnaire, but also that anyone could become cultivated, even intellectual.

The culture of Europe, in the meantime, was in crisis. During the Thirties, the wave of artistic innovation that had swept over the Continent during the first three decades of the twentieth century was subsiding. As undulant economic disease and epidemic barbarism racked the Continent, European culture packed its bags for exile in America. Architects and film directors, artists and sociologists, psychiatrists and art historians, photographers and philosophers—though the numbers were small, their impact was uniquely profound. Many of those intellectual refugees deplored and disdained the features of culture as it had evolved in America: its lack of coherent (especially leftist) ideology; its intimate embrace with money; its consequent emphasis on mass appeal; its persistent, irritatingly successful confusion between what constituted high culture and what was low; its elusive, shifting elite; and, perhaps most poignantly, the absence of salons or cafés where that elite could gather informally to prescribe the nation's cultural regimen.

The Europeans who arrived in America were shocked to find that the native avant-garde often scorned politics. It included people like Edward Hopper and Thomas Wolfe and Martha Graham and George Gershwin, who brought an individualistic vision to their work and who drew on popular art, like jazz, for inspiration. Nor did the American avant-garde always congregate in large cities; rather it was scattered over an unpromising hinterland, from Montana to Mississippi. Moreover, many artistic innovators had regular jobs in offices, in advertising, journalism, or even public relations. And, the Europeans were aghast to learn, some even drew artistic inspiration from vile commerce.

America was the only place in the world where, much to the amusement of European intellectuals, a person could obtain a university degree in home economics or animal husbandry, in physical education, commercial art, accounting, retailing, automotive engineering, drama, early childhood education, social work, nursing, library science, agronomy, or petroleum geology. While such schooling may have been narrow and provincial, the college experience sanctioned further learning. For millions of freshly minted college graduates, the degree confirmed their fitness to pursue America's favorite activity: self-improvement.

But whatever their formal education, the mass media offered Americans the richest menu of informal learning in human history. Within the framework of entertainment, the new channels of communication provided consumers with vivid lessons in manners, morals, hygiene, nutrition, fashion, childrearing, sports, interpersonal relations, community resources, history, nature, science, and technology. The mass media presented their huge audiences with both a window and a mirror: a panoramic view of the great world outside and also a vivid and appealing reflection of themselves as members of one great audience and even as consumers of the same brands of toothpaste and toilet paper.

Firmly focused on the European model, however, most of America's intellectual elite was blind to the educational kernel within the media's entertainment format. Confronted with an unprecedented welter of brash, mostly vulgar diversion, America's tastemakers, like the European emigrés, frequently expressed shame at how their culture was being overrun by the rabble. And yet the American ideal had always stressed its confidence in the common man—in political, social, and economic egalitarianism. So the notion of a culture open to all left America's cultural elite in a painful double bind. Europe, the mother culture, counseled elitism; America, the mother country, proclaimed egalitarianism. The new mass media could disseminate high culture to every Chicago tenement and to each Kentucky cabin. But the hucksters and bookkeepers who dominated media management ensured that cheap tinsel and vile drama dominated the product. Of course, a huge audience flocked to this crude offering. But could *these* people really appreciate art, music, literature, profound ideas, beauty?

Clearly not all of them could. But the opinion polls just then beginning indicated that amazingly large numbers of plain people listened to radio concerts and opera, to lectures on art, to increasingly competent—and ominous—news reports from abroad. They flocked to films that today are considered classics and enthusiastically read the latest from the world of science, literature, and technology. Modern art, which previously had attracted only a small coterie of connoisseurs and collectors, drew a far wider public from among young, college-educated men and women as well-organized, attractive traveling exhibitions appeared at colleges, women's clubs, and even department stores. Van Gogh may not have found patrons among the cultivated elite of his own day, but the crowds that swarmed exhibitions of his work all over America took him to their bosoms in an unprecedented outpouring of affection.

There was no model for the promiscuous mingling of high culture and mass culture that began in America during the Thirties, nor was there any confidence that rough-hewn provincial Americans could actually create an indigenous culture free of the European umbilical cord. However, the infrastructure was in place. For, between 1919 and 1929 America really became "one nation, indivisible." Highways augmented railroads in physically binding diverse regions. Even tighter were the invisible bonds stretching coast to coast: telephone and radio. By 1931, nearly 20 million phones were interconnected and well over a billion long distance calls went through.[3]

Those developments foreshadowed the end of the extreme cultural isolation of America's regional hinterland. To the puzzlement and chagrin of many Eastern intellectuals, American culture went nationwide during the Thirties. From the artists who fanned out into the backwaters to give art lessons and art appreciation courses to network radio, which standardized the fare over the airways, from book clubs to the fat copy of *Fortune* on the executive's desk, a great informal, homogenizing, educational enterprise swept across America.

While the *New Yorker* trumpeted that it was "not for the old lady in Dubuque," it certainly appealed to "the *young* lady in Dubuque"—and Kansas City and Dallas and Atlanta and Seattle and Denver and Minneapolis, and perhaps even in Sauk Center, the narrow, provincial town Sinclair Lewis in 1920 had deplored in *Main Street.*

Just as Washington reached out politically and economically to every corner and region of a vast, diverse America during the Thirties; just as railroads, highways, and budding airlines gathered a fragmented nation into their webs during the Thirties, so did American culture spread across the land. Reflecting the American democratic ideal, it was a popularly oriented culture. It was often cloaked in entertainment, sugar-coated with the publicity agent's razzmatazz and sold, like stomach medicine, with an advertising pitch.

The European mother culture had been exclusive and elitist. Its leaders had read the same texts in the same schools; they frequented the same cafés and pursued the same obscure ideological feuds. By contrast, the American offspring, as it developed during the Thirties, was inclusive and democratic. Some of its leaders may have mingled at Harvard, Yale, or Princeton, but there were healthy infusions from New Orleans, Chicago, San Francisco, Baltimore, and little towns like Sinclair Lewis's mythical Sauk Center; from New York's ethnic ghettos, especially black Harlem and the Jewish Lower East Side; from the exotic rural South as well as the bizarre bohemia flourishing around Hollywood.

Lack of ideology was a sore point for some cultural leaders, but far more dismaying was another characteristic of the emerging culture of the Thirties: its flagrant intercourse with money and money-making. Was it decent for a radio broadcast of the Metropolitan Opera to be sponsored by Texaco? Wasn't it demeaning for a renowned poet like Archibald MacLeish to polish journalistic prose at *Fortune* or for a playwright like Lillian Hellman to trade crude epithets with Samuel Goldwyn, a vulgar immigrant who couldn't even compose a proper English sentence? Could an automobile maker like General Motors be trusted to devise and build a worthy model of Utopia?

Could a world's fair organized by a dapper glad-hander, a salesman like Grover Whalen, convey a meaningful vision of the world of tomorrow? American intellectuals agonized over such questions, but unlike the Europeans they never arrived at a final answer. Many of them, like the writers who went to Hollywood and the would-be novelists who toiled at *Time*, became reconciled to the emerging role of the mass media in shaping a uniquely American culture.

The offspring of the love affair between money and American culture was popular culture, and the question continues to be: Is it legitimate? Time and again, Thirties thinkers wondered about the money-grubbing sow in the garden of elevated ideas. Can a movie that made millions, *Gone with the Wind*, say, also be a work of art fit for exhibition in a museum? Can a magazine that caters to the masses, like *Life*, also publish the greatest photographic art of its time?

Those issues baffled even the sharpest social observers of the Thirties, largely because they were totally new. A new kind of art work was emerging in America, something that attracted enthusiasts from the full spectrum of taste. *Citizen Kane*, for example, appealed to some for its success story, to others for its artful camera work and snappy dialogue, to still others for its grand theme of the emptiness of power. Some listeners savored comedian Fred Allen's dry wit and deadpan delivery, while others enjoyed the broad parody of Senator Claghorn and the other residents of Allen's Alley.

The impact of technology on individual expression was also nettlesome to the leading lights of Thirties culture. In Hollywood, for example, the playwright lost his role as a solitary creator. He became part of a collaborative endeavor orchestrated by a director, who himself had to bow before producers and other "noncreative" types. Sound, which arrived in the late Twenties, transformed the movies from stilted, artificial pantomimes into a different medium, a dramatic genre for which all the world could become the stage. The new technology demanded an even more elaborate cooperative effort. Sound films cost so much more than silents that banks and financiers became the real managers of Hollywood. So compli-

cated was production that it mimicked in many ways the assembly line division of labor in a factory. The film was simply
another product marketed for profit.

Radio also was a collaborative effort, ruled by technology
and much polluted by its immense financial needs. Advertising
money paid for its nonstop outpouring of drama, sports, variety programs, music, news, and commentary. Being a powerful tool for mass marketing of consumer products, much of
it was aimed at the lowest educational and social levels in
society. A guest in the home, as it was often described in its
early days, the radio broadcaster had to consider the needs
and fantasies of a multitude of listeners; otherwise they were
free to ignore the announcer's command: "Don't touch that
dial!"

High-speed presses, cheap coated papers, and reliable rural
mail delivery enabled mass weeklies like *Life* to hit American
mailboxes on schedule. To attract the advertising to finance
that costly technology, publishers had to give masses of readers
a diverse, provocative, habit-forming product. No less than
movies or radio, the weekly mass magazine of the Thirties
was a collaborative effort. While the pages of *Life* featured
the work of the world's best photographers, the production
of the magazine involved armies of editors, writers, researchers, production executives, and advertising and promotion
people.

Never before had technology been so intimately entwined
with culture. Observers wondered whether those mechanized
spawns could be art and, if they were, how they should be
judged. Indeed, the world of machines had often been viewed
as the very antithesis of individual inspiration. And yet Thirties
people understandably placed their hopes in technology, and
not only because it might get America's factories humming
again. Technology meant construction of great dams to open
or reclaim thousands of square miles of farmland. Technology
meant that radio sets were cheap enough for everyone, that
cars, refrigerators, and washing machines were within reach
for every American family. Technology meant that the remotest farm acquired electricity and that airplanes spanned

the oceans. Technology also broadened democracy, liberating the worker from exhausting physical labor and the housewife from her boring, arduous weekly routine.

So great was the impact of technology on Thirties culture that it dominated the New York World's Fair of 1939. Inside buildings so streamlined they looked ready to fly away, many exhibits extolled the wonders of the laboratory and the promise of a mechanized future. Summing up the decade, "The World of Tomorrow" was a technological utopia; life would be better not because humans were better, but through chemistry.

The huge audience gathered by the mass media moved in mysterious ways. It listened to a program on the radio, capriciously turned the dial to something else, or simply switched the danged thing off. On the basis of some inscrutable formula combining movie stars, title, and publicity, it decided whether or not to plunk down ten cents to see a film. (If the theater was giving away dishes that night, all other calculations went out the window.) Bemused throngs reverently filed past poor, scorned Van Gogh's masterpieces and entertained the notion that a handsomely turned ball bearing belonged in a museum. This audience constantly confounded—and still confounds—the most sophisticated public opinion research, a sometime science which itself originated during the Thirties. Precise as a poll might be in assessing the public's views at a particular moment, it is shaky at best at predicting future responses. Nevertheless, the mass media's craving for a mass audience resulted in that audience's becoming an essential partner in the development of American culture.

Nor was a mass audience enough. Those who nurtured the fledgling media quickly realized that their baby was insatiable. While the critics righteously groaned over the trivia and trash poured over the American public, the media managers frantically battled the specter of silent airwaves, dark movie screens, and blank magazine pages. To unheard-of abundance, Thirties critics brought tools forged in past eras of scarcity. Accustomed to a Broadway season, for example, that produced fewer than a hundred plays (only a handful of them memorable), the critics never comprehended the problems faced by Hollywood studios to complete fifty or sixty productions *a month*. Unlike theaters or opera houses, which were often dark and in any event housed the same performance over many weeks or months, mass media wolfed material voraciously. The airwaves cried for sounds twenty-four hours a day, 365 days a year. Tens of thousands of movie houses demanded fare to fill them seven nights a week and with matinees on Saturday and Sunday. A weekly magazine like *Time* or *Life* devoured all the talent that even a genius like Henry Luce could marshal. A quality weekly like *The New Yorker* drove its editor to the brink of insanity in the perpetual hunt for material.

In the thick of the cultural revolution of the Thirties, the critics of mass culture failed to note the gems in the giant dungheap churned out by the new media. Persistently, understandably, they focused on mindless—and endless—soap operas and horse operas. Yet the radio audience for a single broadcast of Arturo Toscanini's New York Philharmonic probably exceeded the entire attendance at the orchestra's live concerts since Carnegie Hall was built. Far more people saw Wendy Hiller and Leslie Howard in the film version of *Pygmalion* than had ever seen the Shaw comedy on the stage. Such observations are commonplace today, but during the Thirties few intellectuals stopped bellowing in indignation long enough to take note.

Today we can witness the outcome of the Thirties cultural revolution as it manifests itself in print and on the screen. We can praise—and more frequently blame—the uses of the electronic media. Strident, tawdry, money-grubbing, distracting, vulgar, tasteless, and seductive, the mass media nevertheless have created the largest audience the world has ever seen for "the finer things in life." More people are attending theater, concerts, operas, dance recitals, and art exhibitions than ever before in the history of mankind. More people are buying books and reading them. More artists are working and finding a clientele. And countless millions more enjoy the best that world culture has to offer on radio and television. Baryshnikov and Beethoven are household words. It was not always so.

Many would argue that the intrusion of the masses has corrupted high culture and that the good art, literature, and music of today smells of the market place and of the masses. But the cultural revolution of the Thirties proved that this market place is expansive indeed, with room for many kinds and levels of product. As for inviting in the masses, in a democracy could there be any other choice?

1

WRITTEN ON THE WIND: THE IMPACT OF RADIO

LONG BEFORE RADIO flowered during the Thirties, it evoked wonderment—and chagrin. Secretary of Commerce Herbert Hoover in 1921 called it "an instrument of beauty and learning." A black cook in a Pelham, New York, home put on earphones, listened, and exclaimed, "That sure is a box full of magic!" Waldemar Kaempffert, who as editor of *Scientific American* had followed the beginnings of radio technology, imagined in 1922 "a radio mother . . . crooning songs and telling bedtime stories" while a future Einstein could elaborate his theories "to a whole world with an ear cocked to catch . . . his voice as it wells out of the horn." The manager of General Electric's pioneering station in Schenectady, New York, hoped in 1922 "that the power to say something loud enough to be heard by thousands will give rise to the desire to say something worthwhile." But even in its infancy, radio drew fire, especially from intellectuals. Bruce Bliven, editor of the *New Republic,* described the emanations from "this magic toy" in 1924 as "outrageous rubbish, both verbal and musical."[1]

To the growing audience, however, whatever meaningful sounds could be discerned above the squawks, screeches, hums, and cracklings of the ether were pure enchantment. Robert Wood, who later became chief engineer of BBC, heard

"Two Emma Tock calling" on his homemade set in 1922 and was "tense with excitement and sick when I had to tear myself away." The sportscaster Red Barber first heard radio in 1924 at the home of a high school friend in central Florida. "A man . . . in Pittsburgh said it was snowing there. . . . Someone sang in New York . . . a banjo plunked in Chicago . . . it was sleeting in New Orleans." Barber walked home at dawn, he recalled, entranced with "intimations of a new life . . . I was excited completely."[2]

So were millions of others on both sides of the Atlantic as they braved ear-rending racket on primitive headsets to catch voices or music issuing from equally primitive studios. Hundreds of manufacturers leaped into production. Sterling Telephone and Electric Co. built a hand-held earphone so that ladies could "listen in without disarrangement of the coiffure." Peto-Scott's Broadcast Baby of 1923 included a signed certificate guaranteeing that each set had been tested on an aerial. But most audio fans of the early 1920s built their own sets from a chunk of germanium crystal hooked to a coiled wire that faintly resembled a cat's whisker, both attached to a "breadboard" (which most were). The most expensive component was the headset, at $1.98. The listener twisted the "cat's whiskers" until he heard a sound. Often whole families would place the headset into a soup tureen and cluster with their ears close to this primitive loudspeaker. What they heard was "AWK . . . RAACK . . . hello out there . . . hello ouBriee . . . crackle . . . snap . . . wee . . . this IS . . . ROAR . . . HISS . . . STAtion 8 xkCRASHhiss . . . ROArrr . . . pop." It was no wonder, therefore, that listeners eagerly awaited a "silent night," an evening when local broadcasters closed shop so that listeners could tune in to stations from other places.[3]

The transmitters were equally crude. The first microphone at WLW in Cincinnati was a huge morning glory horn 8 feet long and 3 feet across. "You shouted into the big end," an announcer recalled, but to be sure of being heard, "you stuck your head halfway down into it." Recorded music, a large component of programming, was transmitted "by putting the morning glory horn of the phonograph player against the morning glory horn that was the transmitter." Similar contraptions were the rule at most of the stations that erupted, like measles, across the American landscape. At the beginning of 1922, twenty-eight stations were operating; by the end of the year, there were 570, all crammed onto two frequencies. Total confusion was averted only because most of them had little power—on the order of 20 to 50 watts—and none of them operated full time. But by 1924, the chaos of American airwaves was complete. Some 1,400 stations polluted the ether with "shrieks and groans, cross-talks, muddled and garbled music and announcements . . . a radio reign of terror." Radio's feeble regulator, Secretary of Commerce Hoover, then declared the license book full and refused to issue any more unless compelled by court order.[4] While the first commercial had already sullied the airwaves on August 28, 1922—a plug for Long Island real estate aired by WEAF New York for $100—most of the industry saw stations as a way of promoting sales of radio sets. Indeed, despite the din on the headphones, the $350 million Americans spent on radios and parts in 1924 accounted for one-third of all spending on furniture.[5]

Clearly, it was the medium, not the message, that entranced the public. In Britain listenership also leaped, despite a sedate menu of music, talks, religious services, and the occasional live celebrity, the Prince of Wales, for example, giving Boy Scouts a pep talk in 1922. Almost a million sets had been licensed at ten shillings each, and 4 million others were thought to be bootlegged. "If the BBC had put out nothing but weather forecasts and hymn tunes," noted one broadcaster, "the rise in listening would probably have been only slightly affected."[6]

In both Britain and the United States, the institutionalization of radio began in 1927. In America, establishment of the Federal Radio Commission ended the chaotic cacaphony on the airwaves, while the beginnings of two major networks set the stage for the orderly, though intensely commercial, development of radio as a big industry. In Britain, the BBC was chartered as a public corporation, run by an independent board of directors and financed through license fees. Firmly in control was John C. W. Reith, a towering and opinionated Scot, who stamped his concepts of righteousness, propriety, and good taste on the BBC until 1940.

The two systems, in their wide divergence, symbolized the

contrasts between American and British society; indeed, a common language was often the only point of similarity. Reference to the British solution thus can profitably be made to highlight American developments and as a reminder that radio in the United States, though it grew into the most pervasive and in many ways the most enterprising in the world, followed a path that was not necessarily the only one open to it.

Radio people everywhere learned almost immediately that what David Sarnoff called "the broad highway of the ether" had a tremendous capacity for traffic. At all points in the cultural spectrum, the need to fill the hours of air time pressed heavily on those involved; no medium of enlightenment, information, or entertainment had ever gobbled up material so speedily. A visitor who watched the writers of a popular comedy program riffling through gag files asked the producer, Carroll Carroll, why those frantic people spent so much time retreading old jokes rather than creating new ones. "There isn't time," Carroll replied. "Radio needs too much material too often. It eats up copy too fast." Nor was the problem much different at a highbrow level. When New York's good music station, WQXR, began broadcasting full time in 1936, it had to fill 7,000 hours with concert music every year. The station's founder, Elliott Sanger, recalled a friendly description of his programming as "excellent turkey—sometimes roast turkey, sometimes creamed turkey, sometimes just the drumsticks, sometimes turkey hash and finally good turkey soup." Sanger agreed, pleased that it was "tasteful, well-seasoned and just the right dish for the time of day you are ready to enjoy it. It must never be what Broadway would call a turkey."[7]

The many and varied notions of how to fill the ravenous maw of the medium led James Thurber to observe that early radio was "like the deck of a sinking ship . . . old timers sound curiously like survivors of disasters." By 1927, however, the *ad hoc* days were largely over. No longer would listeners be startled by the announcer Norman Brokenshire as he desperately sought a noise to fill an unexpected five-minute pause. "Ladies and gentlemen," he said as he thrust the microphone outside the studio window, "we now bring you the sounds of New York City." Nor could those who tuned in to New Jersey's WHN any longer join "an enchanting madhouse," where announcer Nils T. Grandlund would sob out Rudyard Kipling's "Boots" five times a night as listeners requested it and the pianist Harry Richman would repeat and repeat a ditty titled "There's No Hot Water in the Bronx."[8]

Instead, increasingly large chunks of territory were brought into the orderly orbit of two fiercely competing networks: the National Broadcasting Co., established in 1926, and the upstart Columbia Broadcasting System, founded the following year.

NBC was the brainchild of Owen D. Young, board chairman of General Electric and Radio Corporation of America. Half its shares were held by RCA, 30 percent by GE, and 20 percent by Westinghouse; its original purpose was to stimulate sales of radio sets, for which all three corporations held vital patents. By the summer of 1927, the network had forty stations covering major markets across the United States and linked by telephone lines leased from AT&T. Each time a new station joined, as the parent companies had hoped, radio sales in its territory would double within a month. But to the parents' delight, the network programs also attracted commercial sponsors. NBC's very first offering, a four-and-one-half-hour variety show on November 15, 1926, was punctuated by discreet sales pitches for Dodge automobiles. After that, the radio critic Robert J. Landry wrote, "the sponsor system" was never "seriously threatened."[9]

In fact, NBC's feisty competitor, CBS, held no patents and thus had no radio sales to add luster to its balance sheet. Depending entirely on advertising revenue, the twenty-seven-year-old William Paley brought imagination, energy, and brashness to the sixteen-station network he took over in 1928. He had persuaded his father and a few friends to buy the ailing company as an advertising medium for the family-owned La Palina Cigar Co. To succeed, it would have to subsist entirely on sales of time to advertisers.

Executives at both networks were concerned about the audience's tolerance for commercial messages. As early as 1922,

Secretary of Commerce Herbert Hoover told the First Annual Radio Conference that it was "inconceivable" that such a great medium for public service should be "drowned in advertising chatter." In 1924, Hoover told the Third Annual Radio Conference that advertising would be "the quickest way to kill broadcasting . . . if a speech by the President is to be used as the meat in a sandwich of two patent medicine advertisements," he warned, "there will be no radio left." Advertisers themselves were timid about the number and stridency of their messages. Herbert Wilson Smith of the National Carbon Co. told the House Merchant Marine and Fisheries Committee in 1926 that advertising must be "delicately handled," for example: "Tuesday evening means the Eveready Hour, for it is on this day and at this time that the National Carbon Co., makers of Eveready flashlight and radio batteries, engages the facilities of these 14 radio stations to present its artists in original radio creations." Standards of taste, alas, quickly crumbled. In the 1927–28 season, thirty-nine companies sponsored programs on NBC and four on CBS, including the A&P Gypsies, the Fisk Time to Re-tire Boys, and two singers who were billed as Paul Oliver and Olive Palmer for Palmolive. For the 1928–29 season, sixty-five sponsors bought network time. Even more prophetic was N. W. Ayer's founding, during that season, of a separate radio department with a capacity not only to advise clients about radio advertising but to produce whole programs.[10]

Alarmed, the Federal Radio Commission in August 1928 refused to renew the license of one station because it "exists chiefly for . . . advertising of a character which must be objectionable to the listening public." The commission put four other stations on probation, renewing their licenses for only thirty days instead of the customary six months, because their listeners had no alternative to "unwelcome messages . . . entering the walls of their homes." Nevertheless, NBC sold $10 million worth of advertising in 1928 and $15 million in 1929. CBS net sales that year were $4.1 million.[11]

Still, advertising and network executives were exceedingly cautious about offending listeners. Roy Durstine, a founder of Batten, Barton, Durstine & Osborne, believed that the function of radio commercials was to "create good will." NBC president Merlin H. Aylesworth wrote in 1929 that the most effective commercial "creates such a friendly feeling in the listener that when he has occasion to buy, he is very likely to remember favorably the industry that has provided him with good entertainment." The following year, as NBC's advertising revenues leaped to $22 million, he told the Senate Committee on Interstate Commerce that some commercial sponsorship was unsuitable. "I just did not quite like to see the Yale–Harvard game announced through the courtesy of so-and-so." Paley told the same committee that only 22 percent of his network's total air time—twenty-three out of 109½ hours per week—were sponsored and that advertising took up only 0.7 percent of the total. William S. Hedges, president of the National Association of Broadcasters, assured the senators that his own station, WMAQ Chicago, limited commercials to one minute per half-hour and that many NAB members "do not use as much as that." The NAB's standards of commercial practice, promulgated in 1929, forbade commercials between 7 and 11 P.M.[12]

But, as the broadcasters all too quickly discovered, the audience was far less finicky than had been thought and, far from objecting to the rising commercialism of the airwaves, enthusiastically embraced it. By January 1, 1929, an NBC survey by an MIT professor, Daniel Starch, found that one-third of American homes had a radio, a potential audience of 41.4 million people, 80 percent of whom listened daily. Whether rural or urban, their taste in programming was virtually the same. More significant than the findings was the process: Starch was the first of a legion of academics who would be drafted by the radio industry to answer that most pressing question: Who is listening? Only a year before the Starch survey, a trade publication, *Radio Broadcasting,* derided a listener survey proposed by the Association of National Advertisers as "equivalent to determining the number of crickets chirping at any given instant, in a swamp on a foggy summer evening."[13] But the claims and counter-claims of networks and individual stations were often so overblown that advertisers insisted on unbiased audience surveys. Out of this would grow a considerable subindustry serving up enormous doses of scientific-sounding statistics while generally backing the bias of whoever had commissioned the survey.

The size of the audience might be in dispute, but on the value of the medium its executives waxed lyrical. General James G. Harbord, president of RCA, called it "a blessing to all concerned," while NBC's Aylesworth deemed it "an uplifting influence." The literary critic Henry Volkening, on the other hand, berated the commercial system for programs that "tickle the tastes of the mentally deficient." The general level, he charged, was pitched at fifteen-year-olds. William Orton disagreed; he believed programs were beamed at thirteen-year-old minds. He warned in the *Atlantic Monthly* that when mass thought "dominates and colors all activity, civilization itself may . . . be in peril. The redemption of the mass cannot come except from minorities."[14]

Many critics of American radio pointed to the BBC as a model. Indeed, the programming developed at Savoy Hill between 1927 and 1932 and later at Broadcast House seldom catered to the taste of the masses. J. C. W. Reith saw to that. Raised in an impoverished and sternly Presbyterian Scottish middle-class family, he had attained some engineering training before answering a want ad in 1922 for director of the fledgling broadcasting service. By 1927, when the BBC was chartered as an independent public company (and Reith was knighted), he had assembled a staff dominated by public school–Oxbridge–gray flannel trouser types. Reith ordered that announcers remain strictly anonymous, do no outside writing without his permission, and, on their weekly pay of five pounds, wear evening dress after 6 P.M. A guest speaker was greeted at the door of Savoy Hill studios by a commissionnaire who would usher him into the "drawing room." There, Colonel Brand, "a splendid character who looked like a colonel and *was* a colonel with white moustache and hair and a big athletic frame—he was very keen on sport," would greet the visitor, offer him a drink, and then "go along to the announcer and tell him you're here." When John Morris, a veteran BBC employee, was asked whether the announcer's job was that "of a waiter, who brings the food he hasn't prepared and mustn't partake of," he replied, "Not so much a waiter, more of a butler." Sir Tyrone Guthrie, who was an early participant in drama workshops, felt that "the BBC has subordinated the question of popular appeal to Principles of Moral Philosophy, but has nonetheless been moderately adventurous." Indeed, the BBC had pioneered radio drama, presenting the first radio play, an amateur reading of *Cyrano de Bergerac* in 1921. Among the fifty plays broadcast in 1930 were a translation of Ernst Johansen's *Brigade Exchange* and an Armistice Day production of R. C. Sherriff's *Journey's End*. But the "impermanence and appetite" of the medium were evident. In the same year, BBC presented 150 vaudeville programs, but even as the audience complained of repetitions, the music hall talent for such a pace was exhausted.[15]

The complaint against radio in Britain tended to run opposite to that in America: BBC was too serious, too highbrow, too dull. The announcers, despite (or perhaps because of) elocution sessions with professor Lloyd James, sounded like "a sort of superior being, educated at a public school and talking down to you." The BBC practices "pontifical mugwumpery," snapped Winston Churchill. Yet Churchill was supremely conscious of radio's political potency. The announcer Harman Grisewood thought he was "the only politician . . . who consciously showed any intelligent interest in how to make a broadcast effective." He brought a typed script to the studio and asked Grisewood to listen and critique. On the air, Churchill asked Grisewood to "stand in front of me and conduct. I know it by heart and I'll follow the beat."[16]

The severest criticism of BBC was that it never reached the working class, the vast majority of the radio audience. BBC executives, it was charged, were unaware that most Britons ate high tea, not dinner. Furthermore, "the language was so separate that it was always a matter of them and us." Typical of this attitude, as well as Reith's stern sabbattarianism, was the "BBC Sunday," which began no earlier than 3 P.M. with chamber music, followed by a sober children's program at 5:30 P.M. Then silence reigned until 8:30 P.M., when a religious program was followed by light "but not flippant" music, news at 10 P.M., and the final "Good night" at 10:30 P.M. Wags called this "the Reithian Sunday," but the Director General insisted it was "one of the unviolable assets of our existence, quiet islands on the tossing sea of life." Reluctantly, he augmented programming; by 1935, Sunday also might include Bible stories for children, a talk on "How to Read an Epistle," and the Bach *St. Matthew Passion*. Critics also complained about BBC's choice of concert music: "Safe, hackneyed, good," wrote one, but skewed toward "the worst music of the best composers and the best music of the worst composers."[17]

How the audience responded to that austere offering is difficult to say, since the BBC strenuously resisted all proposals for audience research. Certainly the public continued to buy radio sets; more than 2 million were licensed by 1929, and, despite the Depression, licenses increased at rates of 20 percent or more a year through the entire decade. But competition also appeared on the horizon. In 1930, the International Broadcasting Co. was formed specifically to beam commercial programs from France to the British Isles. In June of 1931, the *Compagnie Luxembourgeoise de Rédiffusion,* a French-financed firm, began to blanket Europe with commercial programs on 100-watt transmitters. By October 1931, Radio Normandie at Fécamp covered all of southern England, playing hit records on Saturday nights in what BBC called a "blatant American manner." By April 1933, Radio Paris beamed into the English air for two and a half hours every Sunday; Radio Normandie had twelve hours of English Sunday programming, and Radio Toulouse and Radio Côte d'Azur broadcast in English for an hour and a half each Sunday. What meager surveys were done showed that by 1935 fully 50 percent of British listeners were tuned to foreign stations on Sundays and 11 percent on weekdays. Of the public interested in "light entertainment," 22 percent regularly listened to foreign stations on weekdays and 66 percent on Sundays.[18]

The BBC responded by boycotting those performers who broadcast from abroad and refusing to print foreign program listings in its publications, *Radio Times* and *The Listener.* It also augmented its Sunday schedule to fill the silence before 3 P.M. with uplifting offerings, while vigorously complaining to the International Broadcasting Union about foreign invasion of its airways. Meanwhile, the British Radio Manufacturers Assn. charged that BBC had its "priorities upside-down;" 80 percent of the public wanted entertainment, while those with a "cultivated capacity" for serious drama, opera, talks, and concert music amounted to only 20 percent.[19]

The example of the BBC was not ignored in America. A 1932 Senate resolution authorized the Federal Commerce Commission to study possible government ownership and operation of radio, as well as ways to reduce or even eliminate radio advertising. Comparing the British and American systems in the *Atlantic Monthly,* William Hard found that while private broadcasting "is tempted toward accommodating itself . . . to all levels of popular taste, including those inhabited by the least developed portions of the population, government broadcasting . . . is tempted toward accommodating itself . . . to the temper of persons in power and to the defense of existing institutions."[20]

The renewed criticism of American radio was spurred by a profound change in its huckstering efforts. As *Fortune* noted in 1932, sponsors even two years earlier "still hesitated to put a substantial merchandising pill into their amusement sugar. . . . Radio was polite. Radio was genteel. Radio was the guest in the home, not the salesman on the doorstep. . . . But some 18 months of further Depression have changed all that." On local stations, "the hard sell, repetition and blatancy were standard," one announcer recalled. "Sirens, gongs and even pistol shots frequently introduced announcements." On Detroit's WJR, thirty commercials might be read within forty-five minutes. "Sometimes, while the announcer was going through his stint, a salesman would tiptoe into the studio and sneak another announcement on the bottom of the waiting pile."[21]

On the networks too, commercials proliferated. In 1931, 343 sponsors spent $35.5 million on radio advertising. Sponsors, joined by advertising agencies, were also taking increased interest in program content. The music to be played by Guy Lombardo and His Royal Canadians was selected by the wife of the advertising manager for General Cigar Co. "Men who ran oil companies, drug, food and tobacco corporations," Fred

Allen recalled, "were attending auditions, engaging talent."
A group of Texaco officials sat through an entire Broadway
show with their eyes closed to imagine how the star, Ed Wynn,
would come across on radio. "It was inevitable," Allen ruefully
concluded, "that the sponsors would soon consider themselves
authorities on the tastes . . . of the general public." On his
own comedy program, Allen had to accept an organ solo in
the middle because the sponsor's wife liked organ music. It
was, he snorted, "like planting a pickle in the center of a
charlotte russe."[22]

One could hardly blame advertisers for exploiting a medium
that seemed to have a wondrous effect on sales curves, despite
the Depression. A cosmetics company, for example, sponsored
a program called "Evening in Paris." So many women asked
for the nonexistent perfume of that name that the sponsor
created an Evening in Paris line, which promptly outsold all
competitors combined. By 1934, advertisers were spending
$42.6 million on radio, 15 percent of total advertising budgets;
radio was the only medium with a consistent revenue gain.
Between 1928 and 1934, radio advertising had grown by 316
percent, while newspaper advertising dropped by 30 percent
and magazine by 45 percent. Some 246 daily newspapers had
ceased publication entirely.[23]

Understandably, the print media resented the intrusive new
medium, even though a number of newspapers owned stations
(by 1940, almost one-third of all stations were owned by newspapers). Locked as they were in desperate competition with
radio for advertising dollars, the print media tried to ignore
radio in their editorial columns. Among some four hundred
"radio editors," most simply edited the daily radio log or network handouts. Even the few critics who tried to bring professional judgments to the new medium were soon swamped;
no single human could monitor radio's vast output, much less
offer a considered opinion.

As early as 1929, newspapers had tried to retaliate against
radio news competition, sometimes by deleting the daily program logs, but reader protest discouraged that tack. In 1932
newspapers tried but failed to stop radio access to the United
Press and International News Service; in that year's election,

"radio went to town," Paul White, the CBS news director, wrote. "Newspaper extras, long since doomed . . . became an anachronism." In March 1933, newspapers succeeded in shutting off radio access to wire news, but the result was that White and his arch-rival, the NBC news director Abel Schechter agreed that both networks would carry news so long as either one of them "could (1) read and (2) make phone calls and send cables." Schechter claimed a charter membership in the "Scissors-and-Pastepot Press Assn." Some local stations continued to filch newspaper items, but several lawsuits established that news has a commercial value based, like fish, on its freshness. The life span of a news item was set by various courts at between four and twenty-four hours.[24]

The feud was settled in January 1934, with the establishment of a Press–Radio Bureau, which would sell networks five-minute news summaries to be aired unsponsored after 9:30 A.M. and 9 P.M. In addition, the bureau would supply bulletins for news of "transcendental" importance. "The only saving grace of this agreement," the commentator H. V. Kaltenborn remarked, "is that it won't work." Indeed, during its first year of operation the Bureau issued 4,670 bulletins of "transcendental" importance, including 2,300 about the trial of the Lindbergh baby kidnap defendant, Bruno Hauptmann.[25] By 1935, INS and UP were serving radio more amply than ever; AP, which was owned cooperatively by newspapers, joined them in 1939. The dispute's main impact was that the networks formed their own news organizations, precisely what the newspapers had hoped to throttle.

The press–radio war symbolized the maturing of radio as a full-fledged medium of communication. By 1934, radio was reaching 60 percent of all American homes, and the percentage was rapidly growing; in the previous year, the number of sets had risen from 16 million to 18 million. Among families with incomes over $10,000, 88 percent owned radios, but even among those with incomes from $2,000 to $3,000, 72 percent owned sets. Indeed, Americans owned 43.2 percent of all the radio sets in the world. Network executives were quick to draw a relationship between their commercial success and their contribution to American culture. "Because radio is a sound business enterprise," CBS president Paley wrote, "it is able to make a continuously effective contribution toward our nation's cultural development." In the first nine months of 1934 only 31 percent of CBS's programs were sponsored, he pointed out, while some 810.5 hours were "definitely of educational or cultural interest." Paley's concern was probably triggered by the replacement in 1934 of the Federal Radio Commission with the Federal Communications Commission, whose New Deal majority threatened to scrutinize commercial excesses and public service programming when considering license renewals. Although its most stringent decisions came in the 1940s, the commission's orientation was clear in the middle Thirties, when chairman James Fly described the NAB leadership as resembling "a dead mackerel in the moonlight; it both shines and stinks."[26]

The worst advertising abuses were supposedly controlled by new policies announced by CBS on May 15, 1935, which the network called "a turning point in American broadcasting." The network banned commercials describing "graphically or repellently any internal bodily functions" or "symptomatic results of internal disturbances." Children's programs were not to exalt crime or disrespect for parents or authority or glorify cruelty, greed, and selfishness. Commercials were "limited" to 15 percent of daytime programs and 10 percent in the evening.[27]

The new self-control was a response to a rising chorus of criticism. Radio is no longer "an absorbing adventure," Merrill Dennison charged in *Harper's Magazine;* it had become "industrialized," opening an "era of factory production of entertainment." Advertising agencies controlled programs, judging them only on how they sold goods. "To radio's attitude that it was an industry was added the agency's theory that it was a midway." But the advertising executive Roy Durstine insisted radio filled the needs of typical listeners, "a very tired, bored, middle-aged man and woman whose lives are empty and who have exhausted their outside sources of amusement when they have taken a quick look at the evening paper." He contrasted this bleak couple with the most vocal critics, "people with full lives, with books to read, with parties to attend, with theaters to visit, with friends whose conversational powers are interesting. Radio provides a vast source of delight and entertainment for the barren lives of the millions." He also pointed to surveys showing no relationship "between the popularity of a radio program and the good taste—or lack of it—in its commercial announcements." NBC's president Aylesworth echoed Durstine. The bitterest critic of radio, he said, is "the recluse, the intellectually superior person who voluntarily separates himself from the living, breathing, moving America in which he lives . . . these folk do not belong to the great vibrant mass and soul of America."[28]

Certainly the sacks of fan mail daily arriving at NBC lent support to such statements. Since its early days radio had evoked an intimate relationship with the listener; the receiver was part of the furniture in the listener's home, and its disembodied voice made him feel that it was speaking directly to him. In 1928, NBC received 2 million letters, including one from a Buffalo pharmacist: "Your program is surely wonderful and we enjoy your artists. . . . Have a wonderful business on [your ginger ale]." After a single announcement, 42,000 people sent in cigar bands to get a picture of Kate Smith. Nor did fans care that the situation to which they responded was fictional. When Amos 'n' Andy lamented that they lacked a typewriter, 1,880 machines arrived; listeners sent nearly five gross of pencils when the blackface stars needed one; and when Amos and Kingfish started a bank, hundreds of listeners sent dollar bills for deposit.[29]

Broadcasters by 1934 were using fan mail as a possible answer to the nagging question of who was listening. The BBC, while primly eschewing the direct approach of simply going out and asking people, delighted in using letters to confirm its judgment of what the audience wanted. A psychologist who analyzed a batch of those letters concluded that "an excessive proportion" came from obvious neurotics, "people writing about their own mental troubles or those of their children and friends." CBS claimed that of 10,000 letters to *American School of the Air*, 80 percent came from "persons of a high order of intelligence." NBC even sorted letters by type of paper, grammar, and spelling. But the historian Will Durant, asked to study a sampling, inferred that most came from "invalids, lonely people, the very aged, the very youthful, hero worshipers and mischievous children."[30]

Still, the networks relied considerably on fan mail for program decisions. They often based stars' salaries on how many letters they drew, though the volume of mail fluctuated with the seasons and with the unemployment rate. In 1936, NBC claimed it received 5.55 million letters, 1,015,372 in March alone. In the first six months of 1937, when a business slump swelled unemployment, 5,460,000 letters arrived at NBC. So important had fan mail become that the network in that year spent $300,000 on postage to answer each letter. Those who read and wrote replies had, over the years, collected some choice communications:

> "For the sake of suffering humanity . . . a hot dinner plate placed outside the shirt over a pain will give relief in ten minutes."
> "Last night our baby was born during the Victory Hour. We are going to raise him on radio."
> "Rudy Vallee is more wonderful than Beethoven's Sonatas."

One listener had astutely sensed one of radio's chief appeals. Responding to live coverage of the 1931 London Naval Conference, this gentleman had commended "an enterprise that permits ordinary men to button up their underwear to the accompaniment of an address by a European monarch."[31] Enabling the listener to be present at a news event, as this letter writer realized, was radio's most remarkable contribution to journalism. Previously, even the most detailed printed account was filtered through the mentality and vocabulary of the reporter.

Politicians quickly recognized radio's magic. In the early 1920s, Elihu Root could expostulate, when asked to speak into a microphone: "Take that away. I can talk to a Democrat, but I cannot talk to a dead thing." But by 1928, the Republicans allocated the largest share, 20 percent, of their campaign budget to radio. It was money well spent; the medium "converted a poor platform speaker [Herbert Hoover] into an effective campaigner," one observer wrote, "and nullified the influence of [Al Smith,] a master campaigner." Never before had candidates reached audiences even remotely approaching the size of the throng, estimated at 40 million, who heard Hoover and Smith on election eve, November 5, 1928. (By comparison, the speaker previously thought to have addressed the greatest number of people, the evangelist Dwight L. Moody, had reached some 100 million listeners in a lifetime of preaching.) But politicians had good reason to be wary of the new medium. The old-style hellfire-and-brimstone speech seemed to alienate listeners; radio "has slain the political orator," *The Saturday Evening Post* commented. "The day of the spellbinder is over." Radio coverage of the Hoover inauguration, Paley exulted, "broke all records for the number of microphones used, announcers, technicians, miles of cable and, finally, the size of the audience, estimated at 63 million." Sarnoff was convinced that radio had broken the hold of sectionalism and crowd psychology on American politics.[32]

In the history of radio before and since, 1932 was the classic political campaign. Not only was the nation's interest focused on the contest because of the tragic impact of the Depression, not only were radio sets ubiquitous, but the personalities of the candidates provided sharply contrasting images on the air. Both lavishly used radio. The Democrats bought 51½ hours of network time, the same amount as in 1928, while the Republicans massively increased their time purchases from 42½ hours in 1928 to 73 hours. (For the networks, the campaign was a bonanza. CBS's hourly charge rose from $4,000 to $17,000, while NBC, for its much larger audience, charged $35,000 per hour.)[33]

Nevertheless, Hoover, in addition to projecting a pudgy, colorless and impotent image in the face of massive economic disaster, also suffered from overexposure; some ninety-five of his speeches had been broadcast during the previous four years. If listeners were indeed judging politicians more coolly and logically, Hoover should have had wide appeal. In fact, aside from genuine political issues, many trivial and peripheral events influenced voters. One was a speech Hoover broadcast on Tuesday, October 4, at 8:30 P.M. At 9:30, as *The Nation* described it, "listeners confidently awaited the President's concluding words. Confidently and also impatiently, for at 9:30 . . . Mr. Ed Wynn comes on the air. But Mr. Hoover had only arrived at point two of his 12-point program. The populace shifted in its myriad seats; wives looked at husbands, children allowed to remain up until 10 o'clock on Tuesdays looked in alarm at the clock; 20,000 votes shifted to Franklin Roosevelt. At 9:45, Mr. Hoover had arrived at point four; two million Americans switched off their instruments and sent their children to bed weeping." In New York alone, station WEAF was pelted with eight hundred phoned protests, and the network was so swamped with furious calls that only six thousand got through to be counted.[34]

Roosevelt, by contrast, seemed to be a candidate fashioned for radio. In his campaign speeches, "each word, each phrase, each sentence," wrote the *New York Daily News* radio critic Ben Gross, "seemed to be built . . . with the invisible audience in mind." The millions of the audience consisted of individuals and small groups, so that as Roosevelt was "painting a verbal picture expansive enough for a museum mural, he reduced it to the proportions of a miniature hanging cozily on the walls of a living room." Roosevelt was the first President to address the nation directly by radio, as opposed to simply permitting a speech before a group to be broadcast. The first such talk, on March 12, 1933, impressed even seasoned newscasters. When the President entered the blue-draped White House room rigged as a studio, it seemed to Bryson Rash that "the lights were suddenly turned on because of his cheerfulness and wit and tremendous love of banter." Broadcasters also appreciated that his speeches were timed to end precisely in the time allotted.[35]

In the language of the cash register, CBS crowed about the impact of Roosevelt's speech announcing the bank holiday. "Surely no one thing could have flung radio farther forward . . . than the use of the microphone to sell American sanity." Several claimants appeared for credit in naming Roosevelt's radio speeches Fireside Chats. Gross says it was NBC's president Aylesworth. WJSV manager Harry Butcher says he envisioned listeners at the hearth and came up with the name. The CBS announcer Bob Trout used it first on the air.[36]

At the BBC, the idea of having the King address his subjects at their firesides was considered as early as 1923, when Reith presented George V with a wireless set for the palace. In 1925, some 10 million listened as the King opened the Empire Exhibition at Wembley. The King was finally persuaded that radio was respectable when he broadcast to the Empire, the first of an annual tradition, on Christmas Day, 1932. The audience was said to be of record size, though the BBC's aversion to listener surveys held fast. However, the kind of free-wheeling political coverage practiced by the American networks was impossible in Britain. The BBC charter was a careful compromise among major parties designed to keep radio out of politics. It guaranteed that while the BBC would not become the mouthpiece of a particular Government, it would remain the creature, albeit thinly insulated, of Government. To be sure, an independent board of governors made day-to-day policy and hired a director to carry it out. But, as was typical of all mass media in Britain, those in charge were so close to the Establishment that direct censorship was rarely necessary; they censored themselves. Reith and his wife Muriel were frequent guests at 10 Downing. At one dinner in 1925, Reith offered Stanley Baldwin a radio for Chequers, the Prime Minister's country residence. Asked if he would buy it, Baldwin replied he "did not like spongeing on anyone," Reith noted in his diary, "but quite frankly he would like to have it given to him . . . that he was overdrawn at the bank. He said he used to be quite well-to-do, but there was no money in his present work."[37]

Administratively, the BBC was under the Postmaster General, who collected and disbursed license fees. Its charter required it to transmit whatever a department of government gave it and to suppress whatever the Postmaster General ordered it to. In an emergency, it could be requisitioned by the Government. Only self-restraint by Government in exercising those powers gave the BBC a veneer of independence. A General Advisory Council, set up in 1934, was described as "about 30 Eminent Victorians, leavened with a few Edwardians and presided over by the Archbishop of York." The rickety system worked partially because Reith was such a prickly figure that he naturally steered an independent course. But the disturbing gaps in BBC's coverage also mirror Reith's peculiar attitudes. "I reflect sometimes on politics," he wrote in his diary. "The whole technique should be abolished. Government of a country is a matter of proper policy and proper administration, in other words, efficiency. It need not be different from the government of a business—only in degree. And the policy should be set according to the Christian ethic." Reith's naïveté could be staggering. In July 1934 he confided to his diary: "I really admire the way Hitler has cleaned up an incipient revolt . . . obviously badly needed." In November 1935, during the Abyssinian War, he told radio's inventor, Guglielmo Marconi, that he had "always admired Mussolini immensely and . . . constantly hailed him as the outstanding example of accomplishing high democratic purpose by means which, though not democratic, were the only possible ones."[38]

In the cultural arena, by contrast, Reith had a sure eye for quality. He had hired Val Gielgud as director of drama, which resulted in consistent experiment and considerable brilliance in the development of radio drama as a specific genre. In 1933, when foreign competition and domestic complaints began to prod the BBC into brightening its image, Gielgud was joined by Eric Maschwitz as director of variety. Maschwitz had been editor of *Radio Times* and was the author, the previous year, of a radio musical, *Goodnight, Vienna,* the first of "innumerable operettas about soubrettes called Mitzi, Fritzie and Pitzie." However, despite a trip to America in 1933 to recruit comedians and singers from commercial radio and a reputation, along with Gielgud, for mocking the BBC administration, Maschwitz was by no means a Bohemian or showbiz type. When George VI years later gave him the OBE, the monarch remarked, "It's been a long time since we played tennis together at Cambridge."[39]

In 1933, the BBC began a series called *Scrapbook,* "a powerful whiff of nostalgia," which, though no surveys prove it, was credited with an estimated total of 30 million listeners in 1937. The first program re-created the year 1913, and the series continued to linger often—as BBC-TV did later—in "the golden Edwardian afternoon." In the realm of current events, by contrast, the BBC was timid, if not silent. Along with the rest of the British press, it observed the unofficial embargo on news of the gathering crisis over Edward VIII's romance with Wallis Simpson. While news media in America and elsewhere covered the sensational love affair, often, to be sure, in lurid terms, the British press and BBC maintained the hush of a gentlemen's clubroom. True, the BBC "avoided the prostitution of broadcasting for commercial ends," as in America, as well as its "exploitation . . . for propaganda," as in Nazi Germany, but it was hardly, as William A. Robson of the London School of Economics asserted, "an invention in the sphere of social science no less remarkable than the invention of radio transmission in the sphere of natural science."[40]

Technically, though, the BBC was inventive and often lavish. For the funeral of George V in January 1936, the coverage was by pure sound, uninterrupted by commentators. Listeners heard the rhythmic steps of the navy ratings pulling the gun carriage on which the king's coffin rested, the solemn commands of officers, and the muffled gun salutes as the King was laid to rest. On the evening before the King died, the BBC maintained total silence, except for the sound of a clock ticking and every quarter hour the dignified words of chief announcer Stuart Hibberd: "The King's life is moving peacefully toward its close." Even for the abdication of Edward VIII, the BBC lent maximum dignity to a sordid affair. Reith himself went to Windsor to supervise technical arrangements, while the chief engineer, Robert Wood, rigged a specially draped microphone on a fine wooden stand to add a small measure of pomp to the Prince's pathetic words.[41]

The coronation of George VI brought forth a virtuoso display of BBC technical prowess. Along the parade route fifty-eight microphones picked up crowd noises and music. Inside Westminster Abbey, 472 miles of wire connected 12 tons of artfully concealed equipment—including one microphone tucked under the throne—operated by sixty engineers, all garbed in full morning dress rented for the occasion. One of the announcers, Wynford Vaughan-Thomas, was stunned by "the last splendid parade of the sartorial glories of the *ancien régime*, with all the uniforms outlined in gold braid, medals galore glittering on every breast, generals in plumed hats riding . . . chargers as if they were off to Omdurman, a whole bevy of bedecked and now obsolete royalty preceding the royal coach." A measure of the contrast between British and American notions of news coverage was CBS news director White's suggestion to a BBC official that a radio car accompany the procession, just in case "some crackpot takes a shot at the King." "In that unfortunate event," he was told, "we would consider it a matter for Scotland Yard, not the BBC."[42]

In the stands for the coronation was the twenty-nine-year-old Edward R. Murrow. He had arrived in Britain a few months earlier, a foot soldier for CBS in its often-bitter rivalry with NBC. "Tall without being lanky, darkish without being swarthy, young without being boyish, dignified without being uncomfortable . . . a scotch-and-story man," Murrow immediately called on Reith; he would need the use of BBC facilities for his broadcasts to America. The BBC policy, the Scotsman said proudly, was to give people what they should have. "We are not so daring, Sir John," replied Murrow. "We give the people what they like."[43]

To that end, Murrow soon located "a philosophical cabby named . . . 'Erbert 'Odge," whose comments on events he broadcast from the Spread Eagle, an Essex pub. The British press, never a friend of the BBC, gave wide coverage to Murrow's live broadcasts to America. Though he had no journalistic training or broadcasting experience—he had previously worked for an international student organization—Murrow had a natural talent for turning contacts into friends and news sources into scoops. Sartorially a dandy (his first acquisition in England was a morning suit), he shocked Britons with his informal work style. Murrow's secretary was horrified when he asked her to telephone Churchill. The custom was to write a note requesting an interview, and to phone Churchill at home she thought unforgivable. Not surprisingly, Murrow "received a quick, indeed eager, response."

For American radio listeners, "there seemed to be two histories of Europe," the journalist Alexander Kendrick wrote. "One was the inexorable march of events toward war. . . . The other was the march of American microphones from one foreign vaudeville act to another." But there were priorities.

In May 1932, for example, CBS's sole European correspondent, César Saerchinger, was in Frankfurt arranging coverage of a choral festival when he learned that Chancellor Heinrich Brüning had been forced to resign. Saerchinger rushed to Munich and persuaded Hitler to make a fifteen-minute broadcast (for $1,500). But CBS told Saerchinger to get back to the singers, cabling: "Unwant Hitler at any price."[44]

Even with their loose definition of news, the networks devoted a tiny portion of programming to current events. Though Paley boasted to the FCC that CBS had aired seventy-two foreign affairs programs in the first nine months of 1934, most of them were bulletins or light features. NBC devoted only 2 percent of its programming to news in 1932, and the share had climbed to 3.8 percent by 1939. Included was *The March of Time,* a portentously dramatized re-creation of news events; the sizzle of eggs frying on a sidewalk during a heat wave and a BBC classic, Beatrice Harrison's midnight cello concert in a Surrey forest to lure the nightingale into singing for the microphone. A good deal of energy and enterprise poured into the shoving match between the two networks, with little benefit for listeners. Even so, the networks' idea of interesting programming was often greeted unenthusiastically by member stations. After great expense and effort to broadcast an international yacht race, for example, NBC received this wire from an affiliated station: "The Middle West has never heard of a J-class sloop, has never seen one and never will. Give us music."[45]

Not that everyone loved music. Soon after having a radio installed at home, Gertrude Stein observed that "there is a deplorable amount of music going on in the world. If they would suppress most of it, perhaps the world would be more peaceful." Despite the belaboring of the networks by intellectuals for their vast trash bag of popular music, radio in America also created a huge audience for concert music. The first live network concert, NBC's 1926 broadcast of Serge Koussevitsky conducting the Boston Symphony, attracted a million listeners. In the first year after Walter Damrosch inaugurated his *Music Appreciation Hour* in 1928, he received more than a million fan letters.[46]

While all estimates of listenership or fan mail should be

viewed as orders of magnitude rather than absolute numbers, such figures impressed networks and sponsors. Both networks presented weekly full-dress concerts throughout the Thirties: the Philadelphia Symphony under Leopold Stokowski on CBS and the New York Philharmonic under Arturo Toscanini on NBC. In 1931 NBC had persuaded the Metropolitan that it was technically capable of broadcasting live grand opera and paid $100,000 for exclusive rights; within three years, those broadcasts were the second most popular on daytime radio. By 1938 the opera audience was estimated at 12 million. A 1938 *Fortune* poll showed that 62.5 percent of respondents liked opera or classical music on radio. Even more impressive was that 40 percent had heard of Toscanini; 71 percent of them identified him as a conductor.[47]

In New York, a new independent station devoted solely to classical music and news had successfully entered the crowded airwaves. From a tiny experimental transmitter, WQXR had grown by 1937 into a commercially robust enterprise. John Vincent Hogan Lawless, a radio inventor, and his partner, Elliott Sanger, at first broadcast only from 5 to 9 P.M. Within a year, "big batches" of mail included comments like, "It is too bad you cannot hear us applaud" and "The dial of my radio is rusted to WQXR." The publisher M. Lincoln Schuster called the station "a sanctuary and a way of life. . . . If Keats were alive today, he would write a sonnet on first tuning in."[48] The station's commercial success was based on the assumption that the listener is an intelligent and cultured person, a statement which *The New Yorker* called "the most astounding ever made by radio men." The station never accepted ads for laxatives, corn cures, baby pants, athlete's foot remedies, or deodorants. It wanted no messages, said Sanger, "which would jar the sensibilities of a person who was still in a mood of exaltation after hearing a great masterwork." But Sanger did persuade the New York Yankees to sponsor an afternoon program of good music interspersed with baseball scores and the New York Stock Exchange to pay for a Friday evening symphony. Even the grand curmudgeon of commercial radio, American Tobacco's president George Washington Hill, was impressed by the maverick station. A cowboy hat tilted back on his head, he plunked his boots on the table while listening to a proposal for *The Treasury of Music*, a series that would feature one Caruso record each time. At the end of the presentation, Hill "removed his feet from the table, pounded his fist on the desk and said, 'We'll make Caruso the Charlie McCarthy of this program.' "[49]

One reason for radio's enthusiastic embrace of music on both sides of the Atlantic was a function of the medium's persistent timidity; music seemed uncontroversial. An English critic observed that "the BBC need no longer . . . worry about the dangers of sex or communism or the truth of the Christian religion when they draw up a music menu." In 1935 Toscanini included the BBC Symphony among the world's great orchestras, and the BBC collection of records, scores and manuscript became, by 1942, one of the richest musical collections in the world. More cynically, the BBC was called "the greatest patron of music since Nero."[50]

As for its effects on listeners, the refugee German musicologist Theodor Adorno warned that radio music promoted "retrogressive tendencies," that an "avalanche of fetishism" was burying music "under the moraine of entertainment." Diminished by technical limitations, the music became "a piece of furniture . . . trivialized and romanticized" so that "what is heard is not Beethoven's Fifth but merely musical information about Beethoven's Fifth." Radio, he concluded, was guilty of "the electrocution of symphony."[51] Like most European intellectuals, Adorno was aghast at American radio's indiscriminate mingling of high and low culture. Rather than seeing a Beethoven broadcast as an opportunity to bring good music to the masses, he viewed it as a vulgar invasion of elite turf and found high-minded reasons to denounce it.

Adorno's fulminations, however, neglected a far larger slice of radio programming: popular music. Through the 1930s, the entire music industry was transformed from an entrepreneur-workshop system to a corporate scheme of mass production. In the genesis of a hit song, a group of sociologists found in 1939, "any romantic notion of the creative artist must be excluded. . . . The process must . . . be viewed . . . as very practical, almost cold-blooded . . . carried out according to a standardized pattern based upon past success." Most songs were written by a group to meet criteria set by music publishers: easy to sing and play; lyrics that are "romantic, original and/or tell an appealing story; and a chorus 32 bars long."

Once cobbled, the songs were taken over by "pluggers," a band of "hardy, indefatigable, insistent and relentless individuals whose sole mission in life is to persuade, wheedle, cajole and implore band leaders and singers to 'do' their song." By such pressures (and sometimes by cash payment) a song would be played fifteen to forty times a week for three to six weeks. If successful, as measured by sales of sheet music and records, the song would get two to five weeks of follow-up plugging. If not, it would be "abandoned as a 'dog.' " This was the system by which, in 1938, almost half of all radio programming was selected. An FCC survey during the week of March 6 of the content of 62,000 radio hours found that one-third was advertising, and of the rest, 50 percent was music, largely popular; 9.1 percent drama; 8.8 percent variety; 8.5 percent news and sports; 5.2 percent religious; 2.2 percent special events; and 13.7 percent miscellaneous, mostly talks.[52]

The drama category included a new genre that had spread, like lard, throughout radio's daytime hours. Neither invented nor developed, soap operas appeared to spring full-blown from the ether. They began to wash over the airwaves in 1931, and within two years there were twelve, including such classics as *Ma Perkins* and *The Romance of Helen Trent.* By 1935, there were nineteen, and two years after that, thirty-one, among them *John's Other Wife* and *David Harum.* By 1940, the daytime air was fogged with sixty chronicles of "life's sorrows according to the gospel of Bi-So-Dol, Pillsbury, Camay and Kix."[53]

Like popular music, soap operas emerged from a factory system in which the creative labor was subdivided into simple tasks. In one such plant, the owners Frank and Anne Hummert dictated story plots for some twenty dramas and then farmed them out to writers, called dialogers. The main thrust of a soap opera was that there would be no main thrust. "A man saying goodbye in Friday's episode, is still departing the following Wednesday." The historical weekly serial *Drums and Roses* dragged over more years than the Civil War it described. While intellectuals invested much bile in the ridiculing, dissecting, and denouncing of soaps—and one New York psychiatrist blamed them for the relapses of his patients—their following was small in comparison with evening variety shows and special broadcasts. The record audience during the Thirties, that for the Max Schmeling–Joe Louis bout in June 1938, had a Crossley rating of 57.6. (This meant that 57.6 percent of all those who had turned on their radios that day had heard it.) Roosevelt's Fireside Chats ranged between 30 and 40. By contrast, the leading soap opera, *Ma Perkins,* had 8 to 9, and the average for all soap operas was 4.5, a matter of some 600,000 listeners.[54]

In the waves of hokum, yocks, flim-flam, and sales spiel that rumbled across the American airwaves, it was difficult to see that the golden age of electronic news was on the horizon. To be sure, by 1935 70 percent of all households had at least one set, twice as many as owned telephones, though there were wide regional and class variations; in Washington, D.C., 96 percent of families had a radio, but in Mississippi only 24 percent. Middle-class people listened the most, lower-class next, and upper-class least. By the end of 1939, the number of radios had more than doubled, to 44 million (including 6.5 million in cars); 86 percent of all homes were covered, and listening averaged more than four and a half hours a day. And yet, in the mid-Thirties few listeners considered their radios an important source of news. Furthermore, the conventional wisdom within the five-block radius of Rockefeller Center, where the radio industry had nested, was that for balance sheets, no news was good news. The press–radio agreement of 1934 had stipulated that the networks' two daily five-minute news programs were to be unsponsored. Moreover, when news bulletins of "transcendental" importance interrupted regular programming, sponsors were entitled to rebates. NBC "does not feel that it has a responsibility to its listeners to supply all the news," a network vice president said in 1935. "Radio is an entertainment and educational medium."[55] But the staccato delivery of Walter Winchell and the sober intonation of David Lawrence; Boake Carter's erudite British accent and Lowell Thomas's short sentences and personal anecdotes; Gabriel Heatter's lugubrious "There's good news tonight . . ."—these were some of the personal styles that gradually developed a following for radio news. Billed as "commentators," they tried to interpret the news. And they could—and did—find sponsors.

The dean of commentators was H. V. Kaltenborn, a mature, Harvard-educated journalist who had been free-lancing on radio since April 4, 1922, when, at an experimental station in Newark, New Jersey, he clamped his head into a viselike frame to keep his lips near the crude carbon microphone and gave his views on a coal strike. From that first spoken editorial, Kaltenborn developed a unique mixture of reporting and extemporaneous interpretation. By 1930, when he turned full time to radio, he had traveled the world and had interviewed the likes of Sigmund Freud, Chiang Kai-shek, the warlord Chang Tso-lin, the Philippine nationalists Aguinaldo and Manuel Quezon, Hitler, and the man who, for $12,000, had embalmed Lenin. A "sparse-haired, moustachio'ed six-footer, with friendly eyes . . . an imposing presence, a spic-and-span military air and a manner of speech suggesting a pontificating college professor," Kaltenborn seemed omnipresent—if not omniscient—wherever things were happening. He was "so excited" by Roosevelt's first inaugural, he confessed, that "I delivered a ten-minute extemporized editorial before getting back to the real job of describing the drive back to the White House."[56]

Given such a man and such talents, it was not surprising that when civil war broke out in Spain in 1936, Kaltenborn provided listeners with extraordinary insight into the conflict. First he found a farmhouse located on a thin finger of French territory protruding into the area where the Battle of Irun was raging. Then he persuaded a French radio engineer to run a phone line to the farmhouse and also to a haystack in the line of fire. Wires in place, he cabled CBS in New York that he could report a live battle. "Stand by," he was told, "there were too many commercial programs scheduled." As Kaltenborn waited, fearful that the battle would change direction, the cable broke twice and the engineer each time crawled out into shot and shell to splice it. Then, when the network was ready, the relay engineer in Bordeaux was out enjoying an aperitif. It was 9 P.M. on September 3 when Kaltenborn finally made his pathbreaking broadcast. He spoke for fifteen minutes, pausing to let listeners hear the rifle shots and explosions. For that broadcast CBS paid him its customary fee: fifty dollars.[57]

While that was a clever technical feat, the series of talks Kaltenborn gave upon returning to America had more profound consequences. Not only was he critical of American non-intervention, he also foresaw, as few Americans then did, the likelihood of a more widespread war in Europe. The most crucial convert to his point of view was his boss, William Paley. The CBS president was in the heat of an "upgrading" campaign. Burns and Allen, Kate Smith, Lum 'n' Abner, and Eddie Cantor brought in record income—$28.7 million gross in 1937, more than $3 million net, though still less than NBC's $38.5 million and $3.7 million net—but Paley also hungered for prestige.[58] In the summer of 1935, he had hired an industrial psychologist, Frank Stanton (who would become CBS president), as a $55-a-week research specialist and Edward R. Murrow as "director of talks." The title aped a prestigious one at the BBC, but it was unclear what kind of talk the twenty-eight-year-old (who had added three years to his age to get the job) would arrange.

It was not so much the threatening situation on the Continent as NBC's virtual monopoly and excellent connections that prompted CBS to ship Murrow to Europe as chief correspondent. The first person Murrow hired was a crack reporter with an unfortunate voice. William L. Shirer "sounded timorous and often tended to drone," but he had reported for years from Berlin, and his job, like Murrow's, was mostly to line up other speakers, not to broadcast himself. Before the end of 1937, Shirer was installed in Vienna, where he expected the next European crisis to break. When the Nazis marched into Austria on March 11, 1938, Shirer tried to broadcast but was prodded out of the Vienna radio studios at the point of a bayonet. Paley, sick with the flu in New York, telephoned the head of Austrian radio to arrange a broadcast, but the official broke down and cried, saying it was out of his control. Shirer then caught the first plane out, and at 6:30 the following evening broadcast from London: "I'm here tonight to report what I saw," he said, "not to give any personal opinions." But he made it clear that the Nazis had lied about "violent Red disorders" in Vienna. He told such a vivid story that no one paid any attention to the quality of his voice.[59]

Paley wanted even more. "Can't we get several overseas reports at the same time for the same program?" he asked his engineers. The CBS news director, Paul White, immediately ordered Murrow, who had flown to Vienna when Shirer left, to arrange a live news roundup to be broadcast in eight hours, which would be prime time in America. Thus, on March 13, 1938, at 8 P.M., "The Voice of CBS News," Bob Trout, spoke in Studio 9 on the seventeenth floor of the CBS Building: "The program 'St. Louis Blues' will not be heard tonight," he said. Instead, there would be "pickups direct from London, Paris and such other European capitals as at this late hour abroad have communications channels available." It was 1 A.M. in London when Shirer smoothly came in on Trout's cue. He was followed by Member of Parliament Ellen Wilkinson, Edgar Ansel Mowrer from Paris, Pierre Huss in Berlin, and Frank Gervasi from Rome. Murrow, who had somehow gained access to a circuit in Vienna, concluded the half-hour roundup, his first significant broadcast.[60]

Both technically and journalistically, the program was a landmark. The splicing of firsthand reports on a precise schedule was considered miraculous, though Morrow thought it merely "lucky." Paley trumpeted to stockholders that radio "by merely presenting events as they occurred and the factual but personalized accounts of its own reporters . . . was able to help make up people's minds and to further one side of the biggest . . . question of the time, the rise of Nazi power." NBC's reaction was to downplay radio news; a network executive told the U.S. Chamber of Commerce, "Radio is a show." To prove it, NBC news in 1938 featured an international competition for singing mice and, two months after the *Anschluss*, a talking parrot contest, won by a bird who squawked, "Polly wants a cracker."[61]

The BBC's coverage of the ominous news from the Continent was also meager. "In London, the proper people always know what would or would not please the proper people," the radio critic Edward J. Landry observed. "News is not censored; it is merely omitted." When Anthony Eden resigned as Foreign Secretary on February 20, 1938, in protest against Chamberlain's appeasement policy, CBS broadcast to America his speech to his constituents at Stratford-upon-Avon. The BBC did not, and hundreds of Britons phoned CBS's London office asking if they could hear the broadcast. On the eve of the *Anschluss*, Reith "quite enjoyed" himself at a German Embassy party, where he assured Nazi Foreign Minister Joachim von Ribbentrop the "the BBC was not anti-Nazi." Next day, he serenely noted in his diary: "Germany seems to have annexed Austria!" The Nazis were marching on Vienna at the very moment that Ribbentrop was calling on the King and Queen and lunching with Chamberlain. Foreign Secretary Lord Halifax informed Reith that Ribbentrop "had been told in very clear terms what this country thought of it," Reith recorded. "Before or after lunch, I asked."[62]

Less than six months after the *Anschluss*, when Hitler again was restive, this time over the Sudetenland region of Czechoslovakia, Shirer cabled New York asking for five minutes a day. "The home office thought I was crazy," he recalled, and offered five minutes on a Sunday afternoon. But within a week, CBS was broadcasting daily, not only from Berlin and Prague but also from London, Paris, Rome, Bad Godesberg, and Munich. Since the Austrian invasion, Murrow had "lived in the air and in a suitcase" to fulfill the command from New York: "Give us this day our European sensation." When the crisis broke on September 12, both networks were ready for live coverage at a level never before attempted. Within the next eighteen days, they spent $200,000, more than had ever been spent for coverage of any single sequence of events. CBS carried 151 short wave pickups and NBC 147, at an average cost of $500 each; rebates to sponsors whose programs were canceled also were costly. This time listeners not only heard directly from observers in various capitals, they eavesdropped on spontaneous conversations among all of them.[63]

The hero of those eighteen tense days was H. V. Kaltenborn, as even NBC news director Schechter conceded. During the long crisis, the sixty-year-old commentator lived in Studio 9 at CBS, napping on a cot between bulletins, flashes, running stories, and commentaries. He made eighty-five broadcasts ranging from two minutes to two hours in length. So habituated did Kaltenborn become to instant analysis that when the Archbishop of Canterbury broadcast a prayer for peace, he analyzed that too. "I drew on everything I had learned during my entire lifetime," he wrote, "my travels, my interviews, my knowledge of languages, my close association with current events." Not only correspondents, but the participants themselves became familiar voices to American listeners: Mussolini from Trieste, Premier Milan Hodza from Prague, Pope Pius XI from Rome, Hitler personally attacking President Beneš, and Chamberlain's craven, "How horrible . . . that we should be digging trenches and trying on gas masks here, because of a quarrel in a faraway country between people of whom we need know nothing." Bulletins interrupted so many programs that the joke around CBS was "about bulletins interrupting bulletins." Reporters and commentators were careful to avoid editorializing: "We are trying to provide material on which an opinion may be formed," Murrow explained, "but we are not trying to suggest what that opinion may be."[64]

Nevertheless, the effects of radio coverage during those eighteen days were acute. Kaltenborn went from one or two broadcasts a week, at $100 each, to a weekly income of thousands of dollars from broadcasts, lectures, books and articles; in the spring of 1940 he was lured away by NBC. Murrow's grave "This . . . is London," first heard on September 22, 1938, would become a trademark for his epoch-making broadcasts during the London blitz. Among Americans, "never before had so many listened so long to so much." For the first time in radio history, news drew more listeners than entertainment. CBS alone received 50,000 fan letters and so many phone calls that Kaltenborn lamented that he had never before or since "had a chance to refuse to talk on the phone to so many prominent people."[65]

For both networks, the Munich crisis coverage was a source

of prestige that would soon translate into profits as more news programs found sponsors. It also caused them to augment and professionalize their news staffs, preparing for the war that now seemed inevitable. Their 1938 news coverage had triggered a shift in public attitudes toward radio news: In 1937 and early 1938, Columbia University's Office of Radio Research had found that less than half the public preferred radio to newspapers as news sources; in October 1938, just after Munich, more than two-thirds preferred radio news.[66] Soon after that survey, Congress passed a special bill and, for the first time in history, on April 25, 1939, radio reporters were admitted to the press galleries of the Capitol.

Never in the history of civilized life had there been a medium of communication that could transmit so much information—whether lofty or trash—to so wide an audience. In millions of radio hours, much that was genuinely cultural reached the most isolated citizen. Good music, an occasional treat for a refined urban elite, became the pleasure and inspiration of many millions in small towns and remote rural places. Radio also set a standard for cultivated speech; dialects and regionalisms began to disappear from everyday discourse.

In a larger sense, radio unified the country in speech, tastes, customs and moral standards as no other medium ever had or—until television—ever would. Politically, radio gave the ordinary American unprecedented quantities and varieties of firsthand information: conventions, speeches, debates, forums, and the chats of a President superbly cognizant of the medium's power. For the first time since the Greek *polis*, citizens could gather to hear for themselves the voices and proposals of their leaders. Then, as radio relayed the disturbing reports from Europe, listeners could hear the strident harangues of Hitler, the hysterical cheers of his followers, the cowardly evasions of Daladier and Chamberlain. Fortunately, the correspondents who guided them were among the best-informed, the most literate, clear-headed, and moderate that American journalism had ever produced. While the purpose of this chapter has not been to draw a full-scale comparison between American radio and the BBC, one can conclude that in the realm of world affairs during that one crucial period, the British listener was not well served by radio. By its charter no less than by the social outlook of its personnel, the BBC was nudged toward betraying its chief responsibility to its listeners: to inform. (Only after Britain was at war did the BBC perform with extraordinary distinction.) Whether its failing was a function of public ownership or of an elitist society is difficult to assess, but certainly the competition between the two networks in America brought listeners a wealth of information. For Americans, radio opened a window on the world and laid the foundation for the enormous shift in public opinion away from isolationism, which enabled Roosevelt to help Britain before Pearl Harbor. Murrow's "This . . . is London," night after night, as the bombs exploded in the background, would be more persuasive than a thousand earnest lectures.

Why the networks allowed advertising agencies to usurp so much programming remains unclear. While the print media seldom treated their thriving competitors fairly, their criticism that radio sold its editorial pages strikes a nerve. The networks replied that their formative years were also years of Depression, that they lacked the financial resources to create expensive entertainment on the chance of finding a sponsor. Furthermore, they claimed, their "continuity acceptance departments" screened objectionable programs and commercials. In addition, up to 50 percent of their programming went out on a sustaining (nonsponsored) basis. Nevertheless, advertiser control showered an unconscionable load of trash upon the American public, partly because the medium was so voracious and partly, of course, because greed dictated entertainment that would appeal to the greatest number while offending absolutely no one.

Clearly, no medium has ever captured the imagination—not to mention the leisure time—of the public with the speed of radio. Yet, within the brief time span of less than two decades under study, a periodization suggests itself. The years before 1929 were the Era of Wonderment: Sound—any sound—emerging from a box seemed like a miracle. The years 1927 to 1933 comprise the Era of Institutionalization: chartering of the BBC, development of networks in America, the discovery and exploitation of commercial sponsorship, and rudimentary government control through the Federal Radio Commission. From 1934 to 1936 was the Era of Exploitation: burgeoning incomes from advertising that threatened print media, sophisticated use by politicians, and efforts at tighter government control through establishment of the Federal Communications Commission. Beginning in 1937 and until the advent of television, radio reached the Era of Maturity: a large and growing audience for serious cultural offerings, both music and drama; coverage of current events of a fairness, depth, and sophistication that alarmed newspapers; and an acceptance whereby Americans avidly devoted the largest chunk of their leisure time to this miraculous box and the sounds it emitted.

2

SOUND AND FURY: HOLLYWOOD AND WRITERS

Sound in films: "It's like lip rouge on the Venus de Milo."—Mary Pickford[1]

WHEN SOUND OVERTOOK the movie industry in 1927, it was not simply a refinement or an improvement of an existing product. "Revolution" is the word most often used by those who witnessed the event. The sound revolution brought into sharp relief the many differences between films and all other genres of art invented by man. Many observers noted, along with Bela Balasz, that the sound film was "not an organic continuation of the silent film, but a unique art, just as painting is not a more highly developed form of black and white graphic art, but a different art altogether."[2] One went so far as to call the advent of sound "the sole cataclysmic event in the history of art."[3] Sound films had a geographic link with their silent parents—the center of the industry remained in Hollywood—but in most other aspects—technical, financial, and artistic—sound brought seismic changes to the sun-drenched Lotusland in Southern California. The sheer novelty of the earliest talkies enchanted audiences, but their vapid content dismayed critics. Garbo could talk, but she had nothing to say.

Faced with conversion to sound that could cost as much as $50 million, studio heads were understandably anxious.[4] The entire technical plant, from stages to theaters, had to be completely replaced—and almost overnight. In less than three years following the first sound picture, not one silent film remained in production. "An art had been exterminated at the zenith of its power," one critic wrote breathlessly, "and something without precedent in human history had taken its place."[5] The competition among filmmakers, always keen, waxed feverish, especially since the studio that pioneered sound, Warner Brothers, rode from virtual bankruptcy to kingpin of the industry on the back of its innovation. (From 1928 to 1929, Warner's profits grew 609 percent.)[6] In the midst of the forced-draft changeover to sound, the stock market crash of November 1929 twisted the screw of the producers' anxiety.

The film pioneer Jesse Lasky noted that the panic of conversion lasted only a year, but it altered the industry forever. After talkies were established, he said, "things were running smoothly again, but with many more craftsmen and auxiliary mechanical devices, less teamwork, more complex organization, less pioneering spirit, more expense, less inspiration, more talent, less glamour, more predatory competition, less hospitality, more doing, less joy in the doing."[7] Budd Schulberg, whose father, B. P. Schulberg, was general manager of Paramount between 1928 and 1932, blamed the Depression for the end of an era in Hollywood. "It wasn't only that Wall Street had moved in . . . it was the giants of high finance, RCA and AT&T. Through the patents they controlled, they were now the true bosses of Hollywood." Pioneers like the Mayers, the Warners, and his B. P. Schulberg, Budd Schulberg declared, "loomed big on the local scene, but they were merely junior officers in a much larger war between the Morgans and the Rockefellers for control of what was now the billion dollar industry."[8]

As financial and technical whirlwinds pummeled the industry, the Word, scarcely a respected commodity in a land of images, suddenly became crucial. Executives who could barely read—and who certainly would never consider reading a good book as a way to spend an evening—were pressed to read novels and plays. Directors accustomed to spinning a film from the end of a megaphone now toiled through a mimeographed script; a script, furthermore, which they altered at their peril, since it served as a blueprint, dictating the costs of the film, its scheduling, its stage and costume requirements, and even its posters and promotional blurbs. Now even the ghastliest, most ephemeral, feature required a script, and the quality films to which the moguls pointed when they wanted to represent their industry as an art demanded a superior script.

Not that writers had been totally absent from the silent screen. Well before World War I, a newspaperman named Roy McCardell had dropped by the Biograph office on 14th Street in New York and asked for a job preparing scripts. He was offered ten dollars each, if he could turn in ten scenarios a week, eleven dollars if they were "good." On a borrowed typewriter, McCardell tapped out ten stories in one afternoon. He was hired at the higher rate, the first screenwriter in history.[9] Since then, novels and plays had provided the bulk of Hollywood's grist; in addition to drawing freely—and often grotesquely—from classics in the public domain, the silents had employed such literary talents as Gene Stratton Porter, Somerset Maugham, Rupert Hughes, Gertrude Atherton, and Arnold Bennett.[10] But by the early 1920s there was already a dearth of material, especially material of quality. Of the 10,000 scripts Cecil B. de Mille was reading each year, he winnowed out perhaps twelve with film potential, selected four for possible development, bought two, and produced one.[11] The professional writer was expected not so much to create a script as to write titles that would turn "a clinker into a hit." Herman Mankiewicz, who began his Hollywood career in that vineyard, relished his gems in this genre: "Derely Devore . . . rose from the chorus because she was cool in an emergency—and warm in a taxi" and "Paris, where half the women are working women . . . and half the women are working men."[12]

Along with every other feature of the industry, sound drastically altered the role of writers in Hollywood. In the competitive scramble, the director Josef Von Sternberg wrote, the studio bosses "knew what they wanted, but didn't know how to spell it."[13] The newspaper headline "Herman is Here on the Trail of Genius" alerted the New York literary community that Hollywood was hiring.[14] Mankiewicz was able to share his own experience with hungry recruits: the train ride west with him and his wife Sara ensconced in a private drawing room, while their children and a nurse traveled in another car; the spacious house on upper Vine Street in the Hollywood hills; the closetful of white flannels and black-and-white wing-tip shoes; the country club; the Cadillac convertible, bought from Ernst Lubitsch, driven by a black chauffeur, and equipped with a lap robe monogrammed H. J. M. and an interior window to seal off the driver, though Herman democratically refused to shut it; the two-seater Buick for running about town; the Chrysler for Sara; the $90,000 house they were about to buy.[15]

Word of the rich lode to be mined with a typewriter spread swiftly, and as the Depression deepened a throng of literary Okies trekked west. Julius J. Epstein (the prototype for Julian Blumberg in Budd Schulberg's *What Makes Sammy Run?*), who had migrated to Hollywood during the silent era, recalled that when sound came, "the trains were full of playwrights, novelists, short story writers, poetry writers, people who wrote home for money—anybody who could put a word on paper."[16] The golden rain from Hollywood—even the rumors of such rain—fell not a moment too soon on the parched sidewalks of Broadway; there, the effect of talkies and of the Depression had been disastrous. The 1927–28 season had seen 264 productions; by 1934–35, there were 149. The number of theater-weeks also plummeted, from 2,852 in 1925–26 to 1,110 in 1933–34. Because of the competition from films in those anxious economic times, Broadway producers went bankrupt so briskly that by the end of 1932 banks owned more theaters than the Schubert and Erlanger chains combined. By the fall of 1931, 20 percent of Broadway houses had been diverted to other uses, principally film showings. While live theater languished, audiences were enchanted with talkies, flocking to film palaces more often and more enthusiastically than ever before. Between 1926 and 1930, paid attendance at the movies rose from 50 million to 90 million a week; an average of once a week for every American man, woman, and child.[17]

The quality of what they saw was generally abysmal. Partly that was a result of technical problems. Cameras, which during the silent days were free to roam the set and to shoot scenes from imaginative angles, were suddenly immobilized. Encased with its sweating operator in a soundproof cubicle, the camera recorded nervous actors enunciating stiff lines into flowerpots and cushions where the microphones were hidden. Suddenly the sound man ruled the set, telling actors when to speak and where. Frank Capra, who had directed seven silent films, found his first sound film "an étude in chaos . . . when the red lights went on, everyone froze in his position—a cough or a belch would wreck the scene." Capra was by no means opposed to technical innovation—he was a graduate of Carnegie Tech in engineering—but he believed that sound had "set back film making 30 years."[18]

Stars with squeaky voices or guttural accents floundering through such obvious tripe as *The Godless Girl* (1929) presented a juicy target, but an element of snobbery also tinged the intellectuals' persistent critique of Hollywood movies. The film historian Benjamin Hampton notes that "sophisticated screen critics and professional commentators . . . who had spent years in perfecting themselves in the art of sneering and jibing at . . . silent drama . . . suddenly reversed their positions and poured out paeans of praise to the beautiful art that was disappearing before the onward march of the unspeakable talkies."[19]

Stung by critics centered in New York and goaded by the financiers who were also based in New York, the Hollywood studios naturally looked to New York for writing talent. Not that they respected writers. Irving Thalberg, the creative genius at MGM, reportedly said, "The writer is a necessary evil." S. J. Perelman thought Thalberg might have said "weevil." Still, working in Hollywood, Perelman felt, was "no worse than playing the piano in a whorehouse."[20] The whorehouse was luxurious indeed, and the players of rinky-dink tunes often

ended up with fortunes. Some reaped artistic satisfaction as
well. Ben Hecht answered the call in late 1926 after receiving
a wire from Herman Mankiewicz: "Millions are to be grabbed
out here and the competition is idiots. Don't let this get
around." On $300 per week at Paramount, Hecht wrote his
first gangster movie, *Underworld,* in one week and received
a bonus of $10,000.[21]

Samuel Marx was flabbergasted by the first job offered to
him in Hollywood. His experience conveys the free-wheeling,
frantic, *ad hoc* atmosphere in the studios. Marx had met Irving
Thalberg during a brief stint at Universal. When he met the
MGM head of production again, accidentally, on New York's
West 54th Street in December 1929, Marx was newly married
and supporting himself by writing a throwaway weekly about
Broadway. Thalberg casually suggested Marx try screenwriting. Four months later, Marx appeared in Thalberg's office.
The producer was baffled until Marx reminded him of his
job offer. "One of my department heads resigned an hour
ago," Thalberg said, and sent Marx to take over the office of
a Robert Harris. Still unclear as to his job, Marx called a friend
and mentioned taking Harris's place at MGM. "I'll be
damned," the friend said, "You're the story editor."[22]

By 1932, some 228 writers (including 36 women) were under contract to seven major studios.[23] Five years later, the
studios were still desperate for writing talent. Garson Kanin,
for example, was assistant to the Broadway producer George
Abbott when he was recruited by Beatrice (Mrs. George S.)
Kaufman to work for Samuel Goldwyn. His fare to California
paid, Kanin was signed for seven years, beginning at $250 a
week and rising to $1,500 a week. Kanin's background for
the job was minimal: He was a high school dropout, a mediocre
musician and burlesque stooge, director of one Broadway flop,
a former stock clerk at Macy's, and twenty-four years old.
His first month in Hollywood was euphoric, he recalled. "I
had somewhere to go every morning, a pleasant office and
an efficient secretary . . . the fascinating studio world to play
with; charming, witty, talented colleagues; and a library of
films at my disposal."[24]

"The wise screenwriter is he who wears his second-best suit, artistically speaking."—Raymond Chandler[25]

For experienced writers, Hollywood proffered rewards that were well-nigh irresistible—and not only in financial terms. Hardly a single important literary figure survived the Thirties without spending some time in Hollywood; indeed, a good case could be made for the film studios' role as the greatest patrons of literature in the twentieth century. Yet the myth persisted, often embroidered by those who had fled from film-land, that Hollywood was "a dreary company town controlled by hoodlums of enormous wealth,"[26] that it treated writers with disrespect and exploited them, and—the *coup de grace*— that Hollywood destroyed a writer's talent. The archetype for the myth is F. Scott Fitzgerald, who died of the effects of drink (though some would prefer to blame a broken heart) in Hollywood in 1940.

On his first trip west in 1927, Fitzgerald was hired to write a film about college life for Constance Talmadge. He and Zelda cavorted with such luminaries as Lillian Gish and John Barrymore while squandering his $3,500 advance. *Lipstick,* the script he tossed off during the party, was rejected. "I was a sort of magician with words," he thought.[27] The notion that he could write films without the struggle and pain exacted by fiction was shared by many who tried screenwriting. Many others also believed, with Fitzgerald, that writing for the movies offered a lively challenge to a writer, that the art of screenwriting would enable him to share a personal vision with an audience of millions rather than the mere thousands who read stories or novels. "As long past as 1930," he wrote, "I had a hunch that the talkies would make even the best-selling novelist as archaic as silent pictures."

In November 1931, Fitzgerald returned to Hollywood at $1,200 a week to adapt a Katherine Brush novel, *Red-Headed Woman.* This time, he claimed, "a bastard named de Sano . . . changed [the script] as I wrote. I left with the money . . . but . . . vowing never to go back."[28] Fitzgerald was bewailing the system by which most studios operated: teaming totally uncongenial writers on one film. Worse yet, the producers treated a script like a property, not like a work of art.

However, most writers, certainly Fitzgerald, had no experience in creating screenplays. The producers therefore thought it only reasonable to shelter their investment by teaming a "big name" with a hack who was at least conscious of the tremendous investment of money hinging on the script. Since making films has always been a collaborative art, it seemed reasonable to producers that writers would turn out better work if they had collaborators.

Despite Fitzgerald's vow, by 1937 he was back on the MGM payroll at $1,250 a week. In the next eighteen months, he briefly polished the script for *A Yank at Oxford* and wrote the adaptation of Erich Maria Remarque's novel *Three Comrades*, the only script for which he ever received screen credit. "I'm alone on the picture," he exulted to his daughter Scotty, "That's the only way I can do my best work."[29] But the studio soon assigned an experienced screenwriter, Ted Paramore, to "help with the construction." Even worse butchery, in Fitzgerald's eyes, befell his script after he completed it. Joseph Mankiewicz was brought in to revise it—and to revise it again; in a period of less than three months, six revised versions were circulated. On the final copy, dated February 1, 1938, Fitzgerald scrawled "37 pages mine, about ⅓, but all shadows + rhythm removed." On other portions, Fitzgerald scribbled "so slick—so cheap."[30] To Mankiewicz, Fitzgerald complained, "You *had* something and you have arbitrarily and carelessly torn it to pieces . . . months of work and thought negated in one hasty week."[31]

Even thirty years later, Mankiewicz cringed in recalling that he was treated "as if I had spat on the flag." The actors "could not read the lines," he explained. "It was very literary . . . novelistic dialogue that lacked all the qualities required for screen dialogue." Nor was Fitzgerald's complaint that the revisions ruined his work accurate. *Three Comrades* appeared on many best-ten lists for the year and won for its star, Margaret Sullavan, an Academy Award nomination, a British National Award, and the New York Critics Award.[32]

Despite the studio's alleged mangling of Fitzgerald's work, it paid him handsomely; his last contract at MGM netted him $91,000 for essentially one screenplay, *Three Comrades*, which had to be heavily rewritten. The money enabled Fitzgerald to "rebuild his life without financial cares. Moreover, the locale provided a rich source of subject matter. The writer was especially fascinated with Irving Thalberg. The boy genius, then thirty-three years old, was the model for the "continuity writer not yet broken to Hollywood" in "Crazy Sundays," a short story written in 1932, as well as for Monroe Stahr, the protagonist of *The Last Tycoon*. Hollywood had inspired Fitzgerald from his first trip west, after which he published a potboiler about movie life, *Magnetism*. The hero of his 1934 novel *Tender Is the Night* once worked as an assistant director, cameraman, and cutter for King Vidor, and "all the characters . . . derive their self-image and values from the motion picture." Fitzgerald tried unsuccessfully to sell the book to Thalberg. Ironically, film rights to it were bought from Fitzgerald's estate by David O. Selznick for $17,500 and later resold to 20th Century Fox for $300,000.[33]

In the last fifteen months of his life, Fitzgerald created a series of short stories featuring a Hollywood hack named Pat Hobby. Obvious potboilers, they were published in *Esquire* as quickly as Fitzgerald could crank them out. "They don't want authors," says Hobby about the studios in "Mightier than the Sword," "they want writers—like me."[34] Was Pat Hobby Fitzgerald's bitter revenge against Hollywood? Or did the pathetic, bootlicking hack represent Fitzgerald's self-contempt at being forced to pander to Hollywood's lowlifes by his perennial need for money? An *Esquire* editor, Arnold Gingrich, who wired immediate payment to a frantic Fitzgerald, contends that Pat Hobby must take "his rightful place if not alongside Jay Gatsby . . . then at least between Monroe Stahr and Amory Blaine." But most scholars agree with the literary critic Walter Wells, who calls the Pat Hobby stories "hastily written ephemera" lacking plot complexities or subtleties of character, theme or technique.[35] One of the few fans for Pat Hobby is Scotty Fitzgerald; The hack writer invented by her father, she said, "sent me to Vassar."[36]

Virtually every writer who worked in Hollywood complained as bitterly as Fitzgerald about the crude systems of the studios for developing film scripts. At Warner Brothers, for example, Brian Foy, who was responsible for thirty "B" pictures each year, had a huge pile of scripts alongside his desk. When a writer appeared for assignment, Ring Lardner, Jr., recalled, Foy would hand him the script at the top of the pile and ask him to switch the background. When the picture was completed, its script would return to the bottom of the pile.[37]

But while the veneer of such efficient mass production may have impressed the New York bankers, it was exceedingly thin. Kenneth Macgowan, a veteran studio executive, recalled that MGM's seventy writers were assigned to whatever film needed writing. Having finished a serious drama, a writer might next have to tackle a light comedy. Another common extravagance was to put writers "singly, in double-harness or troika style on story ideas or originals of dubious promise." Of the thirty feature films Macgowan produced for 20th Century Fox from 1935 to 1943, twenty had more than two collaborators, and on eight of them anywhere from six to eleven writers were involved. Only two could be credited to a single writer.[38] Jesse Lasky, Jr., described the tandem system used by Cecil B. De Mille: "Sometimes one talks and the other types. Sometimes they type in separate rooms, then exchange drafts for polishing."[39] Mostly, De Mille simply passed these polished drafts, after a cursory glance, to the next writing team. At MGM, Thalberg instituted a "backup" system for writers, whom he called "ditch-diggers": one writer would follow another, scrapping part or all of what had been written. "Your fame meant nothing," one veteran noted. "Your credit slipped off a film as easily as jelly. This happened to everyone: [Robert] Sherwood, [Aldous] Huxley, Hecht, Faulkner, [Dorothy] Parker: there were no exceptions."[40]

If the director changed, the script would have to be completely revised. If the star objected to the script, it would have to be redone once again. Most galling was the studio executives' general aversion to reading anything. Louis B. Mayer, for example, hardly ever read even a synopsis of a possible film, instead "he had a Scheherezade or two on whose story-telling abilities rested the future" of film projects submitted at MGM.[41] Darryl F. Zanuck's story conferences at 20th Century Fox were "shows in themselves, sometimes more entertaining than the films that came out of them." Usually starting at 10 or 11 P.M., he would assemble "a number of hangers on, yes-men and cronies," perhaps a writer (in this case, Nunnally Johnson), plus his secretary to take down every word. Zanuck "pantomimed, shouted, cursed, sang, danced and plotted with dazzling speed, giving out a hundred variations on both plot and character, while acting out everything." Specialists were imperiously fetched in at a whim and as cavalierly dismissed. Cameron Rogers, a historian of the seventeenth century, was consulted for *Cardinal Richelieu;* when he objected to Zanuck's script, the producer cried, "Aw, the hell with you. Nine out of ten people are going to think he's Rasputin anyway."[42]

Cecil B. De Mille harangued the writers working on *Union Pacific:* "I want train wrecks. I want to see the explosion of steam and bursting boilers! Iron guts! I want to boil on those prairies and freeze in the Sierras. I want to smash through the barricades of mountain ranges of snow and ice. I want a love story that nobody has ever got on the screen and I want human drama! Suspense. Not just 'will they make it or won't they make it?' which any damn fool can write. I want a snake under every bed!" Then his voice would fall to a hoarse whisper: "I want to see Abe Lincoln's dream—come to life!"[43]

Such a pep talk betrays the desperation that producers felt under the pressure to churn out enough films to fill the screens of some 17,000 theaters (in 1938) and the fantasies of 85 million moviegoers each week.[44] For feeding this ravenous maw, the producers' chief criterion was mass appeal. Well-written scripts dealing with mature subjects were suspect. The producer "never worries that the acting may be too perfect for audiences in a New England town, the camera work too fine for Duluth, the sound too well recorded for Natchez, the cutting too subtle for Oshkosh," wailed one bitter writer, "but he is very apt to fear that the story is too good for Tallahassee— or New York."[45] The Production Code Administration's stern censorship further hobbled writers. Many subjects, of course, were taboo, and so were many words, including, in 1933: alley cat, bat, dame, eunuch, fanny, filthy, floozy, guts, hell cat, hellion, hellish, hussy, lousy, nursery, nuts, rump, punk, trollop, virtuous, want you, wench, and house-broken.[46]

Within the studio pressure-cooker bubbled many a bizarre

talent. Bob "Hoppy" Hopkins rambled the MGM lot for years, collaring producers in the commissary or barbershop. Costumed as he thought a writer should be, in a checkered sport coat and baggy gray slacks, he would grab his quarry by the arm or lapel and gabble: "Earthquake—San Francisco—Gable and MacDonald—can't you see it? Clark's on one side of the street. Jeanette's on the other—goddam street splits right between 'em—it's gotta be but terrific!" If a producer showed interest, Hopkins would wave his hand imperiously: "Okay—now put a word-man on it." If a producer asked for more, Hopkins would pummel him furiously: "What more do you need? You stupid son of a bitch! I'll get you a story. I don't need a pencil, I can piss it out! New Orleans! Gable, Shearer, Crawford and Garbo. Can't you see it? My God! You call yourself a producer?"[47]

Producers listened to such drivel because they were desperate for material. Their medium was a monster, insatiably craving plots and stories and fragments of ideas. Like the radio executives, they were haunted by the specter of silence. But unlike radio programmers, the movie producers had no recorded music to fill the gaps in their schedules. Instead, they had to supply endless scripts to occupy their expensive sound stages and to keep the intricate production process flowing. Thus, no idea was too slight to be considered and often handsomely paid for. The eighteen-year-old Budd Schulberg, home from college for the summer, told David Selznick a story over drinks at his parents' Malibu home. "My mother, the agent, made the deal," he recalled gleefully. "$1,500 on delivery of a ten-page outline . . . if David liked what he read, I was to work at RKO for $50 a week to develop the story until I had to leave for Dartmouth."[48] But while a producer would often listen like a child to a story, even the most talented could rarely be persuaded to sit down with the printed word. A seasoned writer, Salka Viertel, met Irving Thalberg at the home of Greta Garbo to discuss a script Viertel had prepared for *Queen Christina*. Thalberg said the script needed "a great deal of work," but his specific suggestions were so vague that Viertel came away convinced that "he had not read the manuscript."[49]

"I didn't want to come out to this God-forsaken country. I
have a beautiful apartment in New York—and friends. But
they hounded me and belabored me and hammered at me,
till you would have thought if I didn't get out here by the
15th of October every camera in Hollywood would stop
clicking . . . And so . . . in a moment of weakness I came.
That was six months ago. I have an office and a secretary and
I draw my check every week, but so far no one has taken
the slightest notice of me. Plenty of good minds come out
here. Why aren't they used? The whole business is in the hands
of incompetents, that's all. But I don't have to stay here and
I'm not going to."—Lawrence Vail in *Once in a Lifetime,* a
comedy by Moss Hart and George S. Kaufman[50]

Time and again, a respected writer was given a ridiculous
assignment—or no assignment at all. In 1931 P. G. Wodehouse
left Hollywood "dazed," he told reporters. "I cannot see what
they engaged me for. They were extremely nice to me [and]
gave me $104,000 for no reason." Outraged by such waste,
Nicholas Schenk, the New York controller of MGM, roared
at Thalberg on the phone: "You are silly boys out there! You
throw away our money." Mildly, Thalberg replied: "Nick, if
you know how to make pictures without writers, tell me
how."[51]

True, writers were necessary, but their talents lay fallow.
Budd Schulberg notes that despite "the finest salaries in the
history of hirelings" not a single unique voice "could be heard
above the insistent general hum of the dream factories." Looking at "the dull stucco bungalows of the Garden of Allah," a
seedy complex of rental apartments, Schulberg wondered "if
there ever had been such an assembly of literary lights all
on the same small hotel register at the same time . . . Yet,
meshed into the assembly line system, almost none of these
genuine writers produced anything genuine, anything
memorable."[52]

From its earliest days, the movie medium had tantalized
novelists. Even Tolstoy had been fascinated by "this little clicking contraption," which he expected to "make a revolution
in . . . the life of writers. . . . This swift change of scene,
this blending of emotion and experience . . . is closer to life.

. . . The cinema has divined the mystery of motion. And that is greatness. . . . I am seriously thinking of writing a play for the screen."[53] Surely, even Tolstoy's enthusiasm for films would have shriveled, had he lived to see the mincemeat Hollywood made of his novel *Resurrection.* After adaptation by Maxwell Anderson and Leonard Praskins, the screenplay was written by Preston Sturges and Thornton Wilder. It starred Fredric March, Jane Baxter, C. Aubrey Smith, Sam Jaffe, and Anna Sten, was directed by Rouben Mamoulian, and was photographed by the master cameraman Gregg Toland. With that constellation of talents hacking at it, there was precious little left of the original, not even the title, which became *To Live Again.*[54] Small wonder that when its producer, Samuel Goldwyn, offered a contract to George Bernard Shaw, the English playwright declined: "The trouble, Mr. Goldwyn," wrote Shaw, "is that you are only interested in art and I am only interested in money."[55]

Many of those who made the pilgrimage to Hollywood could not afford Shaw's archness. William Faulkner, for example, had been working as a janitor and as a deckhand on a fishing boat in Mississippi while writing *The Sound and the Fury* and *As I Lay Dying.* When *Sanctuary* was published in 1931, he attended some New York literary parties, at one of which Tallulah Bankhead asked him to write a picture for her. The idea so appealed to him that he apparently began writing a screenplay immediately. Some months later, reporting to MGM for a six-week contract, he asked to write a picture for Mickey Mouse but, no less absurdly, was assigned to a script for Wallace Beery. Despite the obvious need for trained screenwriters, no studio offered schooling. Faulkner was packed off to a small projection room to watch old movies. Bored after a few minutes, he wandered off for a week in Death Valley, then returned to write four treatments in five days, including one for Beery.[56] He stayed on for six months, earning $6,000, "more money than I had ever seen." Though he wrote to a friend that he was "mad all the time I was in California," he went west again the following year, on a $1,000-a-week contract with 20th Century Fox.

Faulkner returned to Hollywood a number of times throughout the Thirties, writing scripts and later helping to adapt his own novels. His productiveness stunned one collaborator, Joel Sayre, who recalled that producers were delighted when a writer turned in five pages a day, whereas Faulkner would turn in thirty-five.[57] But whether they were cinematic is an open question. The Warner Brothers producer Jerry Wald thought Faulkner had an "excellent sense of story construction," though his dialogue was "rather indifferent." Sidney Greenstreet complained that it was impossible to read a Faulkner speech. Told that it had been written by one of America's greatest writers, Greenstreet replied he didn't care if it was written by Shakespeare.[58]

Unlike many of the writers recruited in New York, Faulkner was far from bitter about his Hollywood sojourns. "It's like chopping cotton or picking potato bugs off plants," he told an interviewer many years later. "You know damn well it's not painting the Sistine Chapel or winning the Kentucky Derby. But a man likes the feel of some money in his pockets." He scoffed at the notion that Hollywood destroyed a writer's talents, asserting that "nothing can injure a man's writing if he's a first-rate writer. . . . Pictures are trying to pay for what they get. Frequently they overpay. But that does not debase the writer."[59]

Over a twenty-two-year period, Faulkner spent a total of four in Hollywood, working on forty-four films, including *Gunga Din, Banjo on My Knee, The Last Slaver, Country Lawyer,* and *Drums Along the Mohawk.* During the same period he also wrote five novels, scarcely suggesting, his biographer Joseph Blottner writes, "a contamination or serious falling off."[60] Faulkner had no illusions about his own screenwriting talents. He insisted, "I will never be a good motion picture writer." But he was also alert to the nature of films as "a collaboration [a] compromise because that is what the word means—to give and to take." Faulkner gave Hollywood six credited screenplays, while taking about $300,000, about half from sales of movie rights to seven of his novels.[61]

What shining phantom folds its wings before us?
What apparition, smiling, yet remote?
Is this—so portly yet so lightly porous—
The old friend who went West and never wrote?

                                    —Edmund Wilson[62]

Eastern critics dwelled extensively on the dreadful fate of writers who succumbed to the lucre of Hollywood. The *New Yorker*'s editor, Harold Ross, found Nunnally Johnson "sickening . . . he has been sucking around the diamond merchants of Hollywood for the last 15 years and hasn't written anything. There is a misspent life." Fitzgerald scolded Johnson for coming to Hollywood because "he had talent, but Hollywood would ruin it." The fact that Johnson was for at least a dozen years the highest-paid writer in America seemed only to underline these verdicts. Nor was he absolved by many first-rate scripts he wrote, not even his stunning adaptation of *The Grapes of Wrath*.[63] S. J. Perelman, who had gone west in 1931 to write *Monkey Business* and *Horsefeathers* for the Marx Brothers and stayed to carpenter such confections as *Sitting Pretty* (1933), *Early to Bed* (1936), *Boy Trouble* (1939), and *The Golden Fleecing* (1940), was sure that Hollywood was "a hideous and untenable place . . . populated with few exceptions by Yahoos. . . . It strikingly resembled the Sargasso Sea—an immense turgidly revolving whirlpool in which literary hulks encrusted with verdigris moldered until they sank." The few live literati Perelman discerned in this swamp were Robert Benchley, Dorothy Parker, and Donald Ogden Stewart. They "had no more connection with the screenwriting fraternity than if they had been Martians," the humorist claimed. They had "never made an accommodation with Hollywood."[64]

One wonders what sort of accommodation Perelman had in mind. Parker first went to Hollywood in 1932 on a three-month contract with MGM, but, she wailed to a newspaper interviewer, "after some weeks, I ran away. I could not stand it. I just sat in a cell-like office and did nothing"—except, presumably collect her paycheck.[65] The following year, she and her husband, Alan Campbell, were back "in a state of semi-destitution to go on a combined salary beginning the following Monday of $5,200 per week. . . . She had no clothes to speak of . . . and everyone was quick to set them up comfortably. George Oppenheimer (a studio executive) loaned them his home; Metro took care of the rest." However, Parker "hated gratitude," and though Oppenheimer also loaned them his silver for the housewarming in their new home, he was not invited to the party.

"I am a Communist," Parker had declared in 1934, but her audience laughed: How could a radical live in a Beverly Hills mansion with a butler and a cook and openly adore Franklin and Eleanor Roosevelt?[66] Parker and Campbell amassed credits for fifteen film scripts between 1933 and 1938, including *The Big Broadcast of 1936, Paris in the Spring, Crime Takes a Holiday, Flight into Nowhere,* and *A Star Is Born,* which was nominated for an Academy Award. Yet "she believed that they were living in Babylonian Captivity, 'working for cretins.' " But while reveling in "huge pink jersey and black lace hats from John Fredericks, handmade lingerie from Emma Maloof in New York, perfume from Cyclax in London," Parker was frequently overdrawn at the bank.[67] As John O'Hara wrote to Fitzgerald in 1936, Parker and Campbell "live in luxury, including a brand-new Picasso, a Packard convertible phaeton, a couple of Negroes and dinner at the very best Beverly Hills homes. Dottie occasionally voices a great discontent. But I think her aversion to movie writing is as much lazy as intellectual. She likes the life."[68]

Had she truly hated Hollywood, Parker could have lived comfortably (if not regally) on her literary earnings. She received more than $32,000 in book royalties between 1935 and 1937. In 1936, critics acclaimed her collected poems, *Not So Deep as a Well.* Nor did she devote the Hollywood largess to left-wing causes; the Friends of the Abraham Lincoln brigade received, according to the check stub, $120, while the Democratic Party got $250. Years later, Parker was still bitter about her Hollywood experience. The place "smells like a laundry," she proclaimed. "The beautiful vegetables taste as though they were raised in trunks . . . the flowers . . . smell like dirty old dollar bills." The money earned in screenwriting "is like so much compressed snow. It goes so fast it melts in your hand."[69]

Robert Benchley also seemed to accommodate himself to Hollywood—while kicking and screaming. He first went West in 1926, while keeping his job as drama critic of *The New Yorker.* Then he stayed, "enchanted," he claimed, "by the idea of [his] mail addressed to The Garden of Allah, Hollywood."[70] He wrote and acted in a number of short subjects, including the classic *The Treasurer's Report,* and *How to Sleep,* which won the Oscar for best short subject in 1935. Yet in 1931 he described Hollywood as "a flat, unlovely plain, inhabited by a group of highly ordinary people . . . turning out a product which, except for certain mechanical excellencies is as unimportant and undistinguished as the mass product of any plant grinding out rubber novelties."[71] At a party in the early 1940s, Benchley was heard to shout, "Those eyes! I can't stand those eyes looking at me!" Guests turned to see Benchley backing away from Robert Sherwood, whose plays had won two Pulitzer Prizes. "He's thinking of how he knew me when I was going to be a great writer," cried Benchley. "And he's thinking *now* look at what I am. . . ."[72]

Donald Ogden Stewart's accommodation to Hollywood took a peculiar form. A graduate of Exeter and Yale, Stewart wrote several whimsically humorous novels during the 1920s and was brought to Hollywood in 1926 at $250 a week to adapt one of them. Stewart reported to work and was assigned the usual small cubicle. But he spent most of the next few weeks playing tennis with Ivy League friends and shopping for a car, which turned out to be a used Buick roadster. Then he was assigned to write an epic called *Brown of Harvard.*

"In the golden climate of California, I began to feel the first faint stirrings of certain financial ambitions," he recalled many years later. "If they really needed good writers in Hollywood as badly as they told me they did, I would be foolish not to think this over carefully—especially as I . . . could cleverly—but with integrity of course—use the movie technique to reach millions!" Presumably Stewart meant millions of people, but dollars could not have been far from his mind. In 1930, having confected a pair of Broadway comedies, Stewart settled in Hollywood for good: "There was all that lovely money."

Always acutely conscious of social distinctions, Stewart resented the low esteem in which writers were held in Hollywood. At dinner parties, he noted, they sat "at the bottom of the table, below Heads of Publicity but above the Hairdressers." However, "when Joan and Jock Whitney entered the arena with an investment of several million in Selznick International," Stewart and his wife "were graciously accepted into the David Oliver Selznick circle. And eventually we reached the Top, the table of Sam and Frances Goldwyn."[73]

Along with social success and a growing reputation as a writer of witty dialogue, culminating in an Academy Award for his screen adaptation of Philip Barry's *The Philadelphia Story* in 1940, Stewart suddenly discovered radical politics. But his fervent leftism was never taken seriously—except, ironically, by the House Un-American Activities Committee.[74] A wag said that he was "hit by a truck as he crossed a street, suffered a concussion and discovered when he woke up in the hospital that he had become a Communist." His ex-wife remembered that he once demanded she turn her fur coat inside out as they attended a Communist rally in New York's Union Square, lest they be taken for capitalists.[75] In 1936, Stewart explained to John O'Hara that "he'd *had* Skull & Bones, he'd *had* the Whitney plantation, he'd *had* big Hollywood money." "He is certainly scared about something," O'Hara wrote to Fitzgerald, "but he is such a horse's ass, it doesn't matter much."[76]

Parker, Benchley, and Stewart belonged to a coterie of glib writers, refugees from the Algonquin Round Table, who had an "aversion to the real toil of authorship," Pauline Kael noted. Screenwriting seemed to be "an extension of what they used to do for fun. . . . They had liked to talk more than to write and this weakness became their way of life."[77]

Herman Mankiewicz was another Round Table fugitive. He had left a job as assistant drama critic of the *New York Times* in 1925 to write scenarios for silents. Though instantly successful, he longed to write a great Broadway play. His only such effort, ironically titled *The Meal Ticket,* was produced in 1937. It died after the out-of-town tryout. The critic for the *Philadelphia Record* expressed the consensus of his colleagues: "A cheaper, more poorly constructed play has seldom been seen on any stage. Its characters are funny only when they are disgusting. It lacks tone, timing, scenario, good lines, acting ability and competent direction." Crushed, Mankiewicz was unable to see himself as a successful screenwriter rather than a failed dramatist, even though he had worked on such important films as *Dinner at Eight* and *Girl Crazy* and was largely responsible for the script of *Citizen Kane,* winner of the Academy Award in 1941. Sitting at the bar in New York's 21 one afternoon in the early 1940s, Mankiewicz got off a classic mock lament: "Oh, to be back in Hollywood, wishing I was back in New York."

His competence swamped by cynicism, he insisted that screenwriting was not "an artistic pursuit, but . . . a very hard-boiled business, which pays well." Success, he maintained, did not require literary skill but rather "a flair for ideas, for situations."[78] Unfortunately—and mostly because of his morose personality rather than maltreatment by the studios—he mingled such insight with contempt for his work, calling it "slop," "shit" and "vomit." When movie attendance fell, after 1932, he advised a studio sales meeting: "Show the movies in the streets and drive the people back into the theaters." Near the end of his life, he was still apologizing for having had a successful Hollywood career: "I came out here . . . for a few months," he said forlornly in 1953. "You start working at something you don't like and before you know it, you're an old man."[79]

Why were these writers so exceedingly defensive about their work in Hollywood? They were enmeshed in the cultural revolution of the Thirties, with its mingling of high and vulgar art. Literary figures had always belonged to the intelligentsia; they did not write for the masses. But with the advent of mass media during the Thirties, the lines were blurred. Broadway may have been the route to respect among the literati, but Hollywood could offer true fame and fortune. And sometimes, among all the trivial horse operas, there would be a true masterpiece, like *Stagecoach* or *I Was a Prisoner on a Chain Gang.*

Flaying Hollywood was a favorite sport of a New York literary establishment which, in its snobbish provincialism, could not believe that any worthwhile literary work was being done in the hinterland. That myth rested on the European model of an intellectual elite based in a metropolis, preferably Paris. But in America, the greatest American novelists of the Thirties—Faulkner, Wolfe, Steinbeck, Hemingway, O'Hara—all worked outside New York. Unlike Paris, which is both the literary and publishing capital of France, New York had never been the literary capital of the United States, only the publishing capital. Yet critics like Edmund Wilson and Malcolm Cowley resented the pull Hollywood exerted on writers. And New York's leading theater critic, George Jean Nathan, waxed positively livid over the sins of Hollywood moguls. "They have bought literature," he thundered, "and converted it, by their peculiar and esoteric magic, into rubbish."[80] In four or five years, Nathan predicted in 1931, "theater will flourish as it has not for a generation."[81] But when the New York theater continued to falter, Nathan in 1936 extolled Ben Hecht, Charles MacArthur, and Laurence Stallings for being superior to "the muckworm spirit of the Hollywood factories" by insisting on writing their screenplays in New York, "3,000 miles safely removed from Beverly Hills Spanish-Yiddish villas, illuminated swimming pools and purple and orange Rolls Royces."[82] That must have been news to Hecht and MacArthur, who thoroughly enjoyed extended sojourns in California. Hecht called his trips west "a plush Bohemian vacation," while MacArthur cynically remarked: "You write stinking scripts but you meet the people you like to be in a room with."[83]

While the New York literary critics indulged in mere spleen against defectors to Hollywood, the theater critics could point to genuine grievances. By the end of the 1930s, films had made drastic inroads on Broadway. Not only had many theaters become film palaces. Not only had Hollywood money lured many good playwrights into writing for films. (No one seemed ready to thank Hollywood for diverting so many dreadful playwrights from careers on the Great White Way.)

Indeed, the beast from Hollywood had practically gobbled up its venerable parent, Broadway.

The career of a puff of stage fluff by Preston Sturges, *Child of Manhattan,* is typical. On opening night, in 1932, the audience included not only New York Mayor James J. Walker and former Governor and presidential candidate Alfred E. Smith, but also Jesse Lasky, Adolph Zukor, Ernst Lubitsch, Jack Warner, Lewis Milestone and Mary Pickford. The critics dismembered the play: "Coarseness and cheapness of thought and expression . . . concerned with vulgarity . . . tawdry gags and nonplussing commonplaces . . . as silly as it is trite." Columbia Pictures bought it for $40,000. Three years earlier, buoyed by a theatrical hit, Sturges had deplored "the great talent drain" from Broadway to Hollywood and swore that he would not become a part of it.[84] It was not so much a measure of Sturges's disloyalty as of changing conditions that the playwright nevertheless settled permanently in Hollywood in 1933.

A myth to which most film executives subscribed was that a play that had appeared on Broadway was "presold." Somehow, it was believed; the approval of the relatively small and localized audience that attended even a long-running Broadway play made its production as a film less risky. However, it seems more plausible that a Broadway play was presold not to any potential film audience but to the film financiers who lived in New York and patronized the Broadway theater. How else might one explain the wholesale importation of Broadway playwrights, many of whom hated everything about Hollywood except its paychecks and were totally—and often militantly—inept at writing for the screen?

Through the decade of the Thirties, the studios developed increasingly sophisticated ways of obtaining Broadway materials. At first they simply bought plays, increasing from 8 percent of all plays produced during the 1927–28 season to nearly 20 percent the following year. Under the pressure of producing talkies, the studios soon developed elaborate scouting procedures. On opening nights, as many as fifty orchestra seats were occupied by people appraising the play's possibilities for the screen. "No sooner does a new head bob up on Broadway," the producer Brock Pemberton lamented in 1936, "than it is knocked westward by a well-aimed bean bag full of gold." Soon, synopses of as yet unproduced plays were rushed to Hollywood; frequently eight or nine studios would bid for plays before they opened.

The next step, given the lopsided financial health and strength of Broadway and Hollywood, was direct studio financing of theater productions. By the 1935–36 season, one of every four Broadway plays had Hollywood money behind it. The *New York Times* theater critic, Brooks Atkinson, condemned several of that season's plays as "unphotographed scenarios." The playwright Sidney Howard, who was president of the Dramatists Guild (and who had also worked in the movies) worried that the studios' financing of plays would result in "the virtual elimination of plays which do not . . . offer promising picture material."[85]

The criticism stung, but far more painful to the studios was a rule by the Dramatists Guild that forbade Broadway producers to take Hollywood money before a play opened and required them to offer the property for competitive bidding after it opened. In 1936–37, the season after those rules were forced on the producers, the studios boycotted Broadway and began buying plays abroad. "If a play was good," the film writer Walter Reisch recalled, "whether written by a Russian, Swiss or Hungarian, it went to America. Every play in any language that had any . . . chance on the screen was purchased immediately."[86] In 1936, seven major film companies set up a Bureau of New Plays to encourage new playwrights with writing contests, fellowships, and scholarships. But the Dramatists Guild, apparently bent on self-destruction, threatened to bar from membership anyone who accepted a grant from the Bureau. By October 1940 a compromise was worked out: Film companies could obtain screen rights for plays they had financed on Broadway. It was no more than what the studios had asked for from the beginning. But the damage was done: In a five-year period, the number of plays annually produced on Broadway fell from 135 to only sixty-nine in 1940–41.

Many felt that the need to tailor plays for screen adaptation compromised the quality of Broadway productions. By 1938, *Fortune* complained of the theater's preoccupation with "safe" subjects, themes of wide appeal to ignorant audiences, and its avoidance of politically or sexually controversial material. While the studios at that time were not financing Broadway productions, they continued to buy screen rights for plays produced on Broadway. Between 1935–36 and 1939–40, the studios bought one-third of all plays, and the average price paid doubled, to $60,000.[87]

Objectively, there was little reason for confidence that a successful Broadway play would make a successful film; quite the contrary. A Yale drama professor, Allardyce Nicoll, who perceptively compared writing for stage and screen in 1936, complained that "authors write for the screen with their left hand." The technique also differed. "A play demands constant talk," he noted, while "a film requires an absolute minimum of words." There is no more relationship between the two, he argued, than between painting and sculpture or music and poetry.[88]

> "It is as hard to make a toilet seat as a castle window, even though the view is a bit different."—Ben Hecht[89]

One suspects that a good deal of dramatists' and novelists' contempt for Hollywood arose from their incompetence in writing for the screen. J. B. Priestley, who first visited Hollywood in 1931, noticed that "many popular and highly paid authors are useless in film work because the stories they invent do not lend themselves to film treatment, they cannot write dialogue that can be heard with conviction and pleasure and remain ignorant of film techniques." But that perception did not dissuade the popular English novelist and playwright from his intent to "creep quietly into Hollywood . . . and discover if they have anything to offer me . . . some extra money would be welcome."[90] William de Mille noticed that Hollywood's dramatic and literary recruits "seemed to take strange pleasure in their utter ignorance of the medium and its demands." Most of them "regarded their studio experiences as literary slumming and delighted to talk about 'prostitution' of their art, not realizing, poor darlings, that . . . the studios were offering . . . honorable marriage."[91]

Robert Sherwood slung the obligatory abuse at Hollywood, even though he found his screen work artistically as well as financially rewarding. A creative person, he warned in 1932, "must either depart at once, before the California climate dissolves the tissues of his conscience, or he must abandon his idealistic pretensions, settle down to a monotonous diet of the succulent fruits of the lotus and live out his days, in sun-kissed contentment, accomplishing nothing of any enduring importance, taking the immediate cash and letting the eternal credit go."[92] To his mother, Sherwood confided that "the work is interesting," but "the stench of stagnation assails the nostrils. It may be ideal for the natives, but it's no place for a white man."[93]

Despite his success at blending Hollywood and Broadway careers throughout the 1930s, Sherwood remained cruelly ambivalent toward film work. Hollywood to him was "a playground" but also "morally corruptive." Yet he contributed much to the success of such films as *Roman Scandals, The Adventures of Marco Polo,* and *Rebecca.* (In 1945 he won an Oscar for *The Best Years of Our Lives.*) In Britain, he wrote scripts for *The Scarlet Pimpernel* and *The Ghost Goes West.* In his lifetime, in fact, he wrote only eleven plays, as against twenty-two screenplays.

Those intellectuals who blamed Hollywood for corrupting writers while turning out trash usually blamed the studio moguls. The movie makers were "not literary people," one fastidious observer wrote in 1937, they were "not even show people . . . They were furriers, tailors, clothiers, glovers."[94] Their commercial origins supposedly explained the meager intellectual content of the films they produced. Their origins also explained why, as was repeatedly charged, they had so little respect for writers. But movies were not like the stage, where the author was the prime mover, the person whose individual vision and message would be faithfully interpreted by the director and actors. Film was a director's medium. Rouben Mamoulian, whose stage career began at the Moscow Art Theater, realized as he directed his first film that "what intrigued me principally was the style and poetry of the visuals . . . dialogue always remained subservient to the language of visual imagery."[95] The novelists and playwrights who were hired to write for movies were not accustomed to thinking in visual terms, nor could they, in the collaborative system essential to film production, enforce their visions on the director, even if the visions had merit. Thus successful playwrights frequently failed in Hollywood.

But conversely, some mediocre playwrights found their calling in writing for films. Robert Riskin, for example, moved to Hollywood in 1931 after creating two mediocre plays for Broadway. Teamed with the director Frank Capra at Columbia, he wrote a series of extraordinary films, including *It Happened One Night,* for which he won an Oscar in 1934, *Lost Horizon, Mr. Deeds Goes to Town, You Can't Take It With You,* and *Meet John Doe.* Talbot Jennings, a graduate of the Yale Drama School, went west after failing on Broadway and became the author of such successful screen adaptations as *The Good Earth, Mutiny on the Bounty, Marie Antoinette,* and *Northwest Passage.*[96]

Dudley Nichols was one of the few 1930s screenwriters who realized that he was pioneering a new art form and whose enthusiasm, talent, and skill carried him to the summit of that new art. Nichols, a former New York *World* reporter, arrived in Hollywood just when sound came. His vision of the perfect screenplay, he wrote in 1937, was "the complete description of a motion picture and how to accomplish the things described." Having tried such a script, he found that, while the set designer and composer greeted it with "shouts of approval," the producer was unimpressed. Nichols learned to avoid the type of producer "who struts himself . . . who airs his ego constantly." He could afford such an independent stance. Shunning collaborators, he prolifically churned out successful scripts. In four years he wrote eleven screenplays. Then his adaptation of Liam O'Flaherty's *The Informer* won Oscars in 1935 for his screenplay, the direction of John Ford, and the acting of its star, Victor McLaglen. (As for O'Flaherty, who received the usual large sum for the novel and then was brought to Hollywood as a consultant, he repaid the favor by adding a tirade called *Hollywood Cemetery* to the long bookshelf of bad novels flogging the movie colony.) Nichols's sure touch as a scenarist is also evident in such other films as *Mary of Scotland, Bringing Up Baby,* and *Stagecoach.* Yet, despite his thoughtful approach to the art of screenwriting, Nichols discovered that "no talent has had more grudging admission through the studio gates than that of the writer."[97] The crucial difference between a playwright and a screenwriter, Nichols found, was that for the stage one writes action, while the screen requires reaction. The camera "automatically" moves to the receiver of lines, he learned, and it is there, in the reaction, that "the hearts of the audience quiver and open in release, or rock with laughter or shrink with pain."[98]

Screen adaptations of hit plays, classics, or best-sellers, Nichols found, were as difficult to write as original screenplays. Fidelity to an original was deadly for a film, but critics pounced when the film deviated from its source, and producers were hopelessly fickle, blaming the screenwriter for a failed adaptation while lauding the author of a work successfully translated to the screen. In filming *Gone with the Wind,* for example, the producer David O. Selznick was obsessed with using not a single word beyond Margaret Mitchell's dialogue in the original novel. The upshot was that the phalanx of wordsmiths— a grand total of seventeen—who hammered on that particular script were reduced to consulting a home-cobbled concordance to Mitchell's book, dragging dialogue out of context, snipping and paring lines to comply with Selznick's demand. So difficult was the task that the script was still being written after shooting had begun.

Tales about producers' quirky judgments of what audiences wanted are legion. Gabriel Pascal, successful after years devoted to worming the film rights to *Pygmalion* out of George Bernard Shaw, loved to tell how, after the usual nonreading, film executives insisted that the play was too highbrow and too talky, had only enough action for a two-reel short, and— the worst—lacked a happy ending.[99] While such snap judgments appear ludicrous in retrospect, they reflect the real dilemmas of producers, faced with mass production of (theoretically) creative goods. The playwright John Howard Lawson, a radical who was one of the organizers of the Screenwriters Guild, observed that the studio heads applied a good deal of ingenuity to the problem of finding a " 'safe' product" that would also be "so original and so lively that it would attract crowds to the box office." " 'Safe' talents with commercial reputations" often produced lifeless work. But artists of originality and integrity "were difficult to control." Lawson rejects the stereotype of Hollywood as "an industry dominated by stupidity and greed." Though many producers lacked formal education, he believed "they were not unintelligent."[100] But they were subject to many pressures.

Exhibitors, reformers, religious groups, parents, and educators made their own narrow demands on films. Writers, along with directors, were responsible for "all the filth of the pictures," The Most Reverend John J. Cantwell, D.D., charged in 1935. Fully 75 percent of Hollywood writers, he claimed, were "pagans," mostly "living lives of infidelity or worse" and caring nothing "for decency, good taste or refinement."[101] From distributors, too, a persistent critical barrage emanated. No costume picture, such as *Marie Antoinette*, would sell in Manassa, Colorado. *The Great Waltz* was "another headache" to the exhibitor in Ligonier, Indiana. Of a Fred Astaire picture, the theater manager in Fertile, Minnesota, wrote: "Just try to kid the farmers this is entertainment." Better to present a rip-snorting serial; "the devotee of *The Lone Ranger* watches his tenth adventure with the same comfortable ease with which the experienced musician hears a new conductor's reading of Beethoven's 'Seventh Symphony.' "[102] That so many films of any quality were produced during the 1930s in the face of such a relentless lowbrow onslaught is a tribute to the studios. That the studios sought out talented people and tried to utilize their genius is a measure of their desperation for material.

> "The only way to turn out 50 or 60 pictures a year was to start a new one every Monday."—Budd Schulberg[103]

No other art form has an economic structure like films. A book publisher can print a small number of copies of a chancy novel and then simply print more if the book catches on; the author's payment is based on sales. In magazines, radio, or television, the product can be quickly changed or canceled to suit the audience's taste. Even in the theater, whose structure is closest to films, the producer can close the play and thus minimize expenses if the play flops. In films, by contrast, the entire cost accrues at the beginning, and there is no way of altering the product if it fails in the market place. When the product happens to be a totally new art form, like talking pictures, which is undergoing transformation of its economic structure in the midst of a tragic Depression, the producers' nervousness appears inevitable. In this light, the gambling neurosis that afflicted so many movie moguls—and which ruined such geniuses as B. P. Schulberg and David O. Selznick—seems an almost reasonable adaptation to an upside-down reality. The wonder is not that the studios could produce such an avalanche of trash; rather, it is that the flow of trash contained so many gems. Those were often the work of writers who recognized not only the power inherent in a well-made film and the important role that a good writer could play in it, but who remained uncorrupted by Hollywood gold and unintimidated by its producers.

Lillian Hellman, for example, had "a clear-eyed, unworshipful view of Hollywood and its personages." She had worked as a story editor at MGM before being hired by Samuel Goldwyn in 1935, following her Broadway success *The Children's Hour,* and refused to let Goldwyn bully her. Though he reportedly hated aggressive women, Goldwyn lunched with Hellman almost daily in his private dining room; their profane shouting matches were also legendary. On her first assignment, an adaptation of a British play, *The Dark Angel,* the story conferences got nowhere. Hellman, who was receiving an exorbitant $2,000 per week, often napped during those meetings, but when they dragged on for six or seven weeks, she left for New York, not even bidding Goldwyn goodbye. For days she refused to answer the phone. When they did speak, Goldwyn promised her that she could stop talking and start writing. She coyly said she'd think about that, packed up again, and went to Paris. When Goldwyn reached her there a week later, she finally consented to a long-term contract with clauses to allow her to work only on stories she liked at the time and place she chose. Only then did Hellman get back to adapting *The Dark Angel.*

Despite Hellman's independence, or perhaps because of it, Goldwyn bought the screen rights to *The Children's Hour,* though he was warned that the play would probably be rejected by the Hays Office because it dealt with lesbians. "Don't worry," he reportedly said, "we'll make them Americans." In fact, Hellman persuaded Goldwyn that she could adapt the play in a manner that would be approved by the censors. She then changed the romance between two women into a heterosexual affair. The film, directed by William Wyler, was eventually released as *These Three.* Later Hellman wrote the screen adaptations for a number of other of her plays, including *The Little Foxes.* Despite glowing reviews of her screenplays, such was intellectual disdain for Hollywood that Hellman barely mentions that important side of her career in her autobiographies.[104]

S. N. Behrman was another writer who successfully wove lucrative Hollywood excursions into a prolific writing career. He recalled the early Thirties in the film capital as "a halcyon period. . . . There were few places in America where you could go out to dinner with Harpo or Groucho Marx, the Franz Werfels, Leopold Stokowski, Aldous Huxley, Somerset Maugham and George and Ira Gershwin." He was lured to the Coast by the chance to adapt *Liliom* at $1,250 per week, plus the usual de luxe compartment on the Century and the Chief. Behrman's friend, the playwright Arthur Richman, advised him to accept such a pittance for six months only and to demand more thereafter. "They'll be happier with you at $2,000 per week," Richman said. "They don't really believe that a writer they can get for $1,250 can be much good." When *Liliom* was finished, the producer Sol Wurtzel suggested Behrman stay and write adaptations of *Life Begins at 40* and Dante's *Inferno.* "I don't know Dante," Behrman demurred. "You don't have to read it," Wurtzel replied. "I'll show you the silent picture." Returning to his hotel after that conversation, Behrman found a new contract in his room. It was for three years, the pay ascending steeply from $2,000 per week. "I sat at the desk and made a rough estimate of what it would come to if I signed and fulfilled its terms," he remembered. "I stared at the result. It came to about $500,000. The next day I went to Sol's office and turned it down."[105]

Throughout the next decades, however, Behrman continued to write both film adaptations of his plays and original scripts. Though he described Los Angeles as "the abeyance of civilization," he also noted that "to make fun of Hollywood is . . . extremely simple . . . almost without aiming, you may fire and scarcely miss."[106] After four years of "itinerant traffic with the ogres and dragons of Hollywood," he gave little credence to the "blood-curdling accounts of atrocities practiced by the cinema barons on virtuous playwrights and novelists." He had found no evidence, he wrote, "of intellectual handcuffs and straitjackets in the cubicles assigned to visiting writers." Instead, he blamed the visitors for much of the mediocrity of films, asserting that screenwriting is "supremely difficult and elusive."[107] "The great freedom of pictures," he wrote in 1934, "the fact that you can go anywhere, is boring and harassing, like a perpetual picnic."[108] And yet, despite his spirited defense of Hollywood, Behrman continued to harbor qualms about the time he spent there. At the age of seventy-seven, lying in a hospital recovering from a stroke, he reproached himself: "I should have devoted that time . . . to studying Latin and Greek."[109]

> The writer . . . develops a sense of guilt about his "betrayal" of his talents and his intelligence. He becomes guilty about the amount of money he is receiving for work for which he has no respect. He cannot suppress the self-indicting feeling that he ought to be writing "something significant."—Leo Rosten[110]

A number of contemporary observers noticed the self-contempt endemic among screenwriters. A USC psychologist who interviewed one hundred studio writers in 1935 concluded that though they were paid $500 to $2,500 a week, all felt themselves undervalued.[111] Perhaps their perception was correct to the extent that they were not treated to the gushing publicity and unfettered adulation poured over movie stars and, to a lesser degree, directors. The more than three hundred Hollywood correspondents who relayed every filmic burp and snuffle to a breathless world seldom mentioned the men and women who wrote the movies. Hardly a book dealing with the history or craft of filmmaking mentions writers. A popular anthology of 1937 that purported to give the inside story of films contained two chapters about film critics and not a word about writers.[112] Critics frequently omitted writers' names; even so sensitive a reviewer as Graham Greene, who commented on films for *The Spectator* avoided mentioning a single writer during his five-year tenure.[113]

The offices assigned to all but the most stellar writers were cramped and isolated. The commissary tables at which they lunched frequently hugged the walls, while stars and directors sat in the central limelight. At a story conference, Raymond Chandler raged, Hollywood wants "a writer who is ready to commit suicide . . . What it actually gets is the fellow who screams like a stallion in heat and then cuts his throat with a banana. The scream demonstrates the artistic purity of his soul and he can eat the banana while somebody is answering the telephone call about some other picture."[114] Nor did the studios treat writers with the respect they longed for after the script was written. Writers were seldom permitted to visit the sets where their screenplays were being filmed. "We weren't even allowed to go to our previews," Julius Epstein lamented. "It took a strike to win that right." Epstein and his brother, also a writer, had once disguised themselves as hillbillies to attend the preview of a film they had written.[115] Chandler was infuriated, a few years later, when the first screenplay he wrote was nominated for an Oscar, "but I was not even invited to the press preview held right in the studio."[116]

The problem with looking at Hollywood writers as a group is that the word "writer" encompasses such a broad spectrum of talents. Among the hundreds who called themselves writers in Hollywood, only a few had anything to say, whether in film or in any other medium. To question such a group about its aspirations is like asking staff members of a large newspaper or public relations agency about their ambitions. Only a few would match the will with the ability to produce great literature, though many would voice such a goal. Few great novels and plays of the Thirties have survived, perhaps fewer than films of the period. The contempt for Hollywood so freely expressed by the New York literary establishment often harbors an edge of fear, a denunciation so shrill that one questions the motivation of those voicing it. Edmund Wilson, for example, even seized upon "the void of the vast Pacific . . . the surf that rolls up on the beach with a beat that seems expressionless after the moody assaults of the Atlantic."[117]

Was Hollywood the graveyard of talent? The answer has as many facets as the definition of talent. Many writers indeed gave up other genres after coming to Hollywood. But the reasons varied. Some, like Dorothy Parker, were such characteristic voices for an era—in her case, the Twenties—that they simply had nothing further to say. It was easy to blame the corrupting effect of writing for the screen when, in fact, the writer simply didn't care any more for the hard work of setting words on paper. Some others, like Herman Mankiewicz, became so entrapped by the luxury of the film colony that they wished to say nothing further. Still others, like Nunnally Johnson and Preston Sturges, were creatively so much more successful in Hollywood than they had been previously that it was obvious they had found their métier. A melancholy subgroup comprises such playwrights as John Howard Lawson and Donald Ogden Stewart, whose financial success and obvious skill as screenwriters foundered on radical politics. Both men were clearly enthusiastic about their work on films but were unable to enjoy what they thought was too easy money.

For many other writers, Hollywood was a golden life preserver during difficult economic times. Faulkner felt no bitterness; rather, he was grateful to take large chunks of movie money home to Mississippi, where his serious writing took place. Wodehouse, Huxley, and Priestley had no compunction about collecting Hollywood cash when the income from other writing enterprises dwindled. All of them had no notion of how to write for films, but they tried to contribute. Passing through a fabulous place, they observed it from the fringes, took what sustenance they could, and moved on.

Among those who found success in films as well as other genres, there were two groups. One, including Robert Sherwood and Maxwell Anderson, worked successfully on numerous films but moaned about the moral implications of their movie work. Few indeed were the successful writers who took pride in the work they did for films. Hellman, Hecht, and Behrman represent the steady professionals who garnered huge sums from writing screenplays, but insisted on choosing what they would work on, where they would work, and how the work would be done. All three were notable for maintaining their integrity, refusing to work on trash, cogently arguing their position, and, if necessary, leaving Hollywood to pursue other creative work.

Nathanael West is often cited as a writer whose work on "B" movies soured his literary talent. But West wrote painfully and slowly before he went west; the spiritual emptiness that characterizes his masterpiece about Hollywood, *The Day of the Locust,* is also apparent in his New York newspaper novel, *Miss Lonelyhearts.* [118] Those who knew him in New York, no less than his Hollywood friends, recalled a solitary eccentric who had difficulty keeping his life together. Nevertheless, West's tragic death in an automobile accident in 1940 is more often ascribed to the alleged torments he suffered in Hollywood than to his acknowledged ineptitude as a driver.

A good deal of the bitterness about how Hollywood treated writers arose from a reality that dawned slowly upon moviemakers: that film was not a writer's but a director's medium. Directing was an art so different from writing, however, that it was impossible to get along without writers. A perusal of the memoirs and autobiographies written by the best directors of the Thirties makes it quite clear that few of them could assemble on paper anything but exhausted clichés and limp prose. Their forte was film, the visual thrust to the audience's gut. But before the cameras could roll, there had to be a script, any script. The abler directors, like John Ford, welcomed the work of talented writers, and the results were great film classics like *The Informer* and *The Grapes of Wrath.* But many other film triumphs resulted from the director's molding of mediocre material into a stunning movie. Josef von Sternberg, for example, brilliantly adapted *The Blue Angel* from Heinrich Mann's indifferent novel, *Professor Unrath.*

Not even the studio heads realized, in the mad monkeyhouse of mass-producing entertainment, that writing films was a specialized art. While they paid handsomely for plays, novels, and even short stories, and then again for the costly and inefficient system of preparing scripts, no one dreamed of training professional screenwriters. While the Academy of Motion Picture Arts and Sciences in 1929 established a school, supervised by Irving Thalberg, to train personnel in the new sound techniques, not a single writer was among the six hundred students.[119] Not being readers, the executives viewed writers as "itinerant, barely respectable odd-job men on the movie assembly line."[120]

> Screenwriting: a horrible ordeal in which sadistic producers torture you almost beyond endurance by holding your jaws open while they drop a monotonously maddening succession of gold dollars into your helpless mouth.—Harry Kurnitz[121]

Of all the brickbats rained on the studios by aggrieved writers, not one complained of niggardliness. Leo Rosten, who scrutinized the film colony as though it were an atoll of aborigines in his classic *Hollywood: The Movie Colony, The Movie Makers,* found that in 1938, seventeen Hollywood writers earned more than $75,000. Having studied the payrolls of three major studios, he concluded that almost 60 percent of their writers earned more than $250 a week and 13 percent received more than $1,000 weekly. The Screen Writers Guild, in fact, refused to allow Rosten to publish the results of a questionnaire detailing writers' earnings for fear, presumably, that the facts would jeopardize negotiations with the studios.[122] The precise amount spent by studios for writers is difficult to calculate, but the anthropologist Margaret Thorp noted in 1939 that about 7 percent of a typical high-budget feature film's expenditure of $1 million went for story preparation, on top of 5 percent for purchase of the story. Writers thus collected roughly 12 percent of the money spent on a film, about the same as the amount allotted for sets and art directors (12.5 percent), more than the director (10 percent) and about half the amount budgeted for the cast (25 percent).[123] When one considers that in 1940 Hollywood turned out more than 450 major films and had 340 writers under contract, the infusion of capital, if you will, into the literary world was staggering; one wonders how literature and theater would have survived the Depression without it.[124]

Why the studios so generously gathered talented writers remains a complex question. In some cases, one suspects, it was pure vanity. Just as Louis B. Mayer enjoyed staying overnight at the Hoover White House and being driven through Hollywood in a block-long Dusenberg, so his vanity was tickled by being the employer of the great F. Scott Fitzgerald, even an aging, unproductive Fitzgerald, even a Fitzgerald who was totally inept at writing films. And it probably did no harm in justifying studio expenses to the New York financiers to point to a famous novelist as working on this or that current film. The playwrights paid so prolifically for their Hollywood labors, moreover, were familiar names to the New York executives. A success on Broadway inevitably brought rich Hollywood offers to the author, no matter that he lacked the ability or even inclination to write a screenplay. On the writer's side, the big offer appealed powerfully to his vanity, and many believed, along with Clifford Odets, that "the movies have taken over the field of entertainment . . . the theater . . . has dwindled to a little squeak that sometimes, but not often, sounds like something cultural."[125]

Believing in such a myth and, even worse, believing that the writer was the key figure in films caused the fiercest condemnation of Hollywood when the truth came out. But the hostility to Hollywood was so diffused that it is difficult to pin down exactly what was considered most horrendous about it. Was it the setting—that "sprawling stucco and neon landscape set precariously in a land of drought, flood and earthquake"?[126] Or the climate, "strangely enervating sunshine which seems to produce flowers without scent and fruit without flavor"?[127] Was it the isolation, "in the middle of a barbarically provincial non-city . . . as if all British films were

made in Tanganyika"?[128] Perhaps it was the quirky crowd,
"which banks in Romanesque churches, eats in derby hats,
opens a fruitstand with searchlights and sirens, gets gas from
polar bears or Cleopatra's Needle."[129]

But then, the people also offered tempting targets: Bernie
Hyman, one of three top executives at MGM, whom the poet
Samuel Hoffenstein described as "like a glass of water without
the glass";[130] the producer who was working with Salka Viertel
on a picture with a Chinese background and who insisted
on calling Confucius "Vesuvius";[131] and Harry Rapf, MGM's
head of production, who, Herman Mankiewicz said, had
"bought a lovely piece of English suiting which will be made
into a jacket especially waterproofed for eating chicken soup
in the MGM commissary." Again and again, the critique rang
a distinctly anti-Semitic note. The film industry's founding
fathers were "a glove salesman, the sons of a butcher, a
bouncer at an amusement park, two furriers, an upholsterer,
two clothing merchants, a jeweler and two drugstore owners,"
while the current studio heads, Mankiewicz said, were "piss-
ants, ragpickers, blintze brains and Jew tailors."[132] *Fortune*
in 1932 described the MGM scenario chief, Samuel Marx, as
"an intelligent Hebrew with a Neanderthal forehead."[133]
George Jean Nathan bemoaned the fate of his beloved theater
at the hands of "Jews who had previously been engaged in
mercantile pursuits."[134]

Of course, a large percentage of studio executives were Jewish, so many that Leslie Fiedler extravagantly called movies
"a creation of Jewish ingenuity and surplus Jewish capital, a
by-product of the Jewish garment industry which began by
blurring away class distinction in dress and ended by blotting
out class distinction in dreams."[135] But if the studios were
dominated by Jews, those executives had already traveled a
long road toward assimilation into American culture. Budd
Schulberg poignantly describes the generational chasm he saw
in the early Thirties when his grandparents arrived from New
York to live in Hollywood:

> Grandfather's friends were the fathers of the other studio
> heads: Old Man Mayer, Old Man Warner, Old Man Cohn and
> so on, all of them from the same Old World mold, all of them
> aged anachronisms in their dark suits and long beards, with

Yiddish as their daily speech and Hebrew for their daily prayers. All of them were mystified that from their loins had sprung
such unlikely offspring as a loud, wise-cracking, sports-jacketed
Jack Warner; a profane, irreverent, mob-oriented strongman
like Harry Cohn; or a crafty ambitious power broker like Louis
Mayer. . . . Somehow the seed of the Old World had produced
these brash, amoral, on-the-make Americans. The sons with
their bankrolls and their girlfriends and their "fuck you's"
would tolerate and humor these old men as relics of the past.[136]

In the light cast by this vignette, the producers' profligate
hiring of great writers begins to make sense. Immigrants and
the sons of immigrants, poorly educated and rich beyond their
wildest dreams, the moguls still felt the pull of the Jewish
tradition of learning and culture. Writers were not the only
victims of the golden guilt gushing from Hollywood's easy
money; studio owners felt its pangs as well. To have a great
writer on the payroll was more than a way of selling the studio's product to the public or to the New York bankers; it
was also a good deed, a *mitzvah*. The luster of genius, even
failed and unproductive genius, like Fitzgerald; even mysterious and incomprehensible genius, like Faulkner, shed its glow
over the compost pit of Hollywood's pedestrian productions.

Nor did the studio moguls' virtue go unrewarded; it proved
profitable as well. Screenplays written or adapted by imported
writers collected Academy Award nominations or Oscars almost every year during the Thirties (and through the Forties
as well). Among them were George Abbott and Maxwell Anderson in 1929–30, with *All Quiet on the Western Front;* Donald Ogden Stewart for *Laughter* in 1930–31; Sidney Howard's
adaptation of *Arrowsmith* and Samuel Hoffenstein's screenplay for *Dr. Jekyll and Mr. Hyde* in 1931–32; Charles Mac-
Arthur for *Rasputin and the Empress* in 1932–33; Ben Hecht
for *Viva Villa* in 1934; Sidney Howard for *Dodsworth* in 1936;
Marc Connelly for *Captains Courageous* and Dorothy Parker
for *A Star Is Born* in 1937; John Howard Lawson for *Blockade*
in 1938; Sidney Howard again for *Gone With the Wind* in
1939; and Bella and Samuel Spewack for *My Favorite Wife*
and Robert Sherwood for *Rebecca* in 1940.[137] Hollywood films
would have been barren indeed without such contributions.

The historian Richard Hofstadter has observed that "it appears . . . to be the fate of intellectuals either to berate their exclusion from wealth, success and reputation or to be seized by guilt when they overcome this exclusion."[138] The long roster of masterpieces by writers who mocked and excoriated Hollywood bears that out. But the record also shows that inside the blizzard of tinsel, from under the blanket of flim-flam, the genuine talent glowed, though appreciation of it would for decades lie dormant. Daniel Fuchs is a novelist who labored in the writers' hutches of Hollywood during the Thirties. "It is a foolish scandal," he would write in 1962, "that we have the habit of deriding these men and their industry. . . . They were a gaudy company, rambunctious and engrossed. What they produced, roistering along in those sun-filled, sparkling days, was a phenomenon teeming with vitality and ardor, as indigenous as our cars or skyscrapers or highways. . . . It's time someone came clean and said so."[139]

LIFE

WORLD'S FAIR: "AMERICAN BEAUTIES"

MARCH 13, 1939   **10** CENTS

3

GIVE ME MEN TO MATCH MY MEDIA: THE PRINT EMPIRES

PUNY, LACKLUSTER AND EXHAUSTED, *Literary Digest* appeared for the last time on February 19, 1938. Despite its 250,000 subscribers, the magazine had starved to death after half a century, the victim of an advertising famine that had reduced its paid space to less than two pages out of twenty-four. Only a year earlier, *Literary Digest* had absorbed the sober, respected *Review of Reviews,* established in 1891. In 1932 *Review of Reviews* had itself merged with another veteran of American periodical publishing, *World's Work,* founded in 1900. Nor were those the only long-established publications to expire during the Thirties. The necrology includes *Century,* 1881–1930; *The Outlook,* 1867–1932; *Judge,* 1881–1932; *Delineator,* 1873–1937; *Scribner's,* 1870–1939; and *Forum,* 1887–1940.

Like *Literary Digest,* some of the doomed periodicals achieved a brief remission by swallowing a colleague or two. Thus, *Forum* absorbed *Current History,* then merged with *Century* before death came. And *Scribner's* had ingested *Commentator* before giving up the ghost.[1] Others were felled in the bloom of seeming health: *Woman's World* perished in October 1940 at the age of thirty-nine, despite a circulation of 1,500,000 farm women, more readers than it had had since the First World War. "We have given our readers a full measure of good, clean, wholesome editorial matter," its publisher, Walter W. Manning, had bragged in 1931, "believing always that the home, church and patriotism were a better diet than sex, sophistication and sensationalism." But advertisers were skeptical. At the bier, *Tide,* the leading advertising publication, noted that while the magazine's circulation had been pushed "by one means or another . . . advertising was harder to needle"; *Woman's World* did not "offer readers the sort of book [magazine] that any considerable advertisers wanted to be represented in."[2]

In the best of times, the magazine world is precarious, a Darwinian melée for advertisers, for subscribers, for space on newsstands, fought inside the iron ring of deadlines, printing schedules, and cost control. So the Depression might well be blamed for the fevers that carried away so many periodicals during the Thirties. Total circulations of magazines audited by the independent Audit Bureau of Circulations dropped but slightly in 1934 from the previous high of 80 million in 1930, then rose steadily to pass 100 million in 1942. While circulation held, advertising revenue plunged from almost $200 million aggregate in 1929 to just under $100 million in 1931, then lurched upward through the decade, reaching $200 million again only in 1942.[3] Of the publications that entered this long, dark tunnel, many vanished and few emerged unchanged.

In 1925 the Curtis Publishing Co., an empire whose flagship, *The Saturday Evening Post,* traced its lineage—tendentiously—to a newspaper founded in 1728 by Benjamin Franklin,[4] had distributed one of the largest stock dividends in history, some $70 million in preferred went to holders of 900,000 shares. By 1930 Curtis's net income had fallen to $19.1 million, and two years later it had sunk to $5.5 million. Despite those reverses, George Horace Lorimer, the editor who since 1897 had brewed the *Post*'s reliable formula of folksy fiction and flimsy fact and who had become Curtis's president in 1931, ordered no changes in the magazine's format or content. Violently anti–New Deal and stunned by the

1936 Roosevelt landslide, he perceived tardily that "somewhere America had turned a corner that he had missed and that his world was ended." He resigned on January 1, 1937.[5]

Lorimer blamed evil political gales off the Potomac, but the winds shaking the house of Curtis originated in profound changes in American society and the way goods were marketed and sold. As late as 1928, John D. Rockefeller's publicist, Ivy Lee, asked the movie magnate Jesse L. Lasky how he spent his spare time. Lasky replied that he read *The Saturday Evening Post* to see what kinds of stories Americans liked to read so as to produce movies in a similar vein. Lee then asked the same question of editor Lorimer, who answered that he went to the movies to learn what types of stories appealed to audiences.[6]

But just as Lasky's silent films were destroyed by sound in a three-year span, so Lorimer's rural vision of America became as outdated as his rocking-chair intuition about what readers wanted. And while he fumed about "that man in the White House," a fresh group of publications unlike any others ever published arrived at news racks and in mailboxes. Some, like *Time, Reader's Digest,* and *The New Yorker,* were founded during the Twenties and flourished through Depression. Others, like *Fortune* and *Life,* sailed boldly into the economic storm after 1929 and emerged as undreamed-of media giants. The changes the editor Lorimer missed had been blurred by the *Post*'s heroic subscription efforts: legions of clean-cut young men earnestly working their way through college door-to-door and packs of ragged urchins hawking the magazine on street corners for five cents. The new magazines charged more and did not engage in high-pressure sales. Nor did they attempt to publish something for everybody, the formula that had served Lorimer for some forty years. To the contrary, they sharply angled their content for a specific population, attracting an astonishingly loyal readership, an audience that saw itself as a community. Yet the older magazines might have survived—after all, America was still growing rapidly— if the advent of the new magazines had not also concided with a revolution in the advertising business.

Advertising agencies had begun as simple middlemen, collecting a commission for preparing and placing advertisements in the media their clients selected. But soon after World War I, advertisers began badgering agencies with questions: Who saw my ad? What kinds of ads are memorable? Where should I advertise? Like Lorimer of the *Post*, agencies had long operated purely on intuition; now their creativity was being challenged by scientific questions. "Under present conditions of ignorance on choosing media . . . all the buyer can do . . . is to make a more or less intelligent guess as to what media are best for him to use," Thomas L. Greer, assistant manager of the J. Walter Thompson agency (JWT), wrote to professors at leading business schools in 1921. "There is an appalling amount of firing wide of the mark."[7]

So pressing was Greer's problem that within two years a horde of JWT investigators was quizzing thousands of Cincinnati subscribers to forty-four magazines as to marital status, income, and occupation. The study divided respondents into three groups, based on occupation but clearly implying income and social status: Group 1, executives, professionals, merchants, and commercial travelers; Group 2, clerical workers and skilled workmen, and Group 3, unskilled workers, domestics, teamsters, and the like. Thus, advertisers began to glimpse whom their ads reached, while agencies stepped beyond simple guesswork in evaluating media. Magazines gave little overt notice to the research, but in the field of advertising the Cincinnati study was considered a landmark; it won the Harvard Advertising Award for 1923.[8]

The implications of that pioneering market study went far beyond peddling extra cigarettes and razor blades. If one could learn what kinds of people ate Grape Nuts or smoked Sweet Caporals, one could custom-tailor advertising to entice large cohorts of new customers. To that end, JWT hired a founder of behavioral psychology, John B. Watson, whose task was to find the advertising appeals that would turn new products into household necessities through advertising. By that route, such luxuries as tooth paste, face cream, toilet paper, mouth wash, shaving cream, and deodorant marched into the American bathroom.

Advertising agencies raced to include the new research methods in their sales armamentarium; their interviewers combed rural areas to ask about stoves and heating systems, to ask who used biscuit mix and who still made soap. Up rutted rural lanes, to the carved portals of suburban mansions, through stinking tenement hallways surveyors trudged, learning that it was "not impossible to enter the home and engage the housewife in conversation for an hour or longer" and thereby discover that, while most women "had not analyzed their methods of skin care," each one enjoyed discussing "her peculiar problem." So crucial were such trivialities to many manufacturers that in 1924 J. Walter Thompson conducted a consumer survey for one client involving twenty cities in nine states, some 1,390 interviews conducted over an eight-week period. The same client also commissioned a survey of 466 dealers scattered over twenty-seven cities in thirteen states.[9]

In the summer and fall of 1924, J. Walter Thompson's research department descended on ten representative American counties to be surveyed in depth for the agency's most ambitious study yet. This time, the survey was not commissioned by a client but was financed by JWT itself as a pure research effort, to learn how Americans lived at the most basic level. The first area studied was Randolph County, Indiana, just 10 miles west of Muncie, the city that four years later Robert and Helen Lynd would study as *Middletown*. A squadron of interviewers visited every store in the county, noting what brands were carried and the sales of each. For 808 consumers who were vaguely representative, they filled in a nine-page questionnaire, including answers to "Do you eat yeast?" and "Do you use home-made cheese?"[10]

The architect of this and many more complex studies that followed was the JWT Research Director, Paul T. Cherington. He had been the Harvard Business School's first professor of marketing for a dozen years before joining the advertising agency in 1922. Lecturing on the new science of "marketing research" in the JWT assembly room, he taught copywriters and account executives about the capricious ways people spent their money and how his questionnaires helped to pierce those mysteries. In rimless glasses and high starched collar, and with all three buttons firmly fastened on his tweed jacket, Cherington and the behaviorist Watson were the advance guard of an army of academics who brought more or less scientific methods to advertising. Cherington continued teaching occasionally at Stanford, Harvard, and NYU while pursuing his research—at a princely salary—at JWT. He became the first president of the American Marketing Association in 1931 and in the same year formed a consulting firm, which would travel into realms undreamed of when Cherington first sent his interviewers into Indiana farm kitchens to ask: "Do you bake your own bread?"[11]

The work of Cherington and his colleagues revolutionized the advertising business during the Twenties and contributed much to making JWT the world's largest advertising agency. But news of those detailed consumer studies had little impact on the magazine industry. As late as 1928, a lengthy article about American magazines fretted over the lack of magazine data. A single book and a few sketchy essays were about all that had been written on the subject, J. E. Drewry wrote in the *Sewanee Review.* He wondered whether readers of "hundreds of magazines . . . have any real reason for reading [them] or do they continue to buy them because of some vague notion that they contain the kind of stories they like?"[12] Calvin Coolidge may have thought in 1926 that "advertising ministers to the spiritual side of trade," promoting "the regeneration and redemption of mankind,"[13] but most magazine editors thought it a necessary nuisance, and many serious periodicals published scathing attacks on it.

"Excessive scientific advertising takes undue advantage of the public," the sociologist Gordon B. Hancock protested in 1926, citing its blatant appeal to the instincts, rather than to reason. Thus, "the guard of the average man is lowered and he is peculiarly exposed to the subtle psychological thrusts and parries of the advertiser"; the insidious pulling power of the ad is not balanced by "a scientific 'resisting power.'" He feared that untrammeled advertising would promote crime by awakening desires that could be fulfilled only by antisocial means.[14]

"Advertising is the really effective literature of this age," Wilson Follett argued sarcastically in 1929. "The tenth muse—

Advertas," was supplying the masses with "evidence of a standard of life unlike their own and, they assume, superior—superior not because it is more free, more leisured, more humanely rich in content, but because it is more conspicuously irresponsible, debonair and spendthrift." The details of "this romantically superior life—its trappings and background, its dress, its drinks, its acceptable standards of speech and writing, its notions of etiquette, its code of conduct and set of social and intellectual interests," Follett wrote, "has come to be, to three-quarters of America, the principal guidance toward what is worthwhile, what is worth mental house-room."[15]

The fear that advertising would seduce the masses was one corner of a deeper terror that had possessed the bourgeoisie ever since mass society had elbowed onto the historical stage in the nineteenth century. Psychologists, including Sigmund Freud, had anxiously pondered the meaning of crowds. The chief civic argument for universal education had not been that it offered individual fulfillment but rather that it somehow inoculated the masses against the upsetting, dangerous milling about that they were prone to. The comfortable classes had witnessed in photos and films a maddened throng storming the Winter Palace in St. Petersburg and the self-proclaimed rule of the proletariat installed there; mobs of French soldiers refusing to fight at Verdun; a revolution barely contained in postwar Germany; the sedate English society immobilized by a general strike in 1926. In America, an endless stream of unfathomable foreigners had poured through Ellis Island, only to clot and swarm in city slums. The rhetoric of the melting pot was one thing, but the reality of deprived, hot-eyed, gibbering men and passive, bundled women was alarming. And what of the internal migrants, marchers in the gathering parade out of rural hills and valleys and into mill towns and railroad hubs and metropolises? How could that mindless multitude be tamed?

It was a question that disturbed many leading minds, perhaps none more articulately than the Spanish philosopher José Ortega y Gasset. In *The Revolt of the Masses,* published in 1930, he reflected grimly on the "one fact which, whether for good or ill, is of utmost importance in the public life of

Europe at the present moment . . . the accession of the masses to complete social power." That disaster, Ortega y Gasset argued, had been foreseen by the greatest nineteenth-century philosophers: " 'The masses are advancing,' said Hegel in apocalyptic fashion. 'Without some new spiritual influence, our age, which is a revolutionary age, will produce a catastrophe,' was the pronouncement of Comte. 'I see a flood-tide of nihilism rising,' shrieked Nietzsche from a crag in the Engadine." By the 1920s, the Spanish philosopher saw "the multitude . . . in possession of the places and the instruments created by civilization." Even in the intellectual milieu "one can note the progressive triumph of the pseudo-intellectual, unqualified, unqualifiable, and, by their very mental texture, disqualified." Thus, Western culture "has been left without a moral code. It is not that mass man has thrown over an antiquated one in exchange for a new one, but that at the centre of his scheme of life there is precisely the aspiration to live without conforming to any moral code."[16]

Abstract philosophical musings did not often occupy the man who would become the most potent (to use one of his favorite words) media tycoon (to use another) in American history. But when Henry Luce read *Revolt of the Masses* in 1932, he found a moral framework for the vocation that had made him a millionnaire before he had reached the age of thirty. In Europe, as Ortega y Gasset emphasized, the masses had overrun traditional elites. But America, which Luce adored with the passion of a man born abroad, would escape the European debacle, the publisher maintained, because its businessmen were a class "especially qualified . . . to lead and assume the role of the moral and intellectual elite."[17] The business elite would be pragmatic, not wooly-minded like the European intellectual elite, and it would have no qualms about using advertising to persuade the unruly masses that salvation lay in serving the right brand of whisky. Then Luce's magazines could bring enlightenment to all.

The son of a Presbyterian missionary, Luce was born in Tengchow, China, in 1898. He was schooled by his mother at home up to the age of ten, then sent to a sadistic parody of an English public school at Chefoo, where boys were birched and caned so routinely that Luce repressed most of his memories of it. Once, Luce was flogged simply for asking about flogging. Yet again, he was whipped for insisting that Ohio was not pronounced "O-hee-o." He may well have sublimated some of his rage at such treatment into militant patriotism and grandiose daydreams. On Independence Day, 1912, he wrote his parents in chagrin that "the Fourth of July passed without a note to sound the glories of our day." Of his own ambition at the age of fourteen, he wrote, "I would like to be Alexander if I were not Socrates."[18]

When Luce arrived in 1913 as a scholarship boy at Hotchkiss, a posh prep school in Connecticut, he was immediately marked as different. He knew no American slang. He wore "a suit oddly tailored by a Chinese who had studied the general drift of American styles in an old magazine illustration." And he stammered. The previous year he had been sent alone to a cathedral grammar school in St. Albans, near London, where the headmaster had a reputation for curing speech defects. But after five unsuccessful months, young Henry wrote home that he was heading for Switzerland to learn French. Then he embarked on a self-designed Grand Tour, visiting Florence, Bologna, Milan, Verona, and Venice on a budget of sixty-three dollars. His fifteenth birthday he spent alone at the Forum in Rome.[19]

Later, Luce said that he detested waiting on tables and cleaning classrooms at Hotchkiss to earn his scholarship, but he was not humiliated. Unlike most of his classmates, who thought the school "a purgatory to be endured between the Christmas, Easter and summer vacations," Luce, after the ordeal that had passed for education at Chefoo, was pleased to find his hard work rewarded with high grades and the grudging esteem of his classmates. Surely he was also impressed by headmaster Hubert Gray Buehler's annual sermon: "There is only one rule in this school: Be a gentleman." Some fifteen years later, asked to define "tycoon," a word coined by *Time,* he said it referred to "a gentleman owing his fortune to a genius adaptable to the age and a careful education and rigorous apprenticeship; a cultivated citizen of the world [who] will take in a few less leg shows and a little more literature."[20]

The description fitted Luce himself as it differentiated him from his friend, rival, future business partner—and the real inventor of the word "tycoon"—Britton Hadden. Luce's classmate at Hotchkiss and later at Yale, Hadden was an eccentric genius whose flamboyant personality contrasted sharply with Luce's earnest, dutiful demeanor. A cossetted only child who dictated stories and poems to his mother before he could read, Hadden was comfortably raised in New York. His mother, widowed soon after his birth, was remarried when he was six to a physician who adopted and deeply cared for the youngster. Spontaneous and extroverted, Britton's intensely competitive streak provoked the equally competitive Luce. "Chink" Luce may have graduated at the head of the Greek class and scored highest in the nation in the Greek college boards, but Hadden would use his Greek in the most creative manner. When they graduated, Hadden won the Senior Declamation competition by reciting "Casey at the Bat"; Luce won the contest for extemporaneous speaking with "Things Learned Outside the Classroom."[21]

The rivalry that glued their peculiar friendship continued at Yale, where they vied successfully for two of the four places on the *Yale Daily News.* To Luce, it was so crucial that he cabled his parents in China: "Successful." Hadden saw it as a lark and taunted Luce's gravity: "Look out, Harry," Brit would shout across campus, "you'll drop the college." Elected *Daily News* chairman, Hadden instigated a vicious exchange of letters between "Divinity Student" and "Old Hatchet Face," both fictitious. Luce, meanwhile, wrote home that he most prided himself "on my small share in pushing Yale to a more intensive war-training."[22]

The war, of course, was already raging in Europe, and by the fall of 1917 Luce and Hadden were drafted. Together they took OCS training; together they learned that their orders for Europe were canceled by the armistice; together they returned to Yale, their relationship more intense than ever. Luce made Phi Beta Kappa. Both made Skull and Bones. When they graduated in 1920, Hadden was voted "most likely to succeed," while Luce was named "most brilliant." Of their relationship, Hadden said "It is like a race. No matter how hard I run, Luce is always there." Luce remarked that "If I can convince Hadden, I know my idea is good."[23]

College inspired the magazine idea Luce and Hadden evolved over the next two years. "People talk too much about what they do not know," the prospectus for what was first called *Facts* asserted, because "no publication has adapted itself to the time busy men are able to spend simply keeping informed." The magazine would be an educational institution, "interested—not in how much it includes between its covers— but in HOW MUCH IT GETS OFF ITS PAGES INTO THE MINDS OF READERS." Their Yale contacts yielded the $86,000 in stock purchases which enabled Luce and Hadden, on March 3, 1923, to produce a flimsy twenty-four-page sheet, now called *Time*. In the organization of its pages, the magazine paralleled the organization of the campus its two young founders had so recently left; among its departments were drama, music, science, art, law, finance, religion, sports, literature, and medicine, as well as current affairs, domestic and foreign. "Curt, clear, concise," *Time* described itself, but beyond brevity, it provided its readers with an entertaining "pony" or "crib-sheet" on the course of the day's news.

But most collegiate—if not downright sophomoric—was the quirky style that Hadden imposed on the infant publication. "As it must to all men, death came last week to . . ." headed the obituaries. The surprise is that the maddeningly bizarre style in which he cloaked rewrites of newspaper clippings attracted such extraordinarily loyal readers. Hadden may have seized on the use of Homeric double-barreled adjectives as an obscure revenge against Luce, the best Greek scholar in Yale history, but his readers eagerly swallowed the perky, irreverent, confidential, feisty way *Time* dealt with the events of the day.

Before Hadden died of a strep infection in 1929, he had peppered the magazine's pages with twin adjectival shotgun blasts like blubber-lipped, black-bereted, weed-whiskered, multi-chinned and kraut-liveried. That those descriptives often attached to the politically potent or the socially grand delighted his growing and enthusiastic audience. He treated readers as "members of a small and intimate circle of admirers," perhaps a fraternity, to whom the magazine's jargon "resembled a code or cryptogram." In his restless addiction to originality, Hadden had also plumbed the remotest crannies of the Thesaurus. Seeking to describe a powerful industrialist, Hadden mercifully had discarded "hospodar," "beglerbeg" and "three-tailed bashaw," but he had no qualms about moloch, mameluke, potentate, oligarch, shogun, and, of course, the tycoon, be he snaggle-toothed, moose-tall, bug-eyed, eagle-beaked, rat-faced, or hog-fat.[24]

Henry Seidel Canby, their English professor at Yale, had advised the two young publishers that their prospective publication required a style "which will exactly suit your purposes." But the scholarly mentor must have swallowed hard upon reading, in a story about Leon Trotsky: "Criticism to the left of him, enmity to the right of him, jealousy in front of him, the Red Army behind him, a high fever within him, all tried to blight him. He resolved to take a trip to the Caucasus."[25] After 1927, Hadden also began to experiment with compound words: Tom Mixture, infernoise, politricks, Vanderbilge, twinsults, filmen, Hindenburglary, socialite, and a whole series on the movies: cinemactor, cinemoppet, cinemalefactors, cinemerger, cinemasses. To an English critic that verbiaxing made "a sentence [that] looks like a railroad accident." It struck the columnist Westbrook Pegler, no mean word-slinger himself, as "a nervous disease of the typewriter."[26] But readers responded by renewing their subscriptions, and eventually *Time* even found a scholarly defender. "The really significant linguistic achievement of the magazine," the linguist Joseph J. Firebaugh wrote in 1940, "is the adaptation of the language, through elements already within it, to the expression of two great democratic ideals—disrespect for authority and reverence for success."[27]

Time's extravagant style clothed a spindly skeleton of fact. Having no correspondents, it blithely rewrote other publications, principally the *New York Times,* in reliance on a 1918 Supreme Court ruling that news older than twenty-four hours was in the public domain.[28] (Luce expressed his gratitude in 1926, when he called the *Times* "the world's greatest unedited newspaper.")[29] Nor did *Time* employ writers with special training beyond what four college years (preferably Yale) imparted. Clearly, it was the impious, extravagant style and departmental format that captivated its audience, a style and a format redolent of college pranks and academic wit. Only three years out of college themselves, Luce and Hadden had created a magazine for the only world they knew. The source of its success, however, lay less in their unquestionable genius than in a drastic realignment of American society.

Between 1920 and 1930, college enrollments more than doubled, from 341,000 to 754,000; so did attendance at public secondary schools, from 2.2 million in 1920 to 4.4 million in 1930. Lawyers and dentists, among others, now required four years of college before professional school. After 1920, state licensing mandated stringent standards for elementary teachers and specialized subject matter schooling for secondary school teachers. As a result, normal schools multiplied their course offerings in a forced march toward full college status. Chico State Teachers College in California, for example, offered 68 courses in 1920, but 265 a decade later; Arizona State Teachers College had 105 courses in 1920 and 284 in 1930; Colorado went from 493 courses to 723; and Wisconsin, from 210 to 317.[30]

Traditional colleges also diversified course offerings during the decade. Harvard increased its courses from 877 to 1,114; Stanford, from 710 to 1,095; the University of Washington, from 561 to 980; Howard University, from 143 to 255; University of Alabama, from 158 to 437. The orthodox world of scholars, a mandarinate based in the classics, history, literature, and mathematics, broadened to embrace sociology and political science, marketing, engineering, and even, as women increased on college campuses, home economics, drama, physical education, and fine art. By the early 1930s, the most comprehensive study ever made of American society concluded that "a college education is no longer thought of as a rare opportunity open only to students of distinctly intellectual tastes . . . For a very large fraction of the population a college education is regarded as a natural sequel to secondary education."[31]

Without fanfare, a college-educated cohort was filling the interstices of the American middle class. Trained nurses and librarians doubled between 1920 and 1930, while dentists, teachers, professors, technical engineers, chemists, metallurgists, editors, designers, artists and art teachers, stockbrokers, insurance agents, real estate brokers, and bankers all increased by more than 50 percent during the decade. Furthermore, the standard of education for business executives increasingly included at least a B.A. Stanley Resor, the J. Walter Thompson president, himself Yale '01, proudly noted in 1928 that his staff of 600 included 150 college graduates and four Ph.D.s, and "we would like to have more of both." By 1931 more than two-thirds of advertising men had attended college, and nearly half held one or more degrees.[32]

Even as it was being flayed by H. L. Mencken, a large segment of the "booboisie" was melting into the educated class. The steeply rising educational level within American society was reflected in its reading taste. Before World War I, for example, a biography of John Hay, Abraham Lincoln's private secretary, sold 18,000 copies in its first year. But in the later Twenties, a two-volume *Life and Letters of Walter Hines Page*, a diplomat and journalist but a far less interesting figure than Hay, sold 86,000 copies in its first year. The publisher Alfred Harcourt saw this as a significant measure of the changing book market. By 1930, he noted, Sinclair Lewis's *Main Street*, published in 1920, had sold 600,000 copies, and "Babbitt," the hero of Lewis's 1922 novel, had entered the language as a generic epithet for the bigoted, provincial American. "The people who reach economic independence now," Harcourt told an audience of advertising people in 1930, "are much more inclined to buy and read books than is the group that dies off each year."[33]

The upscale magazines successfully launched in the Twenties appealed directly or subtly to the newly educated. They rode out the Depression in affluence because their readers considered them an indispensable postgraduate course, providing not only information but also attitudes, style, and the grist of current conversation. *The New Yorker* may have trumpeted in its 1925 prospectus that it was "not for the old lady in Dubuque," but it clearly captivated the *young* lady in Dubuque; by 1934, only 62,000 of its 125,000 circulation was within 50 miles of Columbus Circle.[34]

Hadden touched off a lengthy, hilarious, and yet bitter conflict when he submitted the first issue of *The New Yorker* to an actual old lady in Dubuque. Its editors, *Time* quoted her as saying, "should learn that there is no provincialism so blatant as that of the metropolitan who lacks urbanity."[35] Then, in 1934 *Fortune* published a full-fledged article about *The New Yorker*, revealing its balance sheet, the salaries of its staff, and the details of editor Harold Ross's nervous breakdowns, including a stay at Riggs Sanatarium, where "he fascinated the staff. No stranger hallucination had they ever met than that of this wild hyena from Salt Lake City who thought he was the editor of *The New Yorker*. For a month he was the pet of the place. Then a gentleman from Texas who thought he was pregnant arrived, and Ross was no longer news."[36]

Twisting the knife, *Time* quoted the *Fortune* piece, spreading the juiciest details over five columns, an unusual length for *Time*. It described Ross as "a nervous, profane, broom-thatched wild man from the West . . . he could not write; he knew few writers." Alongside, the magazine printed a gruesome photo in which Ross seemed to have a front tooth missing.[37]

From then on, Ross lusted for revenge, and in 1936 he assigned Wolcott Gibbs, whom *Fortune* had described as the *New Yorker's* best parodist, to profile Luce. In *Time*-style, Gibbs mercilessly lampooned the beetle-browed publisher, concluding with, "Where it all will end, only knows God!"[38] Before printing it, Ross sent a proof for Luce's perusal and pain. The publisher and a *Time* executive, Ralph Ingersoll, marched over to Ross's penthouse, where the perpetrators of the parody waited snickering. The article contained not a single kind word, Luce complained. Ross snapped, "That's what you get for being a baby tycoon."[39]

Though both editors would deny that crass competition for advertising motivated the feud, *The New Yorker* clearly aimed for the same readers—and thus the same advertisers—as did *Time*.

Luckily for both publications, the third great magazine invention of the Twenties did not accept advertising. Like *Time*, it billed itself as an educational institution. "An article a day from leading magazines, in condensed, permanent booklet form" was the slogan heading the first page of the first issue of *Reader's Digest* in August 1923. Like Ross, Luce, and Hadden, its founder, De Witt Wallace sought to uplift the reader's mind. Like *Time,* he aimed for busy people looking for a quick read, but, unlike *Time,* he eschewed wit or style, instead condensing educational articles into a magic bullet, which offered what Americans have always found irresistible—self-improvement.

Wounded at Verdun, Wallace passed the long days of hospital recuperation leafing through magazines. Almost idly, as he would later describe it, he penciled over those articles, cutting words, phrases, and sentences he thought unnecessary. In February 1922, Wallace and his new wife and business partner Lila Bell Acheson published the first issue of *Reader's Digest.* Their office was a rented storeroom under a Greenwich Village speakeasy. Their capital was a borrowed $5,000. Their content, like that of *Time,* came from previously published material, in this case articles they culled during daily sessions in the New York Public Library's periodical room. But instead of rewriting in a unique, if grotesque, style, like *Time,* DeWitt and Lila simply boiled them down and served them up in a diminutive, pocket-size format. Since they sought no advertising and had no stockholders, facts about the *Digest*'s circulation and income remained closely guarded. After less than a year, they were selling 7,000 copies at an unheard-of twenty-five cents each; by 1939 DeWitt Wallace, who owned 52 percent, had a personal income of $286,011, and his wife, with 48 percent, earned $254,816.[40]

Though each would hotly deny it, the affinities among all these successful editors are striking. They all worshiped facts. At *Time* the "research" had from the beginning been delegated to a feminine phalanx dispatched to the public library when *The New York Times* gave out. They painstakingly scrutinized copy, the researcher's red dot over each word a seal of its authenticity. After Hadden's death, Luce indulged his "touching faith" that if only enough facts "can be somehow amassed" as an angry former employee wrote, "the truth will manifest itself."[41] At *The New Yorker,* Ross devoted periodic nervous breakdowns to the search for an editor who could guarantee factual accuracy. A checker there once confided that "if you mention the Empire State Building . . . Ross isn't satisfied it's still there until we call up and verify it."[42] And the Wallaces turned increasingly to commissioned rather than reprinted articles to vouchsafe their readers the facts they considered vital.

All of these media inventors were extremely young, under thirty. None of them had much journalism experience, and they were all raised in the hinterland, where absolute values ruled, far from the often ephemeral cultural commotions of New York. Luce considered it his life's principal deprivation that he had no American home town, but his foreign childhood gave him a sure intuition for the interests of educated provincials.[43] DeWitt and Lila Wallace were both raised in Minneapolis, long before the Midwest developed cosmopolitan aspirations. James Thurber remarked that the early *New Yorker's* "every effort to sound metropolitan in viewpoint and background brought the breath of Aspen, Colorado [Ross's birthplace], to the journal's perspiring pages."[44]

Like many advertising moguls of their day, these strong-minded editors sprang from an intensely religious, missionary, and/or educational milieu. Luce's father had devoted most of his life to founding and expanding Chinese colleges, including Yenching, China's leading pre-Communist university. Wallace's father was a Presbyterian minister and president of Macalester College. The chief influence on Ross seems to have been his mother, a strong-minded, practical, morally unequivocal presence. She had been a schoolteacher in the Oklahoma Indian territory before marrying Ross's father, an Irish immigrant. Visiting her son during the Thirties, she would upbraid him if he came home later than 11 P.M.[45]

But more than religious faith, missionary zeal moved these editors. "As a fervently patriotic American," the *Time* editor T. S. Matthews wrote, Luce "had an almost religious faith in competition and a striving belief that it was man's duty, like his country's, to win." Luce "was probably among the last of the great editors who was moved," Theodore H. White, a *Time* correspondent, reflected, "by the generative, dynamic force of believing Christianity." At the *Reader's Digest,* the backgrounds of the small staff of editors Wallace gathered about him "were more ecclesiastical than journalistic." Ross, meanwhile, devoted himself to a crusade for perfection in fact and aptness of taste so fanatical that it threatened his sanity. "He read the *Oxford English Dictionary* the way other men read fiction," Thurber wrote.[46]

Of course, all three were workaholics, thriving on relentless deadlines, demanding total commitment from their staffs, driven by unquenchable curiosity. Working with Luce, *Time* editor Whittaker Chambers recalled, was "like working directly behind a buzz saw, chewing metal faster than the eye can follow and throwing off an unremitting shower of sharp and shining filings." Luce's mind, another colleague recalled, was "teeming, probing, paradoxical, arrogant and humble, cold and passionate." He once sent a classic memo to an editor: "See me about Hitler." Luce's curiosity "gobbled up fact after fact and wanted more, more," White remarked. Conversation with him "was like a conversation with a vacuum cleaner: he could strip almost everyone clean of all they knew in a first conversation . . . and the next morning he would have more questions; and more questions at the end of the day."[47]

Wallace, by contrast, veiled his arrogance in mild self-effacement. Asked about any aspect of the magazine business, he would blandly retort: "Well, what do you think? You know more about these things than I do." A colleague thought "it was like Einstein asking a schoolboy for help with fractions." But he had no qualms about preaching other than he practiced: Despite the *Digest's* fiery crusade against cigarettes, he consumed at least two packs a day.[48]

Ross read nothing except what went into his magazine, Thurber cheerfully noted. But he read that with fierce devotion. He seldom left his office at night without a briefcase stuffed with manuscripts and proofs, or else returned after dinner to continue the barrage of penciled marginalia with which he pounded all copy. "The blurs and imperfections his scout's eye always caught drew from his pencil such designations as unclear, repetition, cliche, ellipsis," and the famous query: "Who he?" But his ignorance could be shocking; a checker recalled being asked, "Is Moby Dick the whale or the man?"[49]

The publications that issued from these restlessly inquisitive minds reflected an inquisitive age. For the last time, an educated person could comprehend the latest in science and medicine, art and literature, music and engineering, sociology, psychology, politics, and world affairs before most of those disciplines shattered into arcane subspecialties, guarded by the specialist's jargon. That American universities graduated only 532 Ph.D.s in 1920 but 2,024 in 1930 measures the trend.[50]

The reader of *Time, The New Yorker,* or *Reader's Digest* from the Thirties senses the editors' earnest, frantic, even pathetic pursuit of facts. And yet the truth about the times fails to emerge from those yellowing pages. It may be the Sisyphean lot of journalists perpetually to pour their talents into gathering facts without ever achieving the distance of time and space that promotes coherence and possibly truth. Even the beloved facts—especially about central events—are sparse. "Wallace showed as little interest in the riddle of the Depression as in literary art," Frederick Lewis Allen noted. But Wallace knew his readers; in a 1938 poll, executives' wives named *Reader's Digest* the most important magazine published in the United States, and *Time* was a close second.[51]

From its sophisticated perch, *The New Yorker* glossed haughtily over bank failures, mass unemployment, and shrill dictators abroad. Its profiles focused on the successful, its reporting on glitzy trivia. An apple seller or a fray-collared banker might appear in a witty cartoon, but the end of Prohibition in 1933 probably evoked more comment in *The New Yorker* than any other single event in the decade. Its impudent reviews and cheeky comments no less than its superb fiction attracted affluent readers, and, while Ross might inveigh against advertising and chase admen from the editorial offices, the articles and stories over which he slaved neatly meshed with the snob appeal of the advertising pages. They bore out the theme of a long series of advertisements *The New Yorker* ran in various advertising trade publications during 1936. Illustrated with drawings by the magazine's incomparable cartoonists was the slogan: "It sells the people other people copy."[52]

For Luce, the Depression hardly existed. He viewed the masses plunged into misery as perhaps his parents had viewed the masses of Chinese coolies. Fresh from his reading of Ortega y Gasset, Luce could be frankly, even militantly, elitist. Speaking to the Chamber of Commerce in his father's native city, Scranton, Pennsylvania, in 1932, he voiced disdain for "the vulgar, the moronic, the unpleasant specimens of humanity and those who are as poor in spirit as in purse, but whom for some reason beyond our comprehending, Jesus blessed." At this time, Luce lived in a spacious apartment at 4 East 72d Street and had a staff of servants, including two uniformed footmen.[53]

Luce had survived one financial crisis following Hadden's death in 1929. Hadden's 3,361 shares had gone to Hadden's mother; by the terms of a will on which the moribund editor had scrawled an "X" just three weeks before his death, those shares could not be sold for forty-nine years. However, Hadden's executor, his half-brother Crowell, could legally "do almost anything he judged prudent," says Time Inc.'s official history. He decided that Mrs. Hadden's security required that she sell 2,828½ shares for $360 each. Of those, Luce bought 625, gaining working control, while the rest were scattered among *Time* staffers and stockholders.[54]

Since 1924, when *Time* had turned its first profit—$674.15—the upstart magazine had proved exceedingly robust. By the end of that year *Time* had some 70,000 subscribers, verified by the Audit Bureau of Circulation, and by 1930 the circulation had passed 300,000. More than most magazines, *Time* relied heavily on the five dollars a year (or fifteen cents a copy on newsstands) its readers paid. Unlike most magazines, which sold cut-rate subscriptions through clubs or importunate swarms of door-to-door salesmen, *Time* offered no discounts and waged no high-pressure campaigns for readers. Instead, the advertisements for *Time*, which ran in many advertising trade publications, attributed its unequaled circulation growth to "its personality alone, without premiums and without 'stunts.' "[55] As newsstand circulation grew, *Time* advertised for subscribers in its own pages, using testimonials from well-known readers, for example, forty-two college presidents, including Nicholas Murray Butler of Columbia and the presidents of Stanford, Yale, Princeton, and Cornell.[56] The college theme also was stressed in advertisements in alumni publications and in circulation letters mailed by the millions to lists bought from alumni organizations.[57] In its prospectus, *Time* had promised to reach every college graduate in the United States, plus the "thousands and tens of thousands . . . who have not had a college education but who are intelligent and who want . . . to keep . . . posted on the necessary news." So appealing was its college format and so vast was the pool of new collegians and would-be collegians that *Time* was deriving twice as much income from subscriptions as from advertising, an almost incredible ratio.

Not that advertising languished. In the first nine months of 1929, *Time*'s 1,631 advertising pages were second only to *The Saturday Evening Post*'s (which, to be sure, had run 4,622 pages), and gross ad revenues for the year were $1.9 million. The corporation showed a $325,000 profit. On paper, Luce and Hadden were millionaires, a status Luce appreciated only when the bankers gladly lent him the funds to buy Hadden's shares.[58] The new affluence also rewarded Luce for slogging in the financial trenches while his rival had commanded the glamorous editorial side.

From the beginning, the magazine had benefited from the loyalties of many Yale graduates who had gone into advertising, including J. Walter Thompson's president, Stanley Resor; JWT's vice president Samuel Meek, '17, who was a founding stockholder at Time Inc.; and William Benton, '21, founder of Benton & Bowles. Many were the campus yarns these men could swap with *Time* staffers like national affairs editor Manfred Gottfried, Yale '22; business manager Charles L. Stillman, Yale '26; advertising manager Robert L. Johnson, Yale '18; and circulation manager Roy E. Larsen, Harvard '21. Those affinities marked a ramified social change in American leadership. For, while the Ivy League had long played a strong role in the professions and in government, journalism and advertising had been deemed ungentlemanly occupations. When Benton chose a career in advertising, his mother sent him a sorrowful letter asking if he couldn't have picked "something more respectable."[59] When Luce confessed to the Yale professor Amos Wilder (Thornton's father) that he intended to be a journalist, Wilder begged him to reconsider. "It will turn you into a cynic," the teacher predicted, with tears in his eyes, "It will corrupt and corrode you. It will turn your wine into vinegar. You will lose your soul."[60]

But beyond that helpful old boy network, *Time*'s imaginative advertising and promotion, and especially its pathbreaking readership studies, were bound to impress the agencies. The details *Time* gathered about the interests, life-styles, education, incomes, and occupations of its readers toward the end of the Twenties fitted neatly into the kinds of consumer research that agencies themselves were developing. "Do you own a horse?" a 1928 questionnaire asked of a random sample of *Time* subscribers. In such mailings, a response of 10 percent is considered excellent. When more than 25 percent replied, *Time* used that fact alone in its promotion.

Hadden had deplored the necessary intrusion of the countinghouse into his pure, if captious, editorial realm. As he whacked at elevator doors and automobile bumpers with the cane he habitually sported, so he enjoyed ragging those who paid the bills. He frequently vexed the business side by printing stories derogatory of advertisers precisely when they had signed a fat new contract. When Walter P. Chrysler was *Time*'s second annual Man of the Year (Charles A. Lindbergh was the first) in 1928, Hadden generated a crisis by insisting on printing the former mechanic's embarrassing middle name: Percy. No sooner had the *Time* circulation department launched a campaign for Southern readers than Hadden launched a campaign to refer to blacks as "Mr.," a title then unthinkable in print. A year before his death, Hadden had started *Tide*, a *Time*-style sheet devoted to advertising, which he used as a "paddle . . . upon *Time* itself."[61]

Both partners had begun thinking about expansion. The black notebook in which Hadden jotted ideas listed possible future publications devoted to fiction, women, sports, American history, food, and business. Yet when Luce, in 1928, hired an editor and a researcher to explore a business publication,

Hadden ignored them, the researcher Florence Horn recalled.[62] But Luce poured into the developing new magazine all the creative juices that had so long seethed in Hadden's shadow. As the world slid toward the worst economic misfortune in modern history, Luce energetically pushed forward the magazine named *Fortune.*

American business magazines had failed, Luce told Time Inc. directors in February 1929, because they did not "realize the dignity and the beauty, the smartness and excitement of modern industry." *Time* reported that same month on a twenty-one-year-old who had bought a seat on the New York Stock Exchange for a near-record $585,000.[63] Luce saw in the business world "a unique publishing opportunity . . . wars to record, strategy to admire, biographies to write." The story of America was the story of business, he believed; the magazine he was planning would "give business a literature." It would be larger, more beautiful and more costly than any magazine ever published. And it would definitively draw the line "between the gentleman and the money-grubber."[64]

That elusive line fascinated Parker Lloyd-Smith, a Princeton classics major who became *Fortune's* first editor after barely a year's experience as an Albany, New York, reporter. For a possible article about luxurious executive offices, he received a tip about the Illinois Merchants Bank's sumptuous board room at its Chicago headquarters: Two stories high and hung with crimson brocade from Italy, its directors' table was said to have been used by Italian bankers of the Renaissance and had cost the Chicagoans $40,000. "There is a Greek motto running around this room," Lloyd-Smith's informant wrote, "that in times of prosperity one should prepare for the times that will not be so prosperous."[65]

In April, as *Time* was sorting out the carnage following "the biggest stock market crash in Coolidge–Hoover history,"[66] Luce wrote personally to seventy-nine *Time*-subscribing tycoons humbly asking their opinion on "a project for which our enthusiasm has mounted almost to the acting point." He worried because "too often an editor is led astray by the comments of his immediate friends," and therefore solicited the impartial verdict of Edsel Ford, Harry F. Sinclair, L. F. Swift,

E. F. Hutton, Gilbert Colgate, George Eastman, R. M. Weyerhaeuser, Harvey S. Firestone, and Simon Guggenheim.[67]

The tone of the letter strikingly mimics the sort of letters Luce's father regularly sent to American businessmen for contributions to his Chinese colleges. The elder Luce had had to quit China in 1925 because of severe abdominal pain, which turned out to be stomach ulcer. While his thirty-one-year-old son was soliciting America's business aristocracy for opinions— and subscriptions—the father was tirelessly crisscrossing the nation soliciting contributions from many of the very same sources. In 1932, the elder Luce would be voted Most Successful at the fortieth reunion of the Yale class of '92. On campus, he had been editor of the *Yale Courant.* "The Lord's work," Henry would later say patronizingly of his father, "turned out to be raising money, which is, of all jobs, the worst . . . the Lord was not kind to him."[68]

But the young man's intense efforts to court the business community competed, in a sense, with the father's; the flood of article ideas he poured upon *Fortune* planners included "Potent Sons of Potent Fathers." Perhaps the Lord was kinder to the son as he assigned the magazine's mission: "Business takes *Fortune* to the tip of the wing of the airplane and through the depth of the ocean along be-barnacled cables," the Prospectus declared. "It forces *Fortune* to peer into dazzling furnaces and into the faces of bankers. *Fortune* must follow the chemist to the brink of worlds Columbus never found and it must jog with freight cars across the Nevada desert. *Fortune* is involved in the fashions of flappers and in the glass made from sand. It is packed in millions of cans and saluted by boards of directors on the pinnacles of skyscrapers. Mountains diminish, rivers change their course and 30 million people assemble nightly at the cinema. Into all these matters, *Fortune* will inquire with unbridled curiosity."[69]

The wonder was that *Fortune* came so close to fulfilling its grandiose objective. To accomplish it, Luce commissioned a leading graphic designer, Thomas Maitland Cleland, to create an exquisite format; gathered a staff of distinguished writers (not journalists); and hired a twenty-four-year-old Cleveland photographer who had already transformed industrial picture-taking into a fine art, Margaret Bourke-White. Summoned to New York by telegram from Luce, Bourke-White encountered a young man "strikingly powerful in build," she recalled, whose "words tumbled out with such haste and emphasis that I had the feeling he was thinking ten words for every one that managed to emerge. He began questioning me at once . . . leaping . . . from point to point in a kind of verbal shorthand . . . The camera would act as interpreter, recording what modern industrial civilization is . . . Did I think this was a good idea, Mr. Luce asked, pausing for breath."[70]

Late in May 1929, when *Time* reported that 17 million Americans, mostly "new, small, ignorant," were trading stocks,[71] Luce told Time Inc. directors that Stanley Resor seemed genuinely enthusiastic about *Fortune*. Luce's confidential memo to directors concluded with: "One final point: at the moment of writing, there are slight evidences of business decline—although *Time* itself has felt no such indications. Should this kind of consideration," he wondered, "be taken into account?"[72]

The answer came in a July 1929 test mailing, which elicited subscriptions from more than 10 percent of recipients. As *Time* was reporting that corporate earnings for the first six months indicated that 1929 would be "a banner year of bumper prosperity,"[73] the *Fortune* subscription roll gathered many who would be buffeted—and some who would be broken—in the whirlwind gathering just beyond the horizon: B. Jackson, president of the Stutz Motor Car Company; the flour king C. L. Pillsbury; Henry T. Ewald, advertising agent for General Motors; GM vice president Charles F. Kettering; the organ maker Rudolph Wurlitzer; the toothpaste magnate S. B. Colgate; and Alvan Macaulay, president of the Packard Motor Car Co.[74]

In August 1929, as *Time* reported US Steel stock at an all-time high,[75] Luce mailed a personal letter soliciting subscriptions from those considered important enough to be on *Time*'s free list. *Fortune*'s readers, he anticipated, would be "the people for whom the air transport lines run, for whom round the world and Mediterranean winter cruises would be established, for whom yachts are built and $10,000 automobiles assembled. They are the 30,000 whose influence in the industrial and financial community outweighs that of 30,000,000. They are the people in whose hands billions of the national wealth are concentrated. They are, in short, the aristocracy of our business civilization."[76]

In late September 1929, when *Time* was reporting that $17.6 million in new credit was pouring into American business every day, *Fortune* salesmen sold contracts for forty pages of advertising in the first issue, and forty more were firmly promised.[77] As the *Fortune* ads came in, *Time* seemed mesmerized by the business world. Beginning with Man of the Year Walter Percy Chrysler, it featured sixteen businessmen on its cover, including J. P. Morgan, US Steel President Myron Taylor, RCA chief David Sarnoff, Packard's Alvan Macaulay, and Standard Oil of New Jersey president Walter Teagle. In the fall, five businessmen were successive cover subjects: William Wrigley, Jr., Harry Guggenheim, Ivar Kreuger, Samuel Insull, and Thomas W. Lamont. And, as *Fortune* was being born in the first week of January, *Time* chose yet another executive as Man of the Year: General Electric's Owen D. Young.[78]

The magazine that arrived on some 30,000 of America's most prestigious desks near the end of January 1930 was lavish indeed, "sumptuous to the point of rivalling the pearly gates," the *New York Times* reported. It contained 110 pages of advertising: for long, sleek, classic automobiles and yachts, for vacations in Hawaii and resorts in Banff. Time Inc.'s official historian said the ads reflected "the afterglow of a great age of prosperity."[79] Indeed, as the first issue of *Fortune* was closing late in October 1929, *Time* was chronicling Wall Street's agony: "Roaring was the business done by downtown speakeasies. Wild were the rumors of ruin and suicide. . . . What failures loomed, none could say. Would the nightmare, to many tragically cruel, never end?"[80]

The new magazine's 3-pound heft and 184-page girth lent graphic weight to the judgment of twenty-five business editors who, *Time* reported in January 1930, had unanimously declared: "Business is essentially sound."[81] Its comprehensive articles were printed on velvety antique wild-wove paper by a complicated process upon which the designer Cleland had insisted. To ensure quality, the photographs were printed by gravure in East Orange, New Jersey. Then the pages were trucked to Brooklyn for letterpress printing of the borders, text and cover. That costly procedure was so slow (the press run took almost thirty days) and so diffused (the photographs had to be sent to the printer before the text was even written) that each issue, an editor recalled, "drove us crazy."[82]

The first issue contained, as an internal memo described it, "a detailed exposition of how the paint pot has been dumped over everything American . . . illustrated throughout in color—everything from blue locomotives to green pills."[83] It was the first use of color photographs in a mass publication and required cumbersome cameras, endless lab work, painstaking platemaking and, Eric Hodgins, an editor, wrote, "a lot of prayer." The first issue also contained Margaret Bourke-White's stunning photographs illustrating how the Swift Corporation butchered hogs, a serious study of branch banking, and advice on how to live in Chicago on $25,000 a year.

"Many people said the magazine could last only two years," Bourke-White recalled, because "by then all the industries would be covered and there would be nothing left to photograph."[84] But those pessimists had reckoned without Luce's obsessive curiosity and the extraordinary staff he assembled. Luce had envisioned that, for example, Louis Bromfield, Sinclair Lewis, Clarence Darrow, Walter Lippmann, Thornton Wilder, Grantland Rice, Heywood Broun, Edna Ferber, Ernest Hemingway, John Gunther, and Lewis Mumford all would appear in *Fortune.*[85] "There are men who can write poetry and there are men who can read balance sheets," he declared. "The men who can read balance sheets cannot write . . . it is easier to turn poets into business journalists than to turn bookkeepers into writers."[86]

Luce lured Archibald MacLeish (Yale '15, Harvard LL.B. '19) back from Europe with the promise that he could work for *Fortune* half the year to pay his bills while devoting the other half to poetry. "I know absolutely nothing about business," MacLeish demurred. "That's why I want you," Luce replied. The poet, whose long narrative *Conquistador* won the Pulitzer Prize in 1932, eloquently took *Fortune* readers to the dust bowl and into skyscrapers and tried to make sense for them of insane world politics, before becoming Librarian of Congress in 1939. On *Fortune,* he later wrote, "my essential education as an American began." MacLeish was remembered by his colleagues as uniquely organized: He insisted that researchers (all women who, as on *Time,* were condemned to gather facts, check copy, and, in case of mistakes, take the blame) provide all their notes on cards in logical sequence. MacLeish "merely flipped through his cards and wrote in longhand until 5 o'clock, when he left the office."[87]

Dwight MacDonald, who had been editor of the Yale *Record,* was saved from Macy's Executive Training Squad by his job at *Fortune.* "He wrote at his best when he was indignant about something, which he usually was," Eric Hodgins recalled, "although he was not . . . the professional polemicist and horse's ass that he became as the pink beard slowly grizzled."[88]

Ralph Ingersoll had gone through Hotchkiss and Yale two years behind Luce and Hadden. He had worked on the New York *American* and had attempted a novel in Europe. Then *The New Yorker* hired him as managing editor, reportedly after Harold Ross had accidentally dumped a bottle of ink into his lap. While most *Fortune* writers gladly took $10,000 a year, Ingersoll, perhaps because it struck a blow at the hated *New Yorker,* received $15,000.[89]

The staff gave off "a distinct atmosphere of tennis and squash, a bit of Skull and Bones, a lilt of Ivy League," wrote a later arrival, Louis Kronenberger, "the sort of writers who could qualify as glossy Time Inc. emissaries to corporations, rather than as ink-stained wretches." A bulletin board memo cautioned them against wearing unmatched jackets and trousers on assignment. But the man who developed *Fortune*'s unique contribution to periodical journalism, the searching, fact-laden, and meticulously written corporation story, fitted none of those patterns. He was Edward Kennedy, "a tiny gnome, with mumbled speech, tousled hair, untidy clothes and very thick glasses." The leading poet at the University of Cincinnati, he had missed his degree because he failed to attend commencement and seemed "doomed to an intense and underfed life in a garret." The anomaly of finding him at *Fortune*, Kronenberger thought, was "as though John Keats had wound up as [the advertising magnate] Bruce Barton."[90]

Though not a single *Fortune* writer had much training in economics or experience in business, their articles had a profound impact not only on the business community but on the attitudes of thoughtful Americans toward business itself. Ironically, the golden age of the literature Henry Luce had promised to American business came precisely as American business lay bleeding, perhaps dying. In executive dining rooms, in penthouses, and in country clubs, *Fortune* reclined seductively on the coffee tables, even as the world it described was ruined. Many blamed the men so opulently chronicled in the magazine's pages for the Depression and, as the crisis deepened, called for stern control of private enterprise, even the overthrow of the capitalist system. *Fortune* did not shrink totally from reporting the discussion and, to its credit, shunned the optimistic twaddle that, like treacle, clung to most of the financial reporting of the day. But it excelled at dramatizing the very real structural revolution in the American economy that the Depression masked. It was a broad-based revolution, arising on the one hand from the laboratory that produced new technology and, on the other, from aggressive and innovative marketing.

The wonders of the laboratory captivated *Fortune*. American Viscose Corp., for example, regained its 1929 rayon production peak by 1931 and doubled production by 1936. Burlington Mills, which wove rayon fabric, had made only $1.8 million worth in 1927. By 1933, its production was worth $16 million, and by 1936, $25.4 million. US Rubber, which had developed Lastex, a stretch fabric woven of rubber with cotton, rayon, or wool, sold only 32,000 pounds of it in 1931 but 1,200,000 pounds in 1933.[91] Synthetic resins, brought to the United States from Germany in 1930, reversed a trend away from the use of wood products and revolutionized the plywood industry. Production was at $45.5 million in 1937 and reached $80 million by 1939.[92]

"The business enterprisers of the depressed Thirties, placing their faith in a host of struggling new technologies had really saved the day for us," *Fortune*'s editor John Chamberlain concluded in his memoirs. "The Thirties witnessed the proliferation of the airlines, the building of the mult-au-matic turret lathe, the discovery of new alloys, the spread of the continuous wide-strip steel mill, the transformation of the chemical industry, the development of synthetic fabrics."[93] Taking stock in 1937, another observer wrote: "Critics have complained that we have lacked in distribution of goods, but no one can say that we have lagged in production, transportation, and communication." He cited railroads streamlined and electrified, buses spanning the continent, Pan Am Clippers spanning the Pacific (in five days!), and telephones linking the world.[94] Such a boosterish tone smacked sadly of a failing magazine, *Scribner's*, attempting to ape the sunny swarm of the rampant *Reader's Digest*, but the technological miracles developed during the Thirties were real. That they would transform the life of virtually every American was no empty promise, although much of the transformation would have to wait until after World War II.

Like a summer hailstorm, the Depression capriciously flattened some fields while passing others by. Still other economic sectors flourished. The end of Prohibition brought not only legal liquor, a new industry, but a spate of advertisements to publications like *The New Yorker* and *Time*. Like the people in *Middletown* who told the Lynds they did without bathtubs and skimped on food in order to keep their automobiles,[95] American consumers indulged in unexpected tastes during the slump. Based on an index of 100 for 1929, sales of electric refrigerators, for example, rose to 183 in 1930, 440 in 1931, 625 in 1934, and 770 in 1935. Sales of electric toasters reached 125 in 1935. Sales of electric power itself rose steadily to 158 by 1936. Gasoline sales inched upward to 114 by 1936. While furniture, hardware, and building materials suffered grievously after the crash, purchases of food, apparel, and general merchandise held steady.[96]

What really changed during the Thirties was how goods were marketed. The historian Daniel Boorstin has identified a peculiarly American social unit, "consumption communities," comprising "people who have a feeling of shared well-being, shared risks, common interests and common concerns that come from consuming the same kinds of objects." While they are often reluctant to admit it, Americans derive status and relieve alienation by their loyalty to a particular brand of toothpaste, deodorant, or floor wax. The multifarious consumption communities have given immigrants a sense of belonging and have educated the upwardly mobile in the attributes and behaviors expected of them in the social class to which they aspire.[97] While the market researchers for advertising agencies did not describe the consumers of various products as "consumption communities," they had found that brand names had a magical appeal to particular groups of people.

Intellectuals were mystified and angry at what they considered deception—wrapping a staple product in a beguiling package and flogging it nationwide via spurious individuality. But the perpetrators found the results astonishing: By 1930, brand names accounted for 70 percent of coffee sales in Milwaukee, 74 percent for macaroni, 78 percent for soap flakes, and 81 percent for butter.[98] The radio antics of Edgar Bergen and Charlie McCarthy, for example, vaulted their sponsor, Chase & Sanborn Coffee, from selling in only two cities in 1929 to the leading coffee nationwide some thirteen years later. A steady thrum of print advertisements calling attention to the diseases caused by inferior toilet paper ("Often the only relief from toilet tissue illness is . . .") boosted sales of Scott Tissue by 750 percent between 1927 and 1942. Paper towels, introduced in 1931, were staples in almost 3 million homes six years later. And Scott towels ("I don't see how I ever did without them."), launched in 1934, were indispensable in more than 2 million American kitchens by 1942. Miracle Whip salad dressing, born in 1933, had captured half the market by 1942. Sales of Skol suntan lotion, which began advertising in 1937, had increased 400 percent by 1942.[99]

A vital change in how and where people bought goods accounted for many such feats of merchandising. Difficult as it is to sort out cause from effect, the net result of brand-name staple products advertised to an increasingly urbanized population was that country stores were driven out by city stores, small stores by big stores, and individually owned stores by chain stores. By 1933, half of all Americans lived within an hour's drive of a city of 100,000 or more. Metropolitan areas, a new concept, "took on more and more the aspect of a coherent economic and cultural state, more realistic in many ways than the existing political states," one study found. "Measured in time rather than linear space, the old boundaries of cities have shrunk and vast new areas have been brought within the city limits."[100]

That spelled the end of the country store. By 1936, stores with sales volumes of more than $50,000 per year, though comprising only 6.7 percent of all stores, had captured 35.7 percent of total sales. Those urban emporia, often self-service, embryonic supermarkets, and increasingly chain stores, would become the cathedrals of the American consumption community's cult.[101] Advertising, its liturgy, had short-circuited the age-old relationship between seller and buyer. Like every aspect of urban life, shopping became impersonal, solitary, an internal monologue of fantasy and desire on the part of the buyer, triggered by recognition of the advertised brand name. A successful advertising campaign would lock into the consumer's interests, aspirations, wishes, habits, or emotions so firmly that respondents would tell survey-takers about the product in the exact words used in the advertisements. After a six-week campaign, "Use Lux to cut down runs in stockings," for example, was remembered by almost half of all women.[102]

Furthermore, advertising forged a stronger bond between a product and its buyers than the country storekeeper could ever achieve. Choosing from the varied goods in a self-service store gave the buyer the illusion of princely autonomy, the hauteur of a queen conferring her favor upon this or that importunate cartoned biscuit mix or canned coffee. Books, articles, and even Congressional speeches pointed to the flimsy factual foundation behind claims for cure of "pink toothbrush," "halitosis," and "BO," even as those terms of dread were entering the language. No exposés, no fiery speeches, no appeals to reason could divert consumers from their love affair with brand names. Surveys in the late Thirties indicated that "three out of four respondents, men and women, thought that advertising gives them better products. . . . More than half believed that widely advertised products are usually the best."[103] Many businessmen and economists viewed advertising as the Yellow Brick Road to prosperity. The slump had been triggered, many thought, by overproduction; advertising would persuade people to buy the surplus goods. The Depression signaled a shift in the American economy from production to consumption, others reasoned, and therefore advertising educated consumers to their civic duty: Go to your corner grocer now and buy![104]

While critics have charged that advertising played unfairly upon the public's aspirations, fantasies, and dreams, its power to shape popular ideals demands attention. "It is as impossible to understand a modern popular writer without understanding advertising," the historian David M. Potter observed, "as it would be to understand a medieval troubadour without understanding the cult of chivalry or a 10th century revivalist without understanding evangelical religion."[105] But Depression people seemed peculiarly vulnerable to the tin dreams cooked up on Madison Avenue; wounded by hard times, millions sought balm in simplistic cures, whether offered by Huey Long, Father Coughlin, Aimée Semple McPherson, or Ma Perkins. "When the news story of air cooling appeared in the public print, nothing happened," William Allen White wrote. "But when advertisements with prices and descriptions began to present the comforts of air cooling, a new industry developed." He considered advertising a "smooth-running, powerful machine . . . one of the major aids in erecting our civilization." But others saw it as "the flourish of a decadent civilization." Advertising was luring the poor away from lives of "decent simplicity" into "a riot of luxury," one critic charged. The standard of living depicted in the ads was "unattainable . . . in this generation. . . . Dangling such an impossible prize before those who cannot win is not only sardonic cruelty: it has profound and sure social consequences."[106]

Those views on advertising, whether awe, rage, or bafflement, reflect poignantly the upheaval in the world of magazines wrought by the growing sophistication of space buyers at advertising agencies. Though total budgets for magazine advertising were consistently $3.50 to $3.75 per $1,000 of consumer spending,[107] the media to which the advertising flowed changed radically. More and more, agencies aimed advertising at the most likely customers, as identified through research. For magazines, this meant costly studies of their audiences: where and how they lived, their educational levels and incomes, the size of families, their hobbies and attitudes. Inevitably, editors angled their publications' content toward the type of readers advertisers sought.

Esquire, which began in 1933 as a quarterly of men's fashions, became an instant success by using that kind of targeting. Its publisher personally traveled around the country, selling a hundred copies each to 1,000 haberdashers. Cannily combining salacious illustrations with highbrow articles, the glossy publication sold out despite its high cover price of 50 cents. Within four years it became a monthly with a circulation exceeding 700,000. For *Esquire* as for *Fortune,* the high cover price guaranteed advertisers an affluent audience. "Of all the ideas that went into the *Fortune* formula," a competitor wrote, "none struck the public as so extraordinary as the fact that it sold for $1 a copy."[108] Thus it was that in 1931, the mighty *Saturday Evening Post,* which sought to reach "everybody," lost 40 percent of its automobile advertising, while *Time* and *Fortune,* which shrewdly appealed to the moneyed, alone gained auto linage. By 1934, the success of *Fortune's* targeting strategy was even more apparent; the magazine's 90,000 circulation was less than one-tenth that of the *Post,* yet *Fortune* boasted more advertising than any general monthly in the world.[109]

Beneath the magazine's smooth ride to prosperity, however, ran a rutted footpath over which the editors nudged each month's issue to completion. Editor Lloyd-Smith had inexplicably jumped from a tall building in the fall of 1931. The bright article ideas of succeeding editors often became mired in the temperament of their writers. Wilder Hobson, for example, could turn out "reams of smooth rhetoric, but the great love of his life was jazz and anything else—except alcohol—

was an intrusion." Dwight MacDonald wrote so scathingly about the steel industry that Luce had to answer to the House of Morgan. John Chamberlain, who had been a book reviewer at the *New York Times,* was "a pleasant, gentle man, with a deeply hidden streak of hostility," and thus unreliable. Eric Hodgins adjudged him "not an out-and-out disaster—he was an in-and-out disaster."[110]

James Agee, who joined *Fortune* in 1932, a month after graduating from Harvard, was considered by the staff to be its most gifted writer. On paper he was "so lucid, so vivid, such a master of prose modulation, that it came as a wild surprise that this same fellow . . . verbally . . . could scarcely complete a simple, declarative sentence." Emotionally, Agee "commuted between cloud coocooland and hell," Hodgins recalled, compounding *Fortune's* perpetual production crises as he "failed to distinguish between the fifth and the 25th of the month," or, though he wrote everything in a tiny, crabbed longhand, "the difference between the 5,000th and 50,000th word."[111] Agee's classic *Let Us Now Praise Famous Men* originated as an assignment for a *Fortune* article on Southern sharecroppers. Sent south in 1935 with the photographer Walker Evans, Agee stretched his sojourn there into months, while Luce generously paid the bills. But on that assignment, Agee the novelist and poet warred incessantly with Agee the reporter. No article ever emerged from his endless prose-polishing, and the book, which Agee envisioned as part of a much longer work titled *Three Tenant Families,* was finally published in 1940.

None of *Fortune's* articles had by-lines, because Luce believed that the staff was collectively responsible for everything in the magazine. Often that meant that no one was responsible. Kronenberger was shocked to find that there was "nothing in the barrel to replace a disastrous or uncompleted story." Picture captions were "an artistic exercise," as the author struggled to write "catchily, wittily, brilliantly" just as the deadline rush left him "profoundly, profanely, unutterably exhausted." Each month's issue went to press in the midst of "a shrill, stormy farce- melodrama," dragging on past every announced deadline. As an issue closed, "the office did too—

everyone theoretically went to bed for two or three days." Hodgins was stunned when he completed his first *Fortune* assignment at 11 of an evening in 1933 and found that his editor, Ingersoll, not only answered the phone but wanted the completed article right then. Arriving at the fifty-first floor of the Chrysler Building, Hodgins found "every desk occupied and all lights blazing. It was editorial high noon."[112]

Though exceedingly pampered, Luce's poets did not care to dwell long in the realms of coke ovens and old Mr. Bache. Leftists or radicals almost to a man, the *Fortune* staff's interests roved toward Washington, world trade, assessments of Mussolini and Hitler, and studies of Soviet construction; by 1936, only 45 percent of *Fortune* articles dealt with business.[113] With 11 million still unemployed and an additional 3.57 million on work relief, Luce's business aristocracy tottered. The masses, who had been so grossly described by Ortega y Gasset and so coolly dismissed by Henry Luce, were on the march. The common man—what did he think? expect? fear? adore? Advertising agencies knew more about the public's thoughts on dentifrices and deodorants than the President knew about the public's thoughts on political programs and Presidents. On Luce's orders, *Fortune* in 1934 turned to the very same people who had pioneered market research to study ways of "plumbing . . . the public mind." Paul T. Cherington, who had set up a private consulting firm with Richardson Wood and Elmo Roper in 1931, was hired to develop the Fortune Poll, a quarterly feature of the magazine beginning in July 1935 (and monthly after 1938). Ingersoll was astounded by how much the polls cost, yet awed at the prospect of discerning "the curves that history will draw." Hodgins marveled at "a device . . . to find out what people thought, or thought they thought, about all manner of things."[114]

Cherington and his colleagues had so refined their techniques that a carefully constructed sample of 3,000 reliably reflected opinion in the nation at large. Readers were astounded to learn from the first Fortune Poll that three-fourths of the public believed the government would ensure a job for everyone who wanted work. Subsequent surveys uncovered comparable surprises, for example, that a vast majority of Americans not only willingly discussed birth control, which had been considered taboo, but also favored it. Introducing its new feature, *Fortune* hoped that its survey would "enjoy a certain authority as a barometer of that public opinion the importance of which has been so well described—the nature of which has been so blankly ignored." In an internal critique titled "Survey Entomology," its principal author Lawrence Babcock, pointed to a few "bugs"—results skewed because interviewers failed to follow enough dirt roads. That could be cured, he suggested, only by supplying interviewers with "donkeys and picnic baskets." But the survey's impact was immense: President Franklin D. Roosevelt insisted on getting advance copies. And its accuracy was uncanny: In 1936, it predicted FDR would receive 61.7 percent of the vote. He won with 60 percent.[115]

Nor need Ingersoll have worried about the $10,000 Time Inc. was paying the Cherington firm each year. By 1934 the publisher had a $1.7 million net profit, and in the next year the net jumped to more than $2.2 million. The enterprise had moved beyond being, as Luce said, "even a big Small Business and become a small Big Business."[116]

Time contributed handsomely to those figures. By 1934, it passed half a million circulation; by 1937, 650,000. But more striking than the numbers were the intensity and the quality of *Time*'s readers. A 1937 survey found that 75 percent of men and 69 percent of women read it cover to cover; more than 95 percent read the national affairs section, and more than 92 percent read foreign news.[117] Moreover, those were what today would be called opinion makers: 72 percent of male readers and 64 percent of females had attended college, a 1938 survey showed; 54 percent had servants; 53 percent owned listed stock; 63 percent owned their homes—and 18 percent had second homes; nearly 23 percent owned two or more cars.[118]

The weary reader of the bookshelf of memoirs, exposés, and *romans à clef* churned out by *Time* staffers might conclude that the publication those affluent readers perused so thoroughly contained information as weighty as Holy Writ and that the style in which it was presented rivaled Shakespeare. In fact, *Time* during that period had no correspondents and no offices outside New York. The circulation manager, Roy E. Larsen, might brag to readers that each *Time* word cost twenty-five cents for "fact-finding and cable tolls, for travel and confidential reports, for writing, re-writing, checking, condensing and editing,"[119] but in truth *Time* was prepared largely as it had been from the beginning, a bright and breezy rewrite of other publications, especially the *New York Times.* That it addicted so many intelligent readers is largely a testimonial to the execrable newspapers that afflicted America during the Thirties.

On most newspapers, reporters went from high school to an apprenticeship as copyboys. Women earned by-lines only on society and food pages, except for an occasional "sob sister" who escaped to general news columns via sensational—often fictional—accounts of society divorces and other scandals. Disregard—if not downright contempt—for facts appeared to be a basic qualification for a resourceful reporter. Ben Hecht, co-author of *The Front Page,* was himself a master spinner of invented news; he fired the youthful Henry Luce from his first job as a leg-man for being "too naive." (Read: truthful.) Reporters chased ambulances, jostled attractive courtroom witnesses, cracked rude jokes about the mighty, wore hats indoors, tapped out yarns with two fingers on battered Underwoods, and drank too much. They were poorly paid. *Time's* writers, by contrast, came directly from the Ivy League (preferably Yale), had no newspaper experience, yearned to be novelists and/or poets, sipped cocktails with the mighty, kept Brooks Brothers healthy, wrote artful narratives on the news (sometimes in longhand), and drank too much. They were munificently paid.

A typical newspaper story began with who, what, why, when, and where and then elaborated on those bald facts in order of diminishing importance. A typical *Time* story began with a startling construction ("Forth from the White House sallied . . ."), introduced protagonists (bald-pated, beetle-browed, weed-whiskered, snaggle-toothed), who rushed, worried, harassed, stumbled, loped, grinned, frowned as events waylaid them, and left the reader believing he had witnessed history. No one "said" anything: People burbled, gruffed, croaked, snapped, gushed, and sneered. Nor did they walk, but bounced, leaped, strode, stalked. The bogus brevity of word blends—newshawk, Nobelman, sexational, improperganda—assaulted the reader as he plowed through a thicket of pundits, kudos, and neophytes.[120]

The wonder of it was that an entire staff was lashed (anonymously, since there were no by-lines) into this stylistic straitjacket, and the reason can only be that no writer had developed any personal style or point of view. Winthrop Sargeant, for example, came to *Time* from the string section of the New York Philharmonic. "I knew too much about music to write about it with the 'fresh approach' demanded," he recalled, so he was assigned to write on art. "My writing was sent on to editors who rewrote it completely, turned it into sausage meat . . . and then stuffed it into the magazine."[121] Most *Time* writers believed they were meant to be novelists, and eventually all too many of them fulfilled that fantasy by writing fiction based on thinly disguised versions of *Time*. John Brooks described the staff of *Present Day:* "One day they walk in with nothing but a crew cut and a split infinitive. And two years later . . . they stagger out with a dangling participle." On *Beacon*, Charles Wertenbaker wrote, "opinion had become intertwined with fact. Every story had its 'slant.' " Sturges Strong, the publisher of *Facts, the Knowing Weekly*, Ralph Ingersoll, wrote, "got rich too rapidly . . . he made his multiplied millions manufacturing words instead of shoes or electric irons or even loaves of bread."[122]

Those novels reek of the self-importance that enveloped *Time*. Early on, the magazine had offered its readers, "the complete history of 1924"—two bound volumes of *Time*, costing $3.30. In 1928 the magazine boasted it was free of "cheap sensationalism and windy bias . . . edited in the historical spirit." To a reader's complaint about malicious descriptions, a *Time* editor in 1930 replied: "Physical characteristics are an inevitable concomitant of personality. And personalities are the stuff of which history is made."[123]

If *Time* was a historian, as it so often claimed, its chronicle, constrained by time and space, was inevitably long on style and short on substance. *Time*'s cover stories purported to be a complete account of a subject but were mostly written the week before they were to appear by a writer informed by no expertise beyond a folder of clippings and whatever facts his researcher had been able to glean.[124] And while some men of the year were giants (Gandhi, 1930; FDR, 1932 and 1934; Hitler, 1938; Stalin, 1939), others were not (Owen D. Young, 1929; Pierre Laval, 1931; Hugh S. Johnson, 1934; General and Madame Chiang Kai-shek, 1937). For New Year's Day 1940, *Time*'s managing editor, Manfred Gottfried, suggested that the writer Robert Cantwell prepare a searching comparison of the Twenties, "a fool's paradise," and the Thirties, "a thoroughly lousy time," all in 500 words.[125] History implies a measured overview from a distance, not an account hastily gathered from clippings and on the telephone, however artful the narrative might be. Nor can the history of an eventful era be meaningfully compressed into a page or two.

Time's grandiose sense of mission aside, the magazine's achievements were substantial, especially against the bleak backdrop of American newspapers. The editors of most dailies shunned complicated stories, especially if they involved foreigners other than Edward VIII or Bruno Hauptmann. So while Laird Goldsborough, *Time*'s foreign news editor, was reviled by his colleagues for referring to "Jew Blum," the magazine's readers did get a notion of a French Premier and his travails. While Goldsborough was also damned for his pro-Franco bias in the Spanish Civil War, *Time*'s readers, unlike most newspaper readers, learned of a dirty war in Spain and what the stakes were. Likewise, they knew something about Mussolini and the barbarity of Hitler, of dangerous developments in Japan and in China, subjects that seldom received much newspaper attention. Though bespattered with unseemly descriptives, the account of Washington goings-on presented in "National Affairs" avoided the violently anti–New Deal tone of most newspapers. In its business department, *Time* may have dwelled excessively on personalities, but it shunned the drab press releases and meaningless puffery that filled so many gray columns even in the *New York Times*. In its book pages, superb writers like Whittaker Chambers,

Agee, and James Fixx, despite their bitter political tussles, discussed important works intelligently, while few newspapers carried even syndicated book reviews. *Time* could also take pride in never pandering to advertisers, a pox that tainted so many newspapers and other magazines. And when it gossiped, *Time* aimed for the loftiest targets. Its inside reporting on the crisis over Edward VIII's affair with Wallis Simpson contained so many juicy, accurate details that several issues of the magazine were banned in Britain.

Time's finest hour came when war broke out in September 1939. As Americans vigorously debated their role, if any, in European events, *Time* issued a twenty-eight-page booklet, *Background for War,* which reprinted a series of articles on European developments since World War I. It ended with a trumpet call for American involvement: "Regardless of intention, the United States plays a part in power politics—with the responsibilities and risks of a world power." Within six weeks, 4.5 million copies went out to college presidents, businessmen, ministers, civic clubs, headmasters of private schools, teachers, women's clubs, and newsstands, where it sold for five cents. It was the largest distribution of any single-issue periodical in history, a testimonial that thoughtful Americans realized how impossible isolationism was.[126]

The phenomenal distribution of *Background for War* testified to Henry Luce's sway over public opinion, which the columnist Quincy Howe said made him, "the most powerful magazine editor of all time." His trouble, said the novelist Laura Z. Hobson, whose husband worked at *Fortune,* was that he was "torn between wanting to be a Chinese missionary . . . and a Chinese warlord." As he basked in having an elevator reserved for his personal use in the new Time-Life Building at Rockefeller Center, so he demanded status for his staff; his parting words to the correspondent he sent to Berlin in 1940 were: "Remember, you're second only to the American ambassador."[127] By then, *Time* circulation had passed a million, thanks to its purchase, in February 1938, of *Literary Digest.* In the week that *Time* began, fifteen years earlier, its puny twenty-four pages were dwarfed by the *Literary Digest*'s ninety-four. Now, an eighty-eight-page *Time* swallowed a twenty-four-page *Literary Digest,* "a gesture comparable," one of *Time*'s original staffers, Noel F. Busch commented, "to that of an Arab chief who considers himself bound by the laws of hospitality and genetics to play host to the family of a defeated rival."[128]

In addition, *The March of Time,* a re-creation of news events that started in 1931, reached millions of listeners weekly on the CBS radio network. The newsreel version, begun in 1934, was ultimately shown in 9,000 theaters, reaching some 30 million viewers each month. Mingled with fluff about an American motorist in France who refused to pay a traffic fine until France paid its war debts or a tour of former speakeasies on New York's 52d Street was coverage of important news often ignored by newspapers: the victory of the war party in Japan, the demagogues Huey Long and Father Coughlin, and the alarming growth of France's fascist organization, *Croix de Feu.*[129] But the main source of Luce's burgeoning influence was yet another publishing invention, *Life* magazine.

The germ of *Life* lurked in *Fortune* in the same way as the germ of *Fortune* had lain in *Time.* Its purpose, like that of all Luce's enterprises, was to tell people more about more of the world and to do it in an entirely new way. Its origin reaches vaguely back to 1928, when pudgy, balding forty-two-year-old Dr. Erich Salomon, publicity director at Berlin's vast Ullstein publishing empire, picked up a new camera. Salomon, who was not even an amateur photographer, was intrigued with the candid photos the Leica could produce, thanks to its unobtrusiveness and speed. His notion was to catch famous people unawares, yawning, sleeping, eating. He called himself a photojournalist; others soon called him "The Great Leveller . . . the first cameraman to bring to perfection the fine art of clicking his shutter at the exact wrong moment." In 1931 *Time* invited him to cover the Washington talks between the French Premier, Pierre Laval, and President Herbert Hoover. Laval, who was familiar with Salomon's work, animatedly harangued the President in French, while Hoover apprehensively eyed the camera as Salomon's Leica clicked.[130]

Impressed with his unposed, natural-light pictures, *Fortune*'s editors offered Salomon a job, but he elected to return to Germany. (He was murdered by the Nazis in 1944). By then, ideas for picture magazines abounded in the New York publishing community. Clare Booth, a brilliant and brittle blonde whom Luce divorced his first wife to marry in 1934, had written a long memo to her editor at *Vanity Fair* in 1932 suggesting an American version of the Parisian *Vu*, "reporting not *all* the news, nor necessarily the most *important* news, but the most interesting and exciting news, in photographs."[131]

The ninety-six-page picture magazine that appeared on November 23, 1936, had been ripening for almost two years. Its mission, expressed in terms no less orotund than those of *Time* or *Fortune,* was "to see life; to see the world; to witness great events; to watch the faces of the poor and the gestures of the proud; to see strange things—machines, armies, multitudes, shadows in the jungle and on the moon; to see man's work—his paintings, towers and discoveries, to see thousands of miles away, things hidden behind walls and within rooms, things dangerous to come to; the women that men love and many children; to see and take pleasure in seeing, to see and be amazed; to see and be instructed." For Time Inc. it was, Roy E. Larsen modestly wrote to charter subscribers, "truly the greatest, most complex journalistic assignment in history."[132]

It quickly became Time Inc.'s greatest financial and technological challenge. Staff memoirs recount the daring feats of photographers and reporters and the creative coups of editors, but the real heroics of *Life*'s beginnings took place among ledger sheets and printing presses, in the mundane world of paper orders, printing schedules, and sales presentations. To advertisers, *Life* had sold $1.7 million worth of space for its first year, based on a 250,000 circulation. But in its first month *Life* was selling more than half a million copies a week. By March 1937, J. Walter Thompson was among the agencies reveling in a 300 percent circulation bonus for its clients; the JWT house organ noted that at Time Inc. "they are pacing the carpets thin wondering why."[133]

No American magazine had ever sold a million newsstand copies, the chagrined *Life* executives moaned. But while the

printers at R. H. Donnelley in Chicago were straining to produce just over 1 million copies, tests indicated that 3 million
to 4 million copies of *Life* could be sold. As it was, the presses
were running night and day, all week long, and the advance
forms for the following week were being mounted on the
machines five minutes after the previous week's issue was
completed. Even worse, each issue, which sold for ten cents,
was costing thirty-five cents to produce, a hemorrhage to Time
Inc. of $50,000 a week.[134]

In April, a worried Luce addressed the American Association of Advertising Agencies convention at White Sulphur
Springs, West Virginia. He pointed to the dictatorships, which
in more than half of Europe had destroyed journalism. The
American press was still "free—economically—to engage all
the talent in the world, free to commit moral and intellectual
suicide, free to pander to the people and by pandering to
seduce them into their own enslavement," Luce said. "This
is the true poison of our time. And its only antidote is truth."
With the fervor that the Reverend Henry Winter Luce might
have brought to raising the funds for his beloved Chinese
Christian colleges, the son now begged the assembled advertisers, "not for a few incidental pennies; I ask that you shall
appropriate over the next ten critical years no less than $100
million for the publication of a magazine called *Life.*"[135]

Not charity but crassness saved *Life*. Advertisers responded
to Luce's plea and poured money into it because its avid readers proved also to be such avid shoppers. In 1938, some 73
percent of its readers lived in the desirable ninety-four metropolitan market areas, and 59 percent were in the affluent A
and B economic levels, both market criteria that J. Walter
Thompson had by then designated. *Life* also became the first
magazine ever to take in $10 million from circulation and,
partly because it cost twice as much as its competitors, had
more gross newsstand revenue than any two other weeklies
combined. On its second anniversary, *Life* proclaimed "a miracle": it was selling 2.1 million copies a week. It satisfied "a
peculiarly modern hunger for an accurate account of what's
going on in the world today." More loftily, *Life* was "helping

to safeguard America. For, an intelligent, informed public is not likely to stray from the paths of liberty and democracy." As for its sales potency, R. H. Macy's, the world's biggest store, had written, "If you'll do a story on snowballs, we'll sell 'em."[136]

Despite such success, *Life* continued to lose money until January 1939, when it began to deliver handsomely on its financial promise. In the next two years, Time Inc. revenues would leap from $29.3 million to more than $45 million, and before-tax profits would double, from $3.9 million to nearly $8.2 million. By 1940, *Life* was charging more for space than any of its competitors and swallowing 11 percent of all general magazine advertising dollars.[137]

While it remains doubtful that much of that astounding performance was due to *Life*'s serious coverage of a world that was serious indeed, the magazine did, as promised in its own promotion, reveal to America "its folkways, its politics, its arts and sciences, its theater, its styles; its sports, business, education and religion; its leaders and its common people; its history, public opinion, great events and humor; its fears and its pleasures." But, as the critic Bernard DeVoto tartly pointed out, its formula seemed to demand "equal parts of the decapitated Chinaman, the flogged Negro, the surgically explored peritoneum and the rapidly slipping chemise."[138]

Life invented the picture essay: a set of photographs that built suspense, contrast, narrative—the whole adding up to more than the individual parts. The *Life* photographer, as Carl Mydans remarked, was no longer "a helpless chowderhead . . . following his glamorous masterminding reporter and waiting for his command: 'Shoot that!' " Now he was a professional welcomed by kings and presidents, into the cloakrooms of Capitols and—all, of course, in quest of culture—the colonies of nudists. To the staff, yet another group of well-educated amateurs like those who had carried *Time* and *Fortune* to success, the world held no more secrets. "Anyone here an expert on brain surgery?" Mydans recalled an editor shouting. And a young reporter tore the paper from his typewriter and reached for the telephone, saying, "Not yet . . . but give me ten minutes."[139]

A veteran of *Life*'s early days, William Brinkley, broadly depicted in a *roman à clef* its pell-mell grab bag of grandiose purpose and homely detail. The magazine he called *Vital* was

> . . . the country's really big magazine . . . no magazine had such Power. May we repeat that word? *Power* . . . an article in *Vital* has prompted battles in the streets in . . . Pakistan and Paraguay, blood to flow, men to die . . . Many a tale could be told of how *Vital* has affected the course of an advertising sales campaign, the prosperity of a business, the affairs of state of great nations. . . . No publication so shapes out of the raw, raw clay, the raw unknowing clay, what the people of America buy, eat, drive, wear.[140]

Not the least of *Life*'s effects was to weld irrevocably the interests of masses of Americans in sensationalism, self-improvement, or even, perhaps, the state of the world with the concerns of advertisers: to sell goods. Not that it crudely hawked an advertiser's product in its editorial columns, as many newspapers did (and do). Rather, the *Life* merchandising department alerted manufacturers and stores to upcoming stories to which they could tie promotions. In early October 1940, for example, *Life*'s merchandising manager, H. Ford Perine, issued a "special news release" about a forthcoming picture story on sweaters. The release listed the manufacturer and retail price of all the pictured sweaters and offered free full-size reprints of the *Life* cover, which featured that merchandise. This kind of promotion reached gigantic levels: Merchandising promotions during 1940 used more than 6.4 million promotion items bearing the *Life* logotype, including package and letterhead stickers, folders, display cards, and more than a half million copies of the magazine itself. Some 35,000 newspaper ads also featured *Life* tied in with merchandise.[141]

The agencies' groping efforts of the Twenties to ascertain who bought what and why blossomed into Time Inc.'s baroque readership studies of the late Thirties. Six months after its birth *Life* published a 3-pound tome listing precisely how many copies went to every hamlet and city in the United States. A 1938 Roper survey revealed that 76 percent of *Life*'s readers thought "woman's place is in the home," 50 percent thought "all men are created equal," 64 percent thought a picture was worth a thousand words, 67 percent liked horses well enough to own one, but only 33.9 percent liked goldfish that well, and 48 percent liked Brahms enough to listen to his music. The unfathomable masses, which had so frightened Ortega y Gasset, were beginning to be known—and, so the survey continued, 42 percent of them even liked Debussy. A 1939 survey found that *Life*'s readers were financially comfortable, if not affluent; only 62,000 of them (out of 2.3 million) had family incomes under $1,000 a year, while 1,270,000 had annual family incomes over $3,000.[142]

In July 1938, for the most ambitious study of magazine audiences ever attempted, *Life* assembled the grand panjandrums of the art: Cherington, George Gallup, Roper, Archibald M. Crossley, and two academics, Dr. Darrell B. Lucas, associate professor of marketing at NYU, and Dr. S. S. Wilks, professor of statistics at Princeton. Their assignment at first blush sounds farcically trivial: to learn precisely how many people were reading America's leading magazines. But since advertising agencies allocated budgets on the basis of that kind of information, the results spelled health and life for some publications and disease and death for others. The study *Life* commissioned went on for many years, but its earliest findings accurately foreshadowed those that would follow: *Life* reached a colossal audience. The magazine's 3,092,254 copies were reaching 20,450,000 readers, some 19.1 percent of all Americans over ten years old. (Its nearest rival, *Collier's*, reached 13.7 percent.)[143]

Picture magazines like *Life* are "a publishing coup d'etat," the "cumulative result of . . . visual aids gradually infecting the organs of public instruction," Harry Shaw grumbled in *North American Review* shortly before its demise. *Life* is "an infernal contraption which . . . threatens to transform man into a species of goldfish . . . exposing his private life, loves and scandals to public view," J. L. Brown wailed in *American Mercury*, by then a sickly shadow of the magazine founded by H. L. Mecken.[144]

Iron statistics caused more such shrieks of pain from wounded and dying magazines. Advertisers in 1940 were spending some $156 million in magazines, barely more than the $150 million they had spent in 1931 and considerably less than the nearly $186 million spent on magazine advertising in 1929.[145] But their research methods had become so sophisticated and the demands of their clients so specialized that their budgets went for publications that could prove they had a discrete, free-spending readership. The magazines that flourished in this new climate were those which by format and content assembled consumption communities that proved desirable to advertisers and who, through their own resourceful research, promoted this fact to the agencies.

The old-fashioned generalized magazines, still being edited for rural and small-town America, starved, sickened, and often died, because rural and small-town America had died. They deserved to go, Frederick Lewis Allen, argued. Allen was editor of the *Atlantic*, which, along with *Harper's*, came through by dint of vigorous self-examination and drastic face-lifts. "What caused the procession toward the graveyard," he wrote in 1947, "was not a vulgarizing of American taste or even the rise of a mass-production principle in journalism, so much as the editorial—and business—complacency of the onetime leaders of the American magazine world. . . . They had gradually lost touch with American leadership."[146]

More than by jaded or hidebound editors, however, the changing of the guard among American magazines was caused by a changing of the guard within American society. The people who had flocked through colleges in such great numbers during the Twenties and Thirties wanted more than the carefully crocheted—and poorly researched—essays that the older magazines so frequently applied, like antimacassars, over the pressing problems of the day. The new audience worshiped facts as much as the editors of *Fortune, Time,* and *The Reader's Digest* and was equally eager to appreciate the virtues of Pond's ("for the skin you love to touch), Maxwell House ("good to the last drop"), and Lucky Strikes ("not a cough in a carload"). Advertising had an educational function, which its critics, dwelling only on its superficially witless or even misleading content, had overlooked. Beneath its overt, often blatant message was a subtle invitation to join a community of the elect, the tasteful, and the discriminating, just as *Time*'s format and jargon and *The New Yorker*'s supercilious tone conveyed the ambience of an exclusive club.

The success of those magazines during a dark decade pointed to an unexpected—and perhaps unsatisfactory—solution to the devilish scenario Ortega y Gasset had described in *The Revolt of the Masses.* He had feared that, lacking a noble ideology, the masses would turn destructive, and certainly the Russian Revolution, Fascism in Italy, and the rise of Nazism in Germany, all of which the philosopher had experienced, lent weight to his fear. "When the mass acts on its own," Ortega y Gasset wrote, "it does so in only one way, for it has no other: it lynches. It is not altogether by chance that lynch law comes from America, for America is, in a fashion, the paradise of the masses."[147] The Spanish philosopher was wrong in expecting only violence from the masses. But he was right in his description of America. Had he lived, he might have been chagrined by the pragmatic model it devised for taming the masses: Educated out of their brutish state, beguiled by goods, entertained by a resourceful press, courted by advertisements, the American mass split into myriad consumption communities, a docile giant fettered by the silken threads of mundane fantasy and trivial desire.

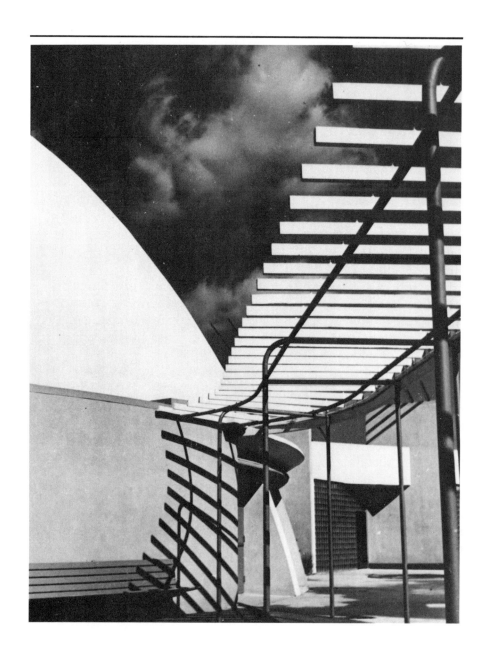

4

"...But Is It Art?"
The Marketing of the Modern

"LOVERS OF MODERN ART have united in unanimous congratulation of a difficult project, magnificently realized. Reluctant admissions have been wrung from the reactionaries."[1] Thus did an editorial in *Art News* greet the Museum of Modern Art's first exhibition, which opened on November 9, 1929. The fashionable crowd in silks and furs that had jammed the preview reception the previous evening included many who had thronged the very first showing of modern art in America, the Armory Show of 1913. Now the camps for and against modern art that had formed sixteen years earlier still skirmished, exchanging barrages of rhetoric as virulent in tone as they were empty of meaning.

"The bones of Edgar Allan Poe, Paul Cézanne, Charles Baudelaire are disinterred and put in consecrated ground," the New York *Sun*'s veteran critic, Henry McBride, who had warmly reviewed the Armory Show, wrote. "People actually whisper prayers for the repose of the souls they had been trying to damn but a short time before."[2] From the opposing trench, Royal Cortissoz, the New York *Herald-Tribune*'s grand critical curmudgeon, who in 1916 had thought Van Gogh's "heavy-handed" daubs "spoiled a lot of canvas with crude, quite unimportant pictures" and dismissed Cézanne as a "sincere amateur," damned with faint praise in 1929. The museum was lucky in "assembling the evidence for a much-discussed school," he allowed. And the show was "admirably hung."[3]

The rise in critical blood pressure that this exhibition could still cause was testimony to Americans' abiding conservatism in the realm of art. The 101 pictures so admirably arrayed through the new gallery's 4,200 square feet were, after all, far less provocative than those shown in New York's 69th Regiment Armory sixteen years earlier. This time, no Marcel Duchamp had sent a *Nude Descending a Staircase* to baffle viewers with its disembodied angles; no Constantin Brancusi had submitted a *Mademoiselle Pogany* to tickle their sexual fantasies. In fact, the four artists whose works evoked such spirited critique in 1929 were Vincent Van Gogh (died 1890), Georges Seurat (died 1891), Paul Gauguin (died 1903), and Paul Cézanne (died 1906). In Europe, those Post-Impressionists had gained the respect of serious critics soon after 1900 and were sold in an international market before World War I. After 1920, the art market's leading scholar, Gerald Reitlinger, noted, "it was useless to expect undiscovered masterpieces." But in New York, the *Post*'s critic urged those who were "instinctively hostile to this art" to "submit yourself to it . . . till you begin at least to comprehend what these 'old masters' of modern art have done."[4]

A tiny band of wealthy Americans had been collecting this kind of old masters for some time; all but fourteen of the works shown were owned by Americans, including Gauguin's *Manao Tapapau,* which A. Conger Goodyear had bought in Paris in 1895 for $216, and Cézanne's *Apples on a Plate,* purchased by Lizzie P. Bliss for $18,500 in New York in 1922.[5] But most art connoisseurs derided modernism, and Goodyear, the new museum's first president, marveled that "for this once and once only, not a finger of scorn was pointed." Indeed, unprecedented crowds often blocked the sidewalk at the southwest corner of 57th Street and 5th Avenue and overtaxed the Heckscher Building's creaking elevators to reach the exhibition on the twelfth floor. In a month, 47,000 passed through, 5,400 on the last day.[6]

The museum director, Alfred H. Barr, pointed to the large attendance as "a declaration of faith in the greatness of these men as artists and in their importance as the 19th century ancestors of the progressive art of our time." It was a quasi-religious theme he would frequently combine with a note of shame: This time he voiced chagrin that seventy of Van Gogh's works were permanently displayed in thirty-four world museums, but none in New York.[7]

The museum aspiring to remedy such native barbarism was the result of some casual shipboard conversations among three New York ladies less than a year earlier. "It seems unlikely that any other cultural organization had as brief a germination as the Museum of Modern Art," its official historian, Russell Lynes, wrote. However, to those "founding mothers . . . wishes were indeed horses." They were "women of spirit, adventurousness and, not unimportantly, of commanding wealth."[8] Lizzie P. Bliss, Mary Quinn Sullivan, and Abby Aldrich Rockefeller impressed their artistic taste not only on the museum they founded but also, through its director and its exhibitions, on millions of Americans in the decade to come.

Sullivan, a former art teacher married to a successful corporation lawyer, had been interested in modern paintings since 1912. She and her husband, Cornelius, had amassed Braques, Picassos, Cézannes, Van Goghs, and Modiglianis along with Georgian silver, rare books, and Early American furniture in their farmhouse in the heart of New York, under the Astoria end of the Hell Gate Bridge. But Mrs. Sullivan was "a church mouse" compared with her friend Lizzie P. Bliss, with whom she had worked in organizing the Armory Show.

The heiress of a New England textile fortune, Bliss was "a submerged maiden lady" who built up an extensive collection of modern art under the tutelage of the artist Arthur B. Davies. The intimate though chaste friendship between Bliss and Davies took the form of daily visits over tea and "intense conversations about art." In 1921 the pair had engineered a show of 127 moderns like Cézanne and Toulouse-Lautrec at the Metropolitan and had stirred a rousing fight. An anonymous circular had called modern art "a form of insanity," part of a worldwide movement aimed at "the breaking down of all law and order and the revolutionary destruction of our entire social system." John Quinn, an attorney and pioneer

collector of moderns, had called the attack "ku klux criticism
. . . rancid with envy . . . its vulgarity equalled only by its
cowardice." Miss Bliss, who had lent many works to the show,
as had Quinn, stayed in the background but began to discuss
a possible separate museum for modern art with Davies and
Sullivan.[9]

It was only talk until the two women broached the idea
to Abby Aldrich Rockefeller during a trip to Egypt and the
subsequent voyage home in the spring of 1929. Davies, who
might have been the new museum's president, had died a
year earlier, and all three women apparently shrank from
heading the museum. However, they had heard of a great
flap over modern art which had rent the board of trustees
at Buffalo's Albright Gallery. Its president, A. Conger Goodyear, had been ousted by the trustees for spending $5,000
for Picasso's pretty, pink period *La Toilette.* In May of 1929
Goodyear received a mysterious invitation to lunch with the
three ladies at the Rockefeller mansion on West 54th Street.
Midway through the simple meal, Mrs. Rockefeller "asked
the two ladies if they felt she should put to me the question
they had in mind," Goodyear recalled.[10] Would he head a
museum of modern art in New York? she asked him. His acceptance led to the commitment of ten years and to an incalcula-
ble increase in the value of his modern art collection.

In his memoirs, Goodyear claims that he had never previously met the three ladies, but Bliss, Mrs. Rockefeller, and
Goodyear had been among the trustees of the Harvard Society
for Contemporary Art, organized by Lincoln Kirstein and John
Walker in 1928. Also on the board of that youthful challenge
to Bostonians' loathing of modern art were Frank Crowninshield, editor of *Vanity Fair,* and Paul Sachs, a Harvard art
professor and curator of the University's Fogg Art Museum.
Both men joined Goodyear and the three ladies as founding
trustees of the Museum of Modern Art. Crowninshield continued to invest small amounts in whatever works Kirstein re-
commended, forming a collection that brought him $181,747
when he sold out a decade later.[11] Sachs, who had abandoned
a partnership in his family's Goldman Sachs investment banking firm in order to devote himself to art, was also an avid

collector. At Harvard in 1923, he had developed the first graduate course for museum curators, imparting to his students
less about art history than about the care and cultivation of
art dealers, collectors, and trustees. He was dubbed "the Felix
Frankfurter of the American art world," because so many
of his students went on to important museum posts. A dwarfish
man given to violent temper fits, with an absolute eye for
quality and intense opinions to match, Sachs proposed a former student as director for the new museum.[12]

After a first interview, Mrs. Rockefeller thought the candidate's "youth, enthusiasm and knowledge would make up for
his not having a more impressive appearance." After their
second meeting, a two-day grilling at the Rockefeller summer
home in Seal Harbor, Maine, she appreciated "not only his
good taste but also his judgment." When the trustees met
in September 1929, the young man was hired—at close to
the munificent salary Sachs had suggested, $12,500 a year.[13]

Slender, serious, a bit rumpled in the unmatched slacks and
jacket he habitually wore, Alfred H. Barr looked to be an
unlikely arbiter of taste. (In the oversize black overcoat he
had bought in Russia, into which his slight frame vanished
with the first snowfall in each of the next fifty-two winters,
he appeared downright bizarre.) Having no gift for small talk,
he fidgeted uncomfortably through the social niceties that
trustees commonly expected of a museum director. His entire
career had consisted of a year at Wellesley, where he taught
the first American course in modern art; a year teaching at
Vassar; and an extended trip to Europe in 1927–28, during
which he had visited the Bauhaus and spent the winter in
the Soviet Union, scouting for innovative artists and buying
the famous overcoat.

Later a composite portrait would emerge: his appearance
"like a defrocked Spanish Jesuit," his smile "suggest[ing] soil
erosion," his aura of "a Svengali," his handling of trustees
with "the diplomacy of a Talleyrand," his management style
a "fine Italian hand."[14] But in September 1929 Alfred H. Barr
tackled the task of creating a new museum for a new kind
of art with the tools provided by his heritage and his upbring-
ing. He was born in Detroit, the grandson of a Presbyterian

minister and the son of the Reverend Alfred H. Barr, a minister and professor of homiletics—the art of writing and preaching sermons. He had discovered art history at Princeton,
where he had received an M.A. in 1923. Enrolling at Harvard
for doctoral work, he stayed long enough to catch the eye
of Paul Sachs before rushing out to preach the gospel of modern art to the young ladies at Vassar and Wellesley. Even
before his museum opened its doors, he was proselytizing New
Yorkers in behalf of his creed. The city "alone among the
great capitals of the world, lacks a public gallery where the
works of the founders and masters of the modern school can
today be seen . . . an extraordinary anomaly," he wrote in
a flyer announcing the prospective museum. Within ten years,
he suggested, "New York, with its vast wealth, its already
magnificent private collections and its enthusiastic but not
yet organized interest in modern art, could achieve perhaps
the greatest modern museum in the world."[15]

Only a man raised in a religious household, where miracles
were dogma, could have believed that implausible promise.
True, the trustees included some wealthy and powerful individuals. But a museum also requires a scholarly pool of curators
to assemble and interpret its exhibits, not to mention a widespread, enthusiastic, and knowledgeable public, neither of
which existed in the United States in 1929. American art jour-
nals were poorly written, sparsely illustrated, and seldom read.
Not a single college course, except for the one Barr had developed at Wellesley, dealt with modern art, while art history
survey courses froze at the brink of Impressionism. No scholars
had applied to modern art the research into schools and influ-
ences, the study of iconography, the search for unknown masters, or the periodization which enhanced appreciation and
lent coherence to the art of the past. Modern art seemed to
have no history, and it certainly had no literature.

Among those who should have been its friends, the collectors and scholars of traditional art, the new art often aroused
bitter loathing. Dr. Denman Ross, for example, a Harvard
professor, Boston Museum trustee, and discriminating collector, was "as determined as Hitler to prevent the dissemination
of what he considered decadent art." Dr. Ross was moved

only to further rage by a 1926 letter to the *Harvard Crimson*, in which Barr had called Boston a "modern art pauper" because it lacked a single work by "men who are honored the world over"—Cézanne, Van Gogh, Seurat, and Gauguin.[16] While abstract art had had a brief vogue in the early Twenties among a few American artists, it sank into obscurity for lack of sales or interest by museums. Galleries routinely removed contemporary works that puzzled or offended any viewer. In the summer of 1929, for example, Ivan Albright, who had been invited to show at the annual survey of contemporary art in Toledo, Ohio, was asked to remove his painting, *Woman*, valued at $8,500, because it did not conform to some viewers' notions of feminine beauty.[17]

Early in the Twenties, an adventuresome New York woman, Katherine Dreier, had collected moderns with more enthusiasm than taste and had even, with the help of Marcel Duchamp and Man Ray, founded a museum of modern art in 1921, playfully called the *Société Anonyme*. Dreier crusaded for modern art with the same zeal she had brought earlier to women's suffrage, a settlement house in Brooklyn, and a vacation home for tired working women. For her modern art collection, Dreier was proud that "we never took into consideration . . . technique, taste, good or bad, or temporary popularity." Her aim was "always to discover the pioneers," but by foreswearing aesthetic standards she guaranteed uneven quality in her collection, even as her earnest Germanic bombast—"I am the reincarnation of Frederick Barbarossa," she once remarked—alienated potential supporters. By 1929 Duchamp and Man Ray were in Paris, and Dreier's collection moldered in her home in Connecticut.[18]

Understandably, those who were gathering modernist works before the paint was barely dry had difficulty distinguishing the lasting works from the more ephemeral. Even the organizers of the new museum often displayed their modern collections in exotic settings, implying that the new art had no ties with the traditional and was perhaps slightly wicked. Lizzie Bliss's spacious flat was furnished with Oriental carpets, Louis XV chairs, Chippendale, and Sheraton, like a thousand other well-mannered Park Avenue apartments. But the best paintings were tucked into an Art Deco gallery around a grand piano. Stephen C. Clark, the Singer Sewing Machine and thread heir, had crammed pictures from the basement to the attic of his gray Gothic mansion on 70th Street between Madison and Park avenues. On the top floor he had remodeled a gym into a Matisse room, with blue curtains, red-checked tablecloths, polka dot pillows, and crockery imitating the paintings on the walls. Shown this room during a visit in 1930, Matisse was appalled to see his pictures used as interior decoration.[19]

In the Rockefeller family, Abby's interest in modern art was considered "an outlandish hobby," her son Nelson recalled many years later. In the early Twenties, with her six children grown, Mrs. Rockefeller had converted their playroom on the eighth floor of the family mansion at 10 West 54 Street into a gallery of modern (or at least contemporary) art. It was designed in the Art Deco style by Donald Deskey and featured changing exhibitions of Mrs. Rockefeller's purchases: paintings and prints by George Bellows and Georgia O'Keeffe, watercolors by Charles Burchfield; abstractions by Alfred Maurer, whose 1932 suicide was blamed on the public's rejection of his work; and examples of most of the French moderns. Tucked under the eaves, those works could not offend the eye of Abby's husband, John D. Rockefeller, Jr., who spent millions restoring the palace at Versailles and Rheims Cathedral and who financed the Metropolitan's medieval showplace, the Cloisters, but who professed bafflement at modern works. Chinese ceramics were his personal collecting passion, and not even Matisse himself, when he came to dinner in 1930, could persuade him that modern art had any relationship to the art of other times and places. "I am interested in beauty," he told his son Nelson, "and by and large I do not find beauty in modern art. I find instead a desire for self expression."[20]

Most of the American art public would have agreed with that wintry judgment. Modern art might be a plaything of the odd millionnaire; paintings or sculptures purchased for a few hundred dollars might even be a speculative investment, as the Impressionists had been in the 1890s. True, the dealer Durand-Ruel had picked up Pierre-Auguste Renoir's stunning

Luncheon of the Boating Party in 1895 for a mere $7,200, but he had to keep it for twenty-eight years before unloading the painting to Duncan Phillips in 1923 for $200,000. And no other Renoir had brought more than $24,000 in the interim (nor would it until 1957). The market for Post-Impressionists was even chancier; in 1920, New York's Montross Gallery had shown thirty Van Goghs without selling one. As Cyril Connolly remarked: "Art is a religion; collecting is a prayer."[21]

As for American modernists, a collector and artist like Gertrude Vanderbilt Whitney might display and purchase their works as a patriotic charity and open a small museum in her Greenwich Village studio because she enjoyed the company of artists, but the public's interest in such art was distinctly marginal. In 1929, Whitney sent her aide Juliana Force to the Metropolitan Museum of Art to offer the entire 600-item collection along with enough money to build and maintain a wing to house it. But the Metropolitan's director, Edward Robinson, declined, saying "We don't want any more Americans. We have a cellar full of that kind of painting."[22]

Among dealers and connoisseurs, whatever market might have existed for the American avant-garde vanished with the stock market crash. Typical of the art public's attitude was the dismay that greeted the Museum of Modern Art's second show, *Nineteen Americans,* which opened on December 13, 1929. The elevators at the Heckscher Building were not overtaxed by throngs pressing to view works by such leading American modernists as Lyonel Feininger, Georgia O'Keeffe, Max Weber, and Charles Demuth, mingled with such traditionalists as Eugene Speicher, Bernard Karfiol, and "Pop" Hart. The choice was "deliberately eclectic," as Barr tactfully phrased it in the catalog foreword, selected by the trustees from their own collections by a complicated system of balloting among themselves. When Alfred Stieglitz, the pioneer exhibitor and collector of American modernists, offered to lend his best Marsden Hartleys for the show, Goodyear declined, saying "We only want the works of men owned by the trustees. That's the only way we can run this museum."[23]

Even friendly Henry McBride thought the museum had gone too far in exhibiting Americans and was pleased with the museum's next show, *Painting in Paris from American Collections*. It featured works owned by eight of the fourteen trustees, paintings by Derain, Bonnard, Braque, and Rouault, as well as *La Toilette*, the early Picasso that had caused Goodyear's ouster as president of Buffalo's Albright Gallery. In the catalog for this show, Barr began to develop the rich blend of scholarly information and summary judgments that he would refine and elaborate for the rest of his career. Unlike most art writings of that day, he dispensed with woolly generalities about compositions, brush strokes, and tonalities. Instead, he provided factual information, intelligent remarks the visitor could himself apply to the works he was viewing, while sharing what for many was still inside information. "If any movement can be said to be out of fashion," wrote Barr, "it is *impressionism* which reached its creative climax 50 years ago and has now degenerated in the hands of a second generation who are already middle aged academicians." For the public, which still wished to imbibe happy scenes, lusciously colored and easily understood, Barr endorsed Bonnard and Vuillard, who, though "of no importance as pioneers," did work "as fine in quality as that of any living painter." For the more adventuresome, Barr placed Derain and Matisse "among the half dozen greatest living artists."[24]

While the 58,575 visitors who stormed the museum during the show's six-week run indicated broad public interest, the preponderance of works owned by trustees seemed to confirm the barbs aimed at the museum before it even opened by the artist Albert Sterner. While the "gropings and experiments" of modern artists were "eagerly sought, appraised, classified and offered for sale for the special consumption of the dilletante collector," Sterner fumed, they were not entitled to "that mark of distinction that a place in a museum has hitherto . . . conferred." For a few wealthy people, modern art might be an "exclusive toy with which they ride the crest of the wave on an exclusive beach, where only the rich and idle may disport themselves." But, Sterner warned, "all waves very quickly turn their crests, merge their waters and disappear in the great and everlasting sea."[25]

Steering the tricky passage between that kind of criticism

and the perennial desire of museum trustees to validate their judgments while enhancing the value of their collections by museum display, Barr arranged a conservative menu for the rest of that first season's exhibitions. In May 1930, he showed American nineteenth-century masters—Winslow Homer, Albert Pinkham Ryder, and Thomas Eakins—painters whose ties to modernism were tenuous and whose ties to each other had never before been explored. For October 1930, he planned a show of Corot (died 1875) and Daumier (died 1879), who were not modernists at all, but who would bring MOMA the prestige of showing the first loans to an American museum from the Berlin National Gallery and the Louvre. Meanwhile, he briskly assigned to the trustees a summer reading list, including a work he considered "fundamental": Thorstein Veblen's *Theory of the Leisure Class.*[26]

To be understood, if not accepted, modern art had to have a history, and Barr saw writing it as one crucial aspect of his mission. Here he faced a paradoxical task, for modern artists and their propagandists had been insisting for at least three generations that their work had overthrown the past, that it was revolutionary. If modern art had no ties with the past, perhaps it really was, as Dean Inge of St. Paul's Cathedral, London, charged, "the delirious hallucinations of an incurable lunatic" or, as the art historian Kenneth Clark observed, an example of "the poverty of human invention . . . the end of a period of self-consciousness, inbreeding and exhaustion."[27]

The wider public beyond a tiny avant-garde coterie could hardly be expected to appreciate a style without roots, without context in the long development of art stretching back to the Renaissance. Furthermore, the lightning leaps of art in the twentieth century perplexed connoisseurs accustomed to the gradual evolution of artistic styles in the past. The Wild Beasts, *Les Fauves,* had barely trampled down the old color harmonies around 1905 when they were shoved aside by the Futurists' stress on depicting movement in 1909. At the same time, Picasso and Braque were exploring Cubism, while an entirely different group of artists, including Derain and Delaunay, claimed also to be Cubists, though their work looked quite different. All those puzzling currents emerged from

Paris in less than a decade; in other places—Munich, Zurich, Berlin, Moscow—all sorts of other experiments bubbled, not only in the realms of painting and sculpture, but in crafts, architecture, and film. Unlike the connoisseur of the past, who could by dint of viewing and study learn to appreciate the grand concepts of Italian Baroque or the domestic intimacy of the Little Dutch Masters, the conscientious amateur of modern art in 1930 was without guidance as he faced a phantasmagoria of apparently unrelated styles, unfamiliar media, and pugnacious manifestos. Alfred Barr recalled only three professors from his students days who had even mentioned modern art; all mentions were derogatory. Before 1931, he could remember only a single American scholarly article dealing with modern art, and it was hostile.[28]

When it came to American art, ignorance reached high into museum staffs. The Metropolitan let the Hearn Fund for purchases of American ($15,000 a year) art grow and grow, because no one knew what to buy; Harry Wehle, Met curator of painting, frankly admitted that while he knew the guidelines for Renaissance art, he had no parameters for American art, especially contemporary works. To educate his colleagues, along with the public, about American art became another missionary challenge for Barr.[29]

For the rest of his tenure as museum director, Barr would juggle more or less successfully the multiple demands of the trustees to exhibit the works of artists in their collections; of American artists, most of whom lived but a five-cent phone call away, to show their works; and of his missionary vocation to extend the museum's role into uncharted territory and to integrate modern art into a coherent history. All that he did while organizing exhibitions, searching for a permanent home for the museum, raising funds in the midst of the Depression, and assembling a permanent collection.

The museum's organizers had few ideas about what the permanent collection might contain. The Museum of Modern Art collection, Goodyear wrote in 1931, "will have somewhat the same permanence that a river has. . . . When a creative artist has not yet attained recognition from other museums . . . this institution [should] give him a full representation." But the MOMA should be "a feeder" to the Metropolitan

and other museums in the same way as the Luxembourg func-
tioned as a waystation for works that might end up in the
Louvre. Thus, "where yesterday we might have wanted 20
Cézannes, tomorrow five would suffice." The anonymous author (presumably Barr) of a 1932 MOMA booklet emphasized
that "the composition of the collection will change; the principles on which it is built will remain permanent. . . . After
an intermediate period in the permanent collection of the
MOMA, many . . . works will find their way into . . . other
museums." So adamant were the trustees about the principle
of an ever changing collection that they originally considered
a rule that the museum could not keep in its permanent collection any work by an artist dead more than fifty years.[30]

The question remained academic for some years, since the
entire collection up to 1933 consisted of twelve paintings and
ten sculptures. However, Lizzie Bliss, who had died in 1931,
willed the museum a magnificent array of thirty oils; thirty-
six watercolors, drawings, and pastels; and fifty prints by such
masters as Cézanne, Gauguin, Matisse, Modigliani, Picasso,
Seurat, Degas, Derain, Pissarro, Redon, and Renoir, all on
condition that a $1 million endowment be raised. By 1933,
the trustees were close to persuading Bliss's brother and executor, Cornelius, that the $600,000 scraped from Depression-
thinned pocketbooks should suffice, and the issue of the museum's collecting policy became more than theoretical. In a
November 1933 report to the trustees, Barr drew a torpedo
to represent schematically the ideal collection: "it's nose the
ever-advancing present, its tail the ever-receding past." In
painting, that would mean the bulk of the collection "concen-
trated in the early years of the twentieth century, tapering
off into the nineteenth." A "propeller" included the diverse
sources from which modern art drew, including Byzantine
panels, Rembrandt, Coptic textiles, pre-Columbian figures, Af-
rican masks, and Scythian metalwork.[31]

Under the fifty-year rule the museum would have to unload
the Van Goghs by 1940 and most of the rest of Bliss's treasures
by the mid-Fifties. That prospect was more than any collector
or curator could bear, the hoarding instinct being a salient
personality trait of such individuals.

In fact, the museum's fifth anniversary show in December

1934 indicated that the Bliss treasures would be around for quite a while, as the museum's focus roved beyond painting and sculpture. Housed in a building on West 53d Street provided at minimum rent by the Rockefellers, the first floors displayed the safe "old masters" of the modern once again, augmented with Picasso, Derain, Bonnard, Modigliani, and Vuillard. Indeed, half the permanent collection went back to the nineteenth century. The Americans were correspondingly uncontroversial—Burchfield, Hopper, Bellows, Prendergast, Davies, Weber. But, as the critic Forbes Watson noted, "the atmosphere chills as one mounts higher" and finds photographs of modern architecture and objects of industrial art. "When the visitor . . . comes upon a kitchen sink in Monel metal he is . . . advised to descend to lower planes before his nose begins to bleed." Still, Watson understood that "this exhibition proposes . . . to write the art history of today."[32]

The photos that startled Watson were the work of a department Barr had started in 1932 on the heels of "Modern Architecture: International Exhibition," organized by Philip Johnson and the architectural historian Henry-Russell Hitchcock. Using models, drawings, and photographs, that exhibition had given Americans their first comprehensive look at the works of Walter Gropius, Ludwig Mies van der Rohe, and Richard Neutra, among others. Along the same scholarly historical lines pursued by Barr in relation to modern painting and sculpture, Johnson and Hitchcock wove the European architects into a coherent historical web and then related their work to that of Americans like Frank Lloyd Wright and Raymond Hood. Just a few months before the fifth anniversary show, Johnson, who headed the museum's architecture department, had scandalized the sedate museum world while drawing abundant publicity and a large public with a show called *Machine Art*. Artfully spread over three floors of the museum were gear wheels and ball bearings, scientific instruments and kitchen implements, all selected for their aesthetic appeal. The museum acquired about a hundred of those objects as the core of its contemporary design collection, the first at any museum anywhere.

Also under way were efforts to start a unique department

that the trustees may not even have realized they wanted. Military history was one of Barr's hobbies, and the strategy and tactics he mustered during his five-year campaign for a film department were worthy of a Napoleon. While the founding trustees refused Barr's request for the department, a motion picture committee, chaired by Edward M. M. Warburg, somehow was started in 1932. The museum *Bulletin* somehow began printing thumbnail reviews of current movies in June 1933. In the next year, Lincoln Kirstein, Nelson Rockefeller, and Frank Crowninshield formed a Film Society for private showings arranged by Iris Barry, an English film critic who had somehow become MOMA librarian. Barr took to sending some of the trustees postcards recommending current films "that seemed to me works of art." By February 1935, he had a committee studying how to fund a film department and polling several hundred colleges on whether they would book MOMA-sponsored film series; 84 percent of those responding said yes. In May 1935 the film department received a $100,000 Rockefeller Foundation grant plus $60,000 from John Hay Whitney, a trustee and principal investor in *Gone with the Wind*. Iris Barry became director of the first film library ever associated with an art museum.[33]

In its first three years, the film library accumulated 288 films, a quantity of footage that would take sixty-eight eight-hour days for a full screening. Most were contributed by studios whose vaults Iris Barry industriously combed. She had also gathered the world's largest library of books about film and was receiving seventy-five phone inquiries, thirty letters, and ten personal visits a day. As Barr was giving modern art its history, Barry was developing the history of movies, assembling programs like "The Development of Narrative" in seven reels, "The German Influence" in thirteen reels; "The Rise of the American Film" in eleven, and "The Film and Contemporary Life" in fourteen. Shipped around the country, those programs attracted enormous audiences: 13,450 for a seventeen-session course at Dartmouth College; 1,800 for five sessions sponsored by the Junior League of Wilmington, Delaware; 500 for one showing sponsored by the Tacoma, Washington, Newspaper Guild; 2,000 for five sessions at the

San Diego Fine Arts Gallery. In its first two seasons, the MOMA film library's programs were viewed by 100,000 people.[34]

Many of those who reveled in their appreciation of modern art by watching movies would hardly have been attracted by a traditional museum exhibit. But the exhibitions that the MOMA began shipping around the country in 1931 also drew unheard-of crowds. The first of these, "A Brief Survey of Modern Painting in Color Reproductions," started modestly with a tour to seven New York City public schools. Packaged in three boxes weighing 638 pounds, complete with instructions for hanging, catalogs to be sold for twenty-five cents, and publicity releases and photos for local newspapers, it then crisscrossed the country for three-week stands at such unlikely habitats of modern art as the Federated Women's Club of Richmond, Virginia; the Junior League of Houston, Texas; the Society of Fine Arts in Evansville, Indiana; the Art Club of Augusta, Georgia; the Kentuckiana Women's Institute, Louisville; and Kresge's Department Store, Newark, New Jersey. The rental for a three-week show cost less than $40, plus freight to the next exhibition point. By May 1939 the show had been exhibited fifty-five times.[35]

Similarly packaged, a collection of photographs of modern architecture had by July 1932 traveled as far as the De Young Museum in San Francisco, the Denver Art Museum, and the St. Paul School of Art. Concurrently, a selection of models of modern architecture had been exhibited at Sears, Roebuck, Chicago; Bullock's Wilshire, Los Angeles; and major museums in Cleveland, Toledo, Milwaukee, Philadelphia, and Boston. In its first ten years, the museum would send ninety-one exhibitions on the road for three- to six-week bookings at 1,363 sites.[36]

From the beginning, the museum basked in publicity. A pamphlet to raise funds in April 1931 gleefully reported that in addition to editorials and articles in all New York newspapers, the new museum had been written up in forty-four others, covering twenty-five states. The museum's sponsorship in 1933 of a nationwide tour of *Whistler's Mother*, a painting whose relationship with modern art was flimsy indeed, garnered nationwide fame. Billed, on no grounds whatever, as "one of the six most popular pictures in the world," James A. McNeill Whistler's *Arrangement in Grey and Black No. 1: The Artist's Mother,* painted in 1872, drew duly gaping throngs. The attendant publicity emphasized how the picture had been spurned in America during the 1880s, only to be snatched up by the Louvre for $400. For the 1933 tour, it was insured for $1 million and "travelled like a returned trans- atlantic flyer, preceded by police escorts and surrounded by armed guards."[37]

The implication was, of course, that many of the works re- jected today would in the future become equally admired and valuable. Nelson Rockefeller recalled that his mother illus- trated "the need for the new museum by citing the tragedy of Vincent Van Gogh . . . who had died at age 37 in an institu- tion for the destitute . . . only to have the greatness of his work recognized years after his death." Abby Rockefeller wanted the new museum "to seek out . . . important new works of art as they were being created—without the benefit of time to test their intrinsic worth."[38] She was echoing an argument Barr frequently used to elicit funds for acquisitions and to justify mistakes in judgment that are inevitable when purchasing works before the paint is dry. "The value of all contemporary art is debatable," Barr had written in 1929, "and much of it is certainly transitory."[39] The trick was in distinguishing the debatable and the transitory from impor- tant new works, a difficulty that continues to bedevil collectors and museums.

The catalog for the fifth anniversary show exulted in the museum's popularity: attendance at its thirty-five exhibitions had been spectacular; almost a million people had paid their twenty-five-cent admission, no mean financial contribution. Barr's guide to the exhibition indicated that he had made considerable progress in creating for modern art the history it needed so badly. He shared with readers his "unfinished conclusion" that the Postimpressionists had assimilated Im- pressionism "into the traditions of European pictorial design." He lumped together the contribution of the painters who fol- lowed, from 1905 to 1920, as disregarding "resemblance to nature and subject matter" while stressing "purely aesthetic values of design." However, he noted a postwar rediscovery of "the traditional values of resemblance to nature and of subject matter." That schema fitted Picasso and Braque and surely pleased the trustees whose collections bulged with paintings from the School of Paris and whose gifts to the museum had skewed its collection in the same direction. But it neatly ignored the persistent abstractionism of such painters as Piet Mondriaan, Paul Klee, and Vassily Kandinsky, none of whose works the museum owned. Nor was Barr able to do much with the Americans in that show, except to note a "spirit of nationalism" as a current tendency.[40]

When consulted by the trustees, Barr gave eloquent lectures to make sense of what he liked. Abby's daughter-in-law Blanchette, who would become the MOMA's president some four decades later, recalled a consultation in Mrs. Rockefeller's private gallery over possible purchases for her collection: "Alfred was a born teacher . . . we . . . listened to him speak about the selection he had assembled, fascinated by his slow, meditative analysis of each work. After considerable discussion, he was careful to see that Mrs. Rockefeller made her own independent choice." But among his peers Barr could be curtly arbitrary. In 1934, he was one of three jurors for the Carnegie International Exhibition Prize. Asked for their criteria, the *New York Times* critic Elizabeth Luther Carey mentioned "merit," and the National Academy painter Gifford Beal said "workmanship and intelligence." Barr answered, "I have no beliefs." Pressed for how he would judge the pictures, he snapped, "By looking at them."[41]

Such was Abby Rockefeller's confidence in Barr that she gave him cash to buy whatever he cared to in Europe in the summer of 1935. And such was the market for modern paintings that for $1,000 Barr came home with three Dada collages, a Max Ernst oil, a Kurt Schwitters collage, an André Masson pastel, an Yves Tanguy gouache, and two Suprematist oils by Kasimir Malevich. That was the beginning of a purchase fund which would swell handsomely with the years. In 1936 Mrs. Rockefeller gave Barr $2,500 for American art and $2,000 for European; in 1938 she gave $20,000, and her son Nelson gave $11,500 in her name.[42]

The Rockefellers seldom invested in failing philanthropies; the many gifts the family made to MOMA testified to the growing respectability of modern art. John D. Rockefeller, Jr., may have relegated his wife's modern paintings to the attic and gently derided what the family habitually called "Mother's Museum," but all the while Abby was pursuing modern art, he was engrossed in creating the most massive real estate development the world had ever seen—Rockefeller Center—and its style was blatantly modern.

In the summer of 1929, while Alfred Barr was being scrutinized by Abby at Seal Harbor, Maine, her husband was consulting there with architects on constructing a new Metropolitan Opera and perhaps other—revenue-producing—buildings on several midtown Manhattan blocks owned by Columbia University. In that summer of prosperity, Junior (as he was universally called) agreed to pay Columbia University $3.3 million a year in ground rent for its land between 48th and 51st streets and Fifth and Sixth avenues. In the fall, when the opera plans fell through and the stock market hit bottom, Junior was stuck with three blocks of ratty brownstones, many of them housing speakeasies, yielding annual rents of $300,000.[43]

On February 3, 1930, Rockefeller approved a preliminary plan for the concept of a development that would be hailed as "one of the most significant architectural enterprises of the 20th century" and would become "the spontaneous core of New York City, just as the agora was in ancient Greece."[44] But, just like the art in Abby's museum, the final plans for Junior's development, when they were revealed in April 1931, were greeted with derision. The *New York Times* feared that it was "designed and will be executed as a big machine." *Pencil Points*, the trade journal for New York's architects, saw it as a test for "functionalists . . . to prove or disprove their theories." The project would "work" and might even be "tremendously useful." It offered "plenty of light and air and every convenience that human ingenuity has been able to devise," the magazine conceded, but it lacked beauty. The public had been promised "something truly monumental . . . that would . . . rank with the great public squares of the world . . . the Place de l'Opéra or the Place Vendôme in Paris . . . With its mouth all made up for frosted cake, the public was

naturally keenly disappointed when the model revealed it
was to get only bread. . . . A great opportunity to beautify
the city has been lost."[45]

Later, Nelson would ascribe his father's decision to go ahead
with the center's construction in 1932 to philanthropic motives: 64 percent of New York's construction workers were
unemployed in that awful winter; some 225,000 would be
employed in the first round of construction.[46] But the buildings' clean architectural design, the complex's functional innovations (such as underground shopping arcades, truck access,
and parking garage, the first in New York), and particularly
the interior decorating schemes indicate that Junior's skepticism about modern art had faded considerably. Perhaps, as
he had told Matisse over the dinner table in 1930, Abby's
"very special gifts of persuasion" had indeed worn his resolution against modernism "down to the consistency of jelly."
It is still more likely that the commercial possibilities of building New York's smartest business address were even more
convincing to the conservative millionaire. While Matisse (and
Picasso) would refuse Nelson's invitation to paint three large
murals for the entrance of the RCA Building,[47] those who
accepted commissions for Rockefeller Center represented the
cutting edge of modernism in America.

A typed summary of themes to be covered explained to
the painters and sculptors who were to do the work that the
complex would be "a monument of human skill and taste
and imagination" which "will be famous throughout the world
of men; none will view it with indifference. . . . It will be
influential . . . upon American taste" because its decoration
"will compel the development of forms of expression which
are novel and which, if successful, will open new avenues to
American art." Expressing the steely Puritanism that ruled
Junior's life, the decorative theme was to show the "social
ideal . . . of human welfare and happiness centering in the
work that we do and not in some incidental wage: if a whole
population, such as Rockefeller City will possess, can be lifted
into a finer life in their working hours, then the economic
democracy of America will have begun its answer to the Bol-
shevist challenge."[48]

Whether Diego Rivera, the artist finally commissioned to paint the RCA building lobby's central mural, read that homily is questionable. His title, *Man at the Crossroads of Life*, seemed nobly ambiguous, and his sketches for the 63-foot-long and 17-foot-high painting included Lincoln and Washington in the midst of an appropriately striving throng of common men. As Rivera began painting, in March 1933, the twenty-five-year-old Nelson Rockefeller sat beside him on the scaffold night after night. What did they talk about? Rivera's friends asked. The artist replied: "Tonight he said, 'I'm of the last generation in which a great fortune will be in the hands of a single family.' " Nelson was then a MOMA trustee and executive vice president of Rockefeller Center. He was dismayed as he watched the artist depart from his sketches to include a portrait of Lenin, the Soviet flag, and Communists gaily dancing in the streets contrasted with scenes of American police brutality, germ warfare, and gross capitalists with running sores. The nightly tête-à-têtes on the scaffolding ceased, and on May 3 Nelson wrote Rivera: "As much as I dislike to do so, I am afraid we must ask you to substitute the face of some unknown man where Lenin's face now appears."[49]

Abby had been an enthusiastic patron of Rivera. In 1927 she had bought three large paintings and a sketchbook of forty-five watercolors, and later she commissioned him to paint a portrait of her daughter Babs. But not even her "very special gifts of persuasion" could save Rivera from her husband's wrath. Nelson could not persuade the artist to permit the mural to be removed and reassembled at the Museum of Modern Art. So Rivera was paid his $21,500 fee and a curtain was hung over his work. At midnight on February 9, 1934, workmen hacked away the offending mural; replacing it would be a work by Jose Maria Sert with a theme aimed straight at Junior's stern belief: "the triumph of man's accomplishments through the union of physical and mental labor."[50]

The brouhaha over Rivera's mural was not the first in that turbulent decade over an artist's graphic political propaganda. The Mexican mural renaissance led by Rivera and Clemente Orozco, with its strong Marxist message, had inspired many American artists. The mural show inaugurating the MOMA's first permanent building, at 11 West 53 Street, in 1932 had featured a Hugo Gellert work depicting John D. Rockefeller, Sr., J. P. Morgan, President Herbert Hoover, and Henry Ford with Al Capone, brandishing a machine gun from behind a pile of money bags and titled *"Us Fellas Gotta Stick To- gether"—Al Capone.* The Advisory Committee, sponsor of the show featuring this polemic, included Lincoln Kirstein, Ed- ward M. M. Warburg, and Nelson Rockefeller among the wealthy young art lovers being groomed for trusteeship. They were horrified, especially since Junior owned the new building and had just reduced the rent. Kirstein argued that if the show were closed it would open elsewhere, so Nelson ended up paying a conciliatory call on his father and Morgan, who, he reported, "didn't mind."[51]

That row had been largely confined inside MOMA, but the Rivera flap reverberated in the newspapers and in the art community. A May 11, 1933, headline in the Boston *Evening Transcript* quipped "Too much 'Red' in his color scheme." Eleven artists protested "cultural vandalism" by withdrawing their works from a municipal art show, which nevertheless opened as planned on February 28, 1934, and filled fifty-three galleries and a sculpture court in Rockefeller Center. For a brief moment, Diego Rivera was a radical hero; threats to remove a provocative mural he had painted in Detroit prompted 12,000 workers there to adopt a resolution that they would "protect the murals with force, if necessary."[52]

But such were the fickle political gales buffeting the Thirties art world that by the end of 1935 even the radical Artists Union was denouncing Rivera. "He isn't a friend of revolution- ary painting and he doesn't paint workers," an article in the union's magazine *Art Front* complained. His "rise to power has an opportunistic stink . . . Rivera has used Communism rather than furthered it." A month later the same publication accused him of "sticking his thick neck into Mr. Rockefeller's noose and then raising . . . a howl when the rope was tight- ened," creating "an illusion that he was a noble martyr of the people." In the best Stalinist tradition, the article then denounced "all the arty humanitarians" who had leaped to the artist's defense.[53]

The Artists Union had grown out of marches and demonstrations, which in 1933 forced the New Deal to include artists in its unemployment relief programs, a step that had far-reaching effects. While most other relief recipients experienced a severe shrinkage in their standard of living during the Depression, most American artists had so long been poverty-stricken that the modest Federal relief payments were a bonanza. Where previously most artists had to support themselves with commercial work or jobs totally unrelated to art, the $23.50 a week that they averaged from relief enabled them to do art full time. Moreover, artists were brought together by the relief agencies' requirement that they regularly bring their creations to central locations and in some instances, as in printmaking, to complete their work in a centralized workshop; by the frequent exhibitions where the Federal agencies attempted to sell the works they had bought; and by the incessant changes in eligibility rules, which required speedy organization of protests.

Few of the 12,000 artists who were aided by various government programs from December 1933 to June 1943 could be called modernists. In the catalog for MOMA's fifth anniversary show, Alfred H. Barr had been hard pressed to integrate the Americans favored by some of his trustees, especially Mrs. Rockefeller, into his developing schema of modern art. The dominant American style during the mid-1930s was American Scene, a celebration of rural and small-town America. A perceptive talent like Grant Wood could mine masterpieces from that idiom, but the majority of the American Scene works "still belonged," as one critic remarked, "to the 'Kiss Mama' school." Yet American Scene had powerful defenders among critics. Such a respected art writer as Thomas Craven hailed "a body of work leading to our cultural independence" and marveled at the "zeal and vitality" with which those painters "dig and delve in the American environment." They were an answer, he thought, to French modernism with its "organized smudges, geometrical patterns and particles of unattached color."[54]

But whatever the style or quality, Federal patronage released a prodigious flood of art in America: more than 2,500 murals, including frescos, mosaics and photo-murals; almost 18,000 sculptures and 110,000 easel paintings; about 250,000 impressions of 11,300 different prints; 2 million copies of 35,000 different posters; half a million photographs. In addition, government support resulted in two widely shown films, one on making frescos and another on mosaics, plus 450 art exhibitions, many of which traveled to remote city halls and schools. Furthermore, the Federal government staffed 103 community art centers and persuaded local governments, clubs, women's groups, chambers of commerce, and art and educational societies to contribute more than $1 million for their upkeep. Altogether the Works Progress Administration/ Fine Arts Project, which included drama, music, and literature, spent $35 million during the eight years of its existence. Other agencies also helped the arts: The Public Works Art Project spent $1.3 million in emergency relief for 3,700 artists from December 1933 to June 1934; the Treasury Department's Section of Fine Arts awarded 1,400 contracts worth $2,571,000 for paintings and sculpture in new Federal buildings, mostly post offices, between 1934 and 1943; and the Treasury Relief Art Project spent $833,784 to employ 446 artists to decorate existing Federal buildings.[55]

Not all artists welcomed Federal aid. When a proposal for a Federal Bureau of the Fine Arts was circulated in 1934, John Sloan replied: "Sure, it would be fine to have a Ministry of the Fine Arts in this country. Then we'd know where the enemy is." Nor was President Franklin D. Roosevelt, under attack by critics of make-work projects, enchanted by the fact that while the average WPA worker received $60 a month, the average artist netted a princely $105.50.[56]

Without question, Federal support not only brought forth an enormous output by an unprecedented number of artists but also developed a vast audience for art. A Public Works Art Project display in March 1934 at the Los Angeles Museum of Art drew 33,000 people, smashing all attendance records for a California exhibition. The critic Forbes Watson hailed a show of 500 PWAP works at the Corcoran the following month as "the greatest art event in this country since the Armory Show." Like the Armory Show, that exhibition stirred the spicy brand of controversy that boosts attendance. The Navy angrily protested Paul Cadmus's *The Fleet's In,* which depicted reveling sailors interacting enthusiastically with questionable ladies. Though the painting was removed, its notoriety contributed much to attracting 26,536 visitors to the Corcoran (as against 11,632 who had entered the gallery in the same period the previous year). After it closed, the works in the show were quickly snapped up by government officials: President and Mrs. Roosevelt picked forty-two items, Secretary of Labor Frances Perkins took 130 oils and water-colors to decorate the Department of Labor, and Congressmen and bureaucrats cleaned up the rest.[57]

The beginning of Federal programs also refreshed the hopes of the few American artists who pursued modernism in the early Thirties. Stuart Davis, for one, hoped that government support would break the "vulgar domination" of the art mar-ket by "a very small class of society with large incomes" and by the dealer who "demanded work he could sell to the money dilettante and the aesthetic connoisseur."[58]

But Davis had not reckoned with the conservative bent of the bureaucrats who managed the government art pro-grams and the narrow views of those who controlled many of the sites where government-sponsored art was displayed. The Treasury Department's Section of Fine Arts, which com-missioned murals in new post offices and court houses, claimed it awarded contracts on the basis of competition. But that claim was largely a shield against Congressmen's attempts to wangle commissions for constituents; the Section held only 190 competitions while awarding 1,271 contracts. The work had to please local juries and therefore often pandered to unsophisticated tastes. Few artists at the time objected to pros-tituting their individual styles to please the bureaucrats of the Treasury Section, because they were desperate to earn the $20 per square foot that the work paid, but later many admitted that they had "learned to 'paint Section.' "[59]

The painter's grand concept often confronted narrow and prejudiced opposition. When the artist James Michael Newell proposed a mural depicting a history of Western civilization around the perimeter of the New York's Evander Childs High

School library, he was dismayed to learn that the school's administrators preferred a history of the Bronx.[60] A Stefan Hirsch depiction of *Justice as Protector and Avenger* in an Aiken, South Carolina, courtroom, which featured a woman who might have been a mulatto, so enraged a judge there that he ordered it shrouded with tan velvet whenever court was in session.[61]

But despite such instances of rampant philistinism, the government art programs reached out to millions of Americans whose lives had never included art. The WPA/FAP established 103 art centers in such remote places as Gold Beach, Oregon; Laramie, Wyoming; and Price, Utah, staffed with professional artists and administrators who had left large cities for this missionary work. Often, the townspeople's support was astonishing. In Helper, Utah, the art center's first show attracted 3,017 visitors out of a population of 3,600, mostly coal miners and railroad people. In Phoenix, Arizona, then a city of 60,000, an opening night crowd overflowed the exhibition building despite a temperature of 120 degrees. Within a week, those who planned to take classes at the center had bought all the charcoal, paint, and paper stocked in the city. In Sioux City, Iowa, the art center developed into a three-and-a-half-story building that attracted 20,000 visitors each year. Many other centers evolved into museums, including those in Roswell, New Mexico; Greenville, South Carolina; and Salem, Oregon, and the Walker Art Center in Minneapolis.[62]

The bureaucrats who commissioned the post office murals may well have seen their mission in the patronizing light of bringing culture to the ignorant hinterland. In their turn, many of the artists who left New York and Chicago for the Kentucky hills may have viewed themselves as pious Marxist emissaries to the proletariat. But both groups seemed unaware that large new segments of American society had considerable education in the arts and were eager to learn more. Between 1920 and 1930, college enrollments in music courses grew by 60 percent and in art courses by 30 percent. Whereas only 541 Harvard men registered for art courses in 1920, 1,217 studied art in 1930, and there was comparable growth of interest in art at Princeton and Yale. During the decade of the Twenties, when college enrollments doubled, professional students of art and architecture increased by 400 percent. When students at Haverford College were asked in 1931 what new courses they wanted, "one-third of the student body placed the arts at the head of their petitions." In New York City high schools, art appreciation became a course required for graduation.[63]

Museums had also grown rapidly during the Twenties; the sixty new art museums opened between 1920 and 1930 were twice as many as had been opened in any preceding decade and brought the total to 167—there was at least one art museum in every American city of more than 250,000 population. In 1933 *Recent Social Trends,* the most thorough survey of American society ever made, found that one of the most striking recent changes in the arts was the museum's new importance in American culture. More people were visiting the Metropolitan Museum of Art in New York than visited the Louvre. Attendance at other museums was equally heavy and would grow even faster as the Depression deprived people of more expensive entertainments. The small museum in Santa Fe, New Mexico, logged 100,000 visitors in 1930, while the numbers who passed through the Toledo (Ohio) Art Museum in a year equalled 75 percent of the city's population.[64]

Audrey McMahon, the editor of an art magazine, *Parnassus,* and director of the College Art Association during the late Twenties, recalled a cultural desert west of the Alleghenies: art courses taught by maiden ladies who had never seen an original painting; a Sacramento museum filled with "*Mona Lisa* by Miss Jones, *Mona Lisa* by Miss Smith, *Mona Lisa* by Miss Raymond"; a Southern museum displaying gilded baby shoes worn by its founder. But the young people whose demand for art instruction was outgrowing classroom equipment and the supply of trained teachers, and the fast-growing attendance at museums foreshadowed an explosion of interest in art and increased tolerance for new kinds of art. "The new and familiar is tending to lose its capacity to shock our susceptibilities," Frederick P. Keppel of the Carnegie Corporation noted in 1932. "It is a new spirit which has so largely removed paintings from the darkened parlor and placed them on the walls of the bank or department store."[65]

So the founders of the Museum of Modern Art had been sailing into a friendly breeze, after all, rather than the whirlwind so many observers had envisioned. In 1934, as MOMA celebrated its fifth anniversary, NBC broadcast nationwide a series of seventeen weekly radio talks on American art, sponsored by the General Federation of Women's Clubs, the Carnegie Corporation, the National Advisory Council on Radio in Education, and the American Federation of the Arts. *Art in America,* the oversize book based on the talks, was written by Alfred H. Barr and Holger Cahill, MOMA director of exhibitions in 1932–33 and adviser to Abby Rockefeller on her folk art collection. Although the radio series had been developed in cooperation with the Chicago Art Institute, the Metropolitan Museum of Art, and MOMA, it followed the sweeping definition of art put forth by Barr. In the book, a popular work that went into at least three printings, Philip Johnson wrote on modern interiors and architecture, Lincoln Kirstein covered photography, and the MOMA film librarian, Iris Barry, wrote on films.[66]

Cahill wrote pessimistically about the future of art in America:

> In the Depression, art seems more a luxury than ever, the artist more divorced from life. And there are no avenues of escape. There is no Europe, no Tahiti, no Bohemia, no ivory tower safe from the encorachments of the world. The Olympus of the observer, detached from the actualities of daily living, has been blasted out of existence. Art for art's sake is a tattered banner which has been blown down by the wind. There is no health in introspection. The cultivation of sensibility is a blind alley.[67]

A year after writing that, Cahill would be named the director of WPA/FAP, organizing the widespread programs that would bring art to every corner of the nation. The tide for modernism was quickening even as he mourned the end of Olympus. Before the decade was out, the crusade for modern art begun by the small band who founded the MOMA, amplified by the Federal art programs, would swell into a mass movement, and New York would begin to replace Paris as the center of the avant-garde.

But in November 1935, MOMA once again reached back for an "old master" of modern art, in quest of nationwide publicity and attendance records. Months before the most comprehensive American exhibition of Van Gogh opened, Sarah Newmeyer, the museum's professional publicist, who had been hired in 1934, was bombarding newspapers with information about the show scheduled to open on November 4, 1935. In July, the press was informed that Goodyear was sailing for Europe to "confer" with Barr on loans for the show from European museums. Later there was news that New York department stores were preparing window displays to tie in with the show and that Van Gogh blue and yellow was the most fashionable color scheme for fall. As the show's opening approached, Newmeyer doled out interesting tidbits to the press almost daily: A Van Gogh sunflower painting for which the poor artist had hoped to receive $100 had recently sold for $50,000; the 127 works to be shown were insured for more than $1 million; when the pictures by "the great modern artist" which had been borrowed from European museums arrived in New York, they would not be examined by customs at dockside but would be taken, "heavily guarded, under customs cord and seal direct to the museum and held unopened until the customs inspector arrives to examine them, a courtesy usually extended when shipments are particularly valuable and fragile."[68]

When the public responded to this publicity drumbeat by swamping 53d Street and formed a queue averaging 3,000 people waiting in the cold to enter the museum, further publicity went out. One release gave tips on how to pronounce the artist's name, explaining that an average of ninety people a day were phoning the museum for information, but "many seem reluctant to say the name of the Dutch painter and phrase their questions in such a way that the operator must say it." After frequent updates on the throngs in attendance, the museum announced that a record 123,339 had passed through the exhibition in six weeks. Most of the paintings then traveled around the country for almost a year, drawing record crowds—and further publicity—wherever they went: more than 100,000 at the Boston Museum of Fine Art; 227,540 in San Francisco; and similarly unprecedented crowds in Chicago, Philadelphia, Detroit, Toronto, Minneapolis, and Kansas City. When the exhibition returned to New York for a farewell viewing, 19,002 visitors crammed the MOMA within two weeks. Altogether, 878,709 Americans had paid twenty-five cents each to see the works of an artist so maligned and so unappreciated in his day that he had failed to sell a single painting in his lifetime.[69]

The implied message of the Van Gogh show was that a great, innovative artist could easily be ignored, perhaps even driven to suicide, by an uncaring public. Its corollary was a warning that the public scorned difficult or puzzling art at its peril: Distorted or abstract work by contemporary artists, scorned today, might well be hailed by future generations as masterpieces. "In the recent past, it has been the lot of innovators among artists to work for posterity, since most of their contemporaries have refused to accept them and the general run of conservative museums have not shown much interest in them until after they were dead. If there are any unrecognized Van Goghs about," *Fortune* noted in a lengthy tribute to MOMA written anonymously by Alfred H. Barr, "they should not be forced to starve and commit suicide and the public should not be denied the opportunity of enjoying their work."[70]

In two monumental exhibitions during 1936, Barr persuasively followed that reasoning to promote modern art. The catalog he wrote to accompany the first, an unprecedented survey of "Cubism and Abstract Art," featured on the jacket a schematic diagram that interconnected the dozens of confusing movements constituting twentieth-century art and carried them backward to the familiar "old masters": Van Gogh, Seurat, Gaugauin and Cézanne. The exhibition included 386 items—not merely painting and sculpture, but also architecture, industrial art, photography, theater, films, posters, and typography. So now modern art had a history and also an expanded content, both developed by Alfred H. Barr.

His catalog was a model of clarity, scholarship, and subtle persuasion. Again and again, he related the unfamiliar art confronting viewers with unquestionable masterpieces of the past. The first two paragraphs in his introduction describe the revolutionary nature of Renaissance art and smoothly contrast the Flemish and Florentine artists' "passion for imitating nature" with the early-twentieth-century artists' "common and powerful impulse . . . to abandon the imitation of natural appearance." Like a subtle preacher, he anticipates his audience's cavils, hesitations, and puzzlements about modern works. "Abstract," he admits, is a confusing and arbitrary description for many of the works in the show. He then quotes Socrates on "the beauty of shapes," which are "not beautiful for any particular reason or purpose . . . but . . . by their very nature beautiful, and give pleasure of their own, quite free from the itch of desire; and colors of this kind are beautiful, too, and give a similar pleasure." Using less than a single page, he relates the polarities developed by the ancient Greeks to the two major streams of modern art: the Apollonian—intellectual, geometrical, rectilinear, structural, classical—and the Dionysian—intuitive and emotional, organic, curvilinear, decorative, romantic, exalting the mystical, the spontaneous, and the irrational. Thus, he concludes, "the shape of the square confronts the silhouette of the amoeba."[71]

More than a tract, Barr's catalog was a mine of solid information, including a chronology of every important modern art movement, 223 illustrations, biographical data on the artists, and a bibliography listing 444 items. Along with many of Barr's subsequent catalogs, this one is still in print after fifty years, a model, the art historian Meyer Shapiro has said, of "lucid, well-illustrated and documented [art writing] with a scholarly scruple free from pedantry and hermetic allusions."[72]

For the thousands who visited the "Cubism and Abstract

Art" exhibition in the spring of 1936, the catalog made sense of works so puzzling that nineteen of the sculptures were refused admission by U.S. Customs on grounds that they did not represent an animal or human form. By 1936, blockheaded philistinism on the part of government officials had been a frequent source of notoriety for modern art. This time the museum's publicity department was prepared: Release after release pounded the Customs Service, spread word of Goodyear's letter to other museums asking for their support in removing aesthetic judgments from people mundanely charged with collecting tariff duties, deplored a week's delay in the show's opening because of those officials' idiocy, and triumphantly announced the nineteen works' release from bureaucratic bondage. After a well-attended, but not record-breaking, six-week run in New York, the exhibition toured nationwide, bringing the largest collection of abstract art ever seen in America to San Francisco, Cincinnati, Minneapolis, Cleveland, Baltimore, and Boston. The participating museums paid just $400 plus freight for a month's rental.[73]

Barr's second blockbuster of 1936, "Dada, Surrealism, and Fantastic Art," also toured widely in the following year, after garnering reams of publicity upon opening in New York on December 9. The most notorious item in the exhibition was Meret Oppenheim's *Fur-lined Teacup,* an object so dubious that Barr didn't dare purchase it outright. Instead, he paid $50 to keep it "on extended loan"; nine years later it entered the "study collection," whence it passed quietly into the permanent collection.[74]

Fomenting scandals had been an intrinsic ingredient of Dada and Surrealist art; the antics of the artists intertwined with their shocking works. At a New York party in 1935, for example, Salvador Dali had eaten the buttons off his hostess's dress. "Permit me to do this," he had said, "as a token of my paranoiac esteem." With his black cape and corkscrew moustache, Dali had lectured at MOMA in January 1935: "How could anyone expect to understand my paintings, when I myself, I regret to say, do not understand them either. . . . I am but the automaton which registers . . . the dictates of my subconscious, my dreams . . . my paranoiac hallucinations and, in short, all those manifestations . . . of that sensational and obscure world discovered by Freud . . . the only difference between myself and a madman is that I am not mad." America's newspaper editors lapped up as much of Dali as they could get, so the Dada and Surrealist show was greeted by delicious notoriety. A woman attending the show had fainted, one story reported, moaning, "Those awful pictures! Those awful pictures!" Another person had offered to attend the show "in any desired costume and pose as an exhibit." *Newsweek* described the founders of Dada in 1916 as "a group of war-weary Zurich artists [who] drank too much and decided art has no place in civilization." The magazine dwelled, with some confusion, on the show's naughty Freudian undertone: "too much symbolism hitting below the belt for even the most out-and-out extrovert not to feel some quiver of the unconscious." In June 1937, Sarah Newmeyer, the publicity director, reported to members that the MOMA had been "exceptionally fortunate," having been mentioned in the *New York Times* "at least once every three days" and receiving "frequent notices in most of the leading newspapers." *Life* magazine had run three- to five-page stories in nine issues during the 1936–37 season, and both Paramount and Universal had shown newsreels of "Dada, Surrealism, and Fantastic Art" in theaters nationwide.[75]

As the show toured around the country in the spring of 1937, local publicity amplified the fanfare. Unlike earlier MOMA traveling exhibitions, which consisted mostly of loans, many works in this show were for sale: an André Breton collage cost $5; a Kandinsky watercolor, $75; René Magritte's *Mental Calculus*, $275; Henry Moore's lead *Reclining Figure*, $250; and Paul Klee's *Mask of Fear*, $1,000. But often the newspaper publicity dwelled on the more sensational items: "insane art" and "psychopathic watercolors" at $40 each and "psychopathic embroideries" at $125 each. When the tour ended after one-month runs in Philadelphia; Boston; Springfield, Massachusetts; Milwaukee; the University of Minnesota; and San Francisco, the *Fur-lined Teacup*, the art journalist

Russell Lynes thought, "was probably the best-known single object in the country."[76]

That fact was particularly galling to the American modernists, who were emerging with the financial, if not ideological, support of government programs. Between the two 1936 blockbuster surveys of modern European art, the MOMA had shown "New Horizons in American Art," which emphasized the popular American Regionalist style while its catalog failed to reproduce any of the few abstract works in the show. The catalog also lacked the kind of scholarly explanation and historical schema Barr had developed so brilliantly for European art. Later in the year, the New York Municipal Art Gallery, a WPA/FAP institution, showed the work of thirteen abstract painters. Eleven of them organized in November 1936 as American Abstract Artists. But, as was typical of the cultural scene in the Thirties, no unity developed within even the tiny, esoteric sect of American abstractionists. Unknowns like Burgoyne Diller, Rosalind Bengelsdorf, and Byron Browne were joined by the newly arrived German refugee artist Josef Albers, but Arshile Gorky and Willem de Kooning who attended the organizing meeting, declined to join. A competing group of modernists who styled themselves "The Ten" included Adolph Gottlieb and Mark Rothko, who would later become leading Abstract Expressionists.[77]

None of these artists were receiving much critical or financial success. Reviewing a show by The Ten at the Montross Gallery in December 1936, *New York Times* art critic Edward Alden Jewell wrote that he could not understand their work "at all. Often they look to me like silly smudges." At an AAA show in the Squibb Galleries in April 1937, the artists had difficulty selling lithograph portfolios containing thirty-nine original works for a total price of fifty cents.[78]

Those who commissioned murals through the government relief programs were only slightly less hostile to modernists than the arbiters of taste in the places where the murals were to be painted. "Immorality became the popular, working definition of modernism," Karal Ann Marling, the historian of Depression post office murals, comments. "Calling someone a modernist was tantamount to calling him a communist."

Thus, a mural showing a bevy of middle-aged ladies in one-piece bathing suits was "yanked off the wall" of the Kennebunkport, Maine, post office "on the grounds that it was un-American, modern, 'Red' and stuffed with 'naked hussies.'" In Belleville, Illinois, citizens forced the artist Arthur Lidov to remove a mural because they thought its Abraham Lincoln resembled Lenin. Even at Bellevue Hospital in presumably progressive New York, doctors permitted murals in the waiting room only after artists promised not to paint "items disembodied, broken, angular or incomplete," to use only "soft colors," and to avoid showing women in any "suggestive" poses.[79]

Of 1,371 murals commissioned by the Treasury Department, only one was overtly abstract. Aware of the hostility to modernism within the Treasury Section of Fine Art, the artist Lloyd R. Ney had somehow wangled letters approving his project from leading citizens of New London, Ohio, where the post office was slated for a mural. Edward Bruce, the Section chief, reluctantly approved Ney's sketch, rationalizing that "it isn't a bad idea to have one experimental picture in the project, as this abstract stuff is certainly getting a lot of attention these days." Balancing the mural's provocative style was its reassuring, humdrum subject: *Delivering the Mail.*[80]

That was in 1940, and by then the battle for modern art had largely been won. But the Americans ranked low among those accepted and admired as avant-garde painters, and none were considered innovators. In contrast with its well-organized shows of European art, the Museum of Modern Art's exhibitions of American painting and sculpture throughout the Thirties often reeked of provincial pride and pity, with the works carelessly selected and catalogs to match. They lacked a coherent aesthetic statement; the criteria for selecting works to show had changed little from the title one critic had suggested for the museum's first American show in 1929: "Some Pictures We Thought Good and Some that Have Been Bought by the Directors."[81]

American art had been seen as derivative and second-rate for so long that it was inconceivable that true innovation could spring from native soil. Moreover, apart from those artists who aped or adapted European styles, American art attracted no scholars. It had no written history. Perhaps even more unappetizing to connoisseurs was the close connection of American art to crass commercialism.

The monumental survey *Recent Social Trends* had stressed that connection as early as 1933. Writing on the arts, Frederick Keppel acknowledged the "very powerful" and generally "wholesome influence" of advertising, packaging, and department stores on American aesthetic standards. To illustrate how commercial art linked up with fine art, he cited the syllabus of a high school art appreciation course that included such topics as "Can Signs be Beautiful?"; the lunchroom as a problem in design; design a container for an article sold in the school; and select and discuss magazine title pages and their design. Such was the demand for information about good design, Keppel wrote, that 180,000 copies of a government pamphlet on furniture selection were distributed in the first month after it was issued. Keppel may have taken pride in the thoroughgoing redesign of the American kitchen and bath during the Twenties—"the sink is no longer a sink of iniquity"—but almost a decade later the MOMA was still complaining about poor taste in the design of everyday objects. In the catalog for a 1939 exhibition of "Useful Objects Under $10," the design curator, Elodie Courter, decried the lack of good-looking clocks and of table lamps "which were not spoiled by frivolous decorations and poor handling of materials or were not frankly imitative of Greek urns, colonial candlesticks or gas lamps."[82]

One of Alfred Barr's most difficult innovations had been his insistence on including commercial design—advertising, packaging, posters, and all objects of everyday life—in his definition of modern art. His views originated from his admiring visit to the Bauhaus, which during the Twenties had gathered artists, architects, designers, and craftspeople into a school and workshop at Dessau, Germany. But the entire art establishment strenuously resisted the mingling of commercial art with fine art. Many reasons were given, but the unspoken one was the low money value of commercial objects. Ultimately, worth in art derives from scarcity, hence no market could develop in milk bottles, no matter how sleekly made. No collector could derive status from hanging one of 100,000 identical steamship posters over the mantel or tax benefits from donating a collection of handsome baking powder tins to a museum. Few museum directors could exercise the rarefied connoisseurship in which they had been trained on the graphic design of *Fortune* magazine. No self-respecting art critic cared to survey the crockery at the five-and-dime; if he did, no art publication would print his findings. And no art dealer could support a posh establishment by selling kitchen stools. Far from achieving status through their successful commercial work, American artists like Edward Hopper and Stuart Davis tended toward reticence about the fact that advertising agencies were their principal patrons.

The *Fur-lined Teacup* in the MOMA Dada and Surrealist show of 1936 had created such a scandal because it made such a shocking statement about the nature of art. Here was a utilitarian object rendered useless and unique by the addition of valuable fur. As such, it raised provocative questions about all sorts of other items in private collections and in museums: altarpieces, jeweled reliquaries, portraits of the rich and powerful, illuminated manuscripts, urns, candelabra, votive figurines, and burial caskets, all of which had once served a utilitarian purpose, only to be wrenched out of their natural context and displayed as works of art when they became rare. Artemas Packard, a Dartmouth art professor and consultant on the future of the MOMA, in 1935 deplored the esthetic confusion of the American public

> . . . by the false sentimentality and snobism which, in the name of "art" exalts a bad etching hanging in the parlor above a first-rate saucepan in the kitchen. . . . Until we, as a people, have become aware of beauty in well-designed saucepans, arm chairs, electric light fixtures . . . or filing cabinets, our interest in etchings or the latest "ism" is bound to remain as inconclusive a symptom of cultural integrity as an adenoidal accent or an artificial diamond; in other words, our fine arts will con-

tinue to be cultivated as expensive baubles to amuse the idle moment and the general public will remain profoundly indifferent to their claims as genuine nourishment for the human spirit.[83]

Virtually no one associated with America's traditional art establishment—not museums, critics, collectors, or dealers—contributed to the acceptance of the doctrine of functionalism that had been embraced so enthusiastically in the world of American advertising and industrial design. There, the successful redesign of a refrigerator showed up in increased sales, and streamlined office furniture resulted in higher productivity. But, beginning in the mid-Thirties, functionalism and the broadened definition of art espoused by Barr received powerful reinforcement from Europe.

The Nazis had closed the Bauhaus within weeks after coming to power in 1933. Simultaneously, they began a vicious persecution of modernists, whether designers, painters, architects, or craftspeople. Barr, who was in Europe on sabbatical during that period, watched in horror as the Nazis purged Germany's leading art scholars and museum directors, including Dr. Max Friedländer, director of Berlin's Kaiser Friedrich Museum and the world's leading expert on fifteenth- and sixteenth-century Dutch and German Painting, and Dr. Georg Hartlaub, director of the Mannheim Museum and originator of the term *Neue Sachlichkeit* to describe German painting of the Twenties. "These changes appeared one by one in tiny news items," Barr reported sadly. But no news items at all announced the disappearance of hundreds of paintings by modern artists or the closing of galleries of modern art. Barr attended the first Nazi meeting on art in Stuttgart and was aghast at hearing the Wurttemberg minister of education rant that "art is not international . . . nor is there any such thing as international science. . . . If anyone should ask 'What is left of freedom?' he will be answered: there is no freedom for those who would weaken and destroy German art." Barr also was present to record how swiftly the Nazis acted on their ideas about art. On March 12, 1933, barely a week after they took control of the Württemberg government, they closed a show of Oskar Schlemmer paintings at the Stuttgart Civic Gallery, after a review in the local Nazi newspaper called the pictures "unfinished . . . decadent" and saw no reason for exhibiting them except "to show the insolence of the 'artist' who has sent such half-baked rubbish on tour." The paintings were hidden away in the basement, an example, Barr wrote, of treating works of art like "persons who, politically or racially anathema to the regime, are put in jail, in *Schutzhaft*" (protective detention).[84]

The outrages he described spread virtually unopposed throughout Germany, triggering the emigration, over the next few years, of the entire modernist establishment. Until the exits from Europe slammed shut following the outbreak of World War II, only 717 European artists and 380 architects arrived in the United States. But their impact far outweighed their numbers. "In no other period in American history were our thought and art and culture more deeply stirred or more grandly shaped by currents from abroad," the historian Daniel Boorstin wrote. "Nor had American civilization in any comparable period been more enriched by new currents." While Boorstin credited the subsequent "flowering of an American art of international stature" to the influx of those European exiles, theirs would have been cries in the wilderness had not enough Americans become educated to appreciate new currents in art, or had no institutions been built to disseminate them.[85]

As the tide of immigrant artists swelled, the crusade for modern art began to encompass political as well as artistic freedom. Those who deplored Nazi barbarism made room for its victims at American schools and colleges, multiplying their influence through a spreading web of students. John Sloan, president of New York's Art Students League, invited George Grosz to teach there in 1932–33, even though a director, Jonas Lie, thought the caricaturist's art was "not a healthy influence on American youth." The Bauhaus painter Josef Albers found a job at experimental Black Mountain College near Asheville, North Carolina, after Philip Johnson, Edward Warburg, and perhaps Abby Rockefeller got him a nonquota visa. Later he would attract the sculptors Jose de Creeft and Ossip Zadkine, and the architect José Luis Sert, among others, to form a progressive bastion in the Southern hills. One of the most influential refugees was Hans Hofmann, a Munich art teacher who had already served several stints of teaching in America before the Nazi triumph. After 1933 Hofmann opened an art school in New York and Provincetown, Massachusetts, and rapidly became the paramount art teacher in America. By 1937, nearly half of the charter members of Abstract American Artists had attended his classes. He would become the principal mentor of such successful modernists as Larry Rivers, Helen Frankenthaler, and Louise Nevelson.[86]

By 1939, when the MOMA assembled its comprehensive survey, "Bauhaus 1919–1928," many of the participants in that pathbreaking enterprise were on hand to amplify and explain what they had done. By then, the architects Walter Gropius and Marcel Breuer were teaching at the Harvard Graduate School of Design, Ludwig Mies van der Rohe was at the Illinois Institute of Technology, the sculptor and photographer Laszlo Moholy-Nagy had started a New Bauhaus in Chicago, and many lesser names had brought the Bauhaus's aesthetic of sleek, stripped functionalism to remoter academic outposts. As a group, they had invented a new species of architecture, but it was their then distant apostle Alfred H. Barr who in 1934 had christened it the International Style.[87] Through the winter of 1939–40, throngs of Americans turned out in such unlikely places as Tallahasse, Florida; Shreveport, Louisiana; and Oakland, California, to see for themselves what these Germans had done. Perhaps some of the visitors wondered, during that first winter of European war, how the same nation that had produced these pristine, crystalline, thoughtful structures and those humane, noble objects could now follow a raving maniac and devastate European civilization.

Wherever it went, the "Bauhaus" show was amply publicized. It is a measure of how confident the MOMA was that modern art was firmly established in America that its own publicity release quoted a gamut of critical New York reactions to it. The *New York Times* had called it "chaotic"; *Art News* found the textiles in it "magnificent," while the *New York Sun* thought them "unfortunate"; one letter to the *Times* called the exhibition "a final danse macabre," while another termed it "the finest thing in existence."[88]

Within a ten-year span, Americans had not only accepted modern art in its broadest definition as including architecture; interior, industrial, and graphic design; films; and photography, but they had become the world's staunchest devotees of the new aesthetic canon. Alfred H. Barr and the MOMA had played a leading role in that upheaval in taste, probably the sharpest change ever recorded in a single decade. Higher levels of education had prepared Americans for new visual ideas, and the evolving design of advertising, publications, packaging, appliances, and furniture had made them more conscious of how things looked. The movies had given them glimpses of modern interiors and sleek sets and costumes. Ironically, the suffering and deprivation of the Depression had not crippled the new ideas but rather had accelerated the change, as government relief programs supported artists, freeing them to experiment and sending them into the hinterland to spread their ideas. Moreover, the hard times prompted people to visit museums, government-sponsored art centers, and exhibitions in record numbers, partly in search of free entertainment. Finally, the exiled Europeans provoked further interest in modern art.

As it celebrated its tenth anniversary with an ambitious survey, "Art in Our Time," President Roosevelt called the MOMA "a citadel of civilization." While the museum's fifth anniversary show had included works lent by galleries and collectors only from the New York area, the tenth anniversary show included works from museums in Paris, London, Brussels, Antwerp, Chicago, Boston, Detroit, Philadelphia, and Cleveland and collectors who spanned the continent: Edward G. Robinson and Mr. and Mrs. Ira Gershwin from Beverly Hills; Frank and Robert Oppenheimer from Berkeley; and others in Cleveland, Baltimore, St. Louis, Wilmington, Delaware, and Germantown, Pennsylvania. While the fifth anniversary show had dealt uncomfortably with Americans, the tenth anniversary exhibition proudly included works lent by Stuart Davis, Alexander Calder, Isamu Noguchi, and William Zorach. While the museum's founding members were all New Yorkers, ten years later half the membership lived elsewhere; membership committees (all women) were active in twenty-one places, including Houston, Louisville, Montreal, New Haven, New Orleans, Palm Beach, Pittsburgh, Providence, Rochester, St. Paul, and communities in Colorado and Vermont.[89]

As the trustees toured the show installed in the museum's brand-new building, the architecture itself a strong modernist statement, they were "greatly impressed," as Abby Rockefeller wrote in a note to each staff member, "with the arrangement of the galleries, the decorations and furnishing, the lighting and the perfection of workmanship throughout." Enclosed with each note was a month's salary. It was, perhaps, symbolic that Mrs. Rockefeller had singled out all the features of the new building except the exhibition hung therein. Somehow, over the previous decade, "what had been a missionary church in a Philistine jungle with a small band of passionately devoted proselytizers dedicated to making converts," the MOMA official historian, Russell Lynes, wrote, "began to look curiously like, and take on the airs and graces of, a cathedral of the new culture."[90]

Addressing the trustees during the tenth anniversary festivities, Paul Sachs urged them to deemphasize sculpture and painting even more than they had, and to concentrate on training scholars, who were still weak in modern art, as well as the public. The museum should hire "a real educator," he proposed, selected "as if we were choosing a college president." In his final report as president, A. Conger Goodyear echoed the museum's goal from the beginning as, primarily, "an educational institution." He reviewed for his successor, Nelson Rockefeller, the first decade's achievements, including 112 exhibitions attracting 1.5 million visitors, and reiterated the original purpose of its collections: to "be permanent as a stream is permanent—with a changing content."[91]

That original idea, however, began to fade with success.

Before the Bliss bequest in 1933, the museum had owned only twelve paintings and ten sculptures. By 1937, after multiple purchases from the Cubist and Surrealist shows, the collection had swelled to 937 items. On its tenth anniversary, the collection included 175 oils; 260 watercolors, gouaches, pastels, and drawings; 100 sculptures; 1,800 prints; 400 photographs; and 140 "objects," insured for $700,000. In the following year, the museum's "most important single gift" was not an exciting new work by a young artist but rather an established masterpiece by one of the quadrumvirate honored in its very first exhibition: Van Gogh's *Starry Night.*[92]

The collection had grown so large that even with the spacious new building, most of it had to remain out of sight in storerooms, a mounting hoard of valuable goods inaccessible to the public. The museum would continue to break attendance records and to circulate ever more impressive exhibitions—alas, at ever more exorbitant rentals, thus ruling out showings at small colleges, women's clubs, or department stores and other chapels that had been strong links in its missionary chain. By 1943, there would be a total of ninety catalogs and other publications containing Barr's loving and scholarly history of modern art. Since the beginning, the museum had sold 274,000 copies of those publications and had distributed 173,000 more to members, making it by far the world's largest art book publisher.[93]

But by then a brief, extraordinary moment in the modern history of tastemaking in art was over, as the revolution sponsored by the museum went the way of all the other artistic revolutions of the previous 150 years. Ever since public museums began in the nineteenth century, the art public's taste had been channeled by an interlocking complex of collectors, dealers, critics, and museums. The Impressionist rebellion, which began in 1867, was not merely a revolt against traditional styles of painting but also an attempt to overturn the traditional art market. The dealers, collectors, and critics who bought Impressionism early enough saw their enlightened taste validated handsomely in the auction rooms after museums accepted the newer works, so that admission of an artist's work into a museum meant not merely a gratifying bow to his talent but a rich profit to his patrons.

As newer styles followed Impressionism in ever quickening succession, not only pure love of art but an underlying entrepreneurial impulse motivated collectors, including the public-spirited citizens who founded the MOMA in 1929. The trustees who generously loaned their Cézannes, Van Goghs, Gauguins, and Seurats to the museum's early exhibitions were often rewarded manyfold when those works reached the market place a few years later. Cézanne's *Portrait of Mme. Cezanne,* which Mrs. Sullivan had bought in France for less than $12,000 during the Twenties, for example, fetched $27,500 in a forced sale in December 1939. (Twenty years later, the same picture would bring $160,000.) Those who had bought earlier and were able to hold on longer reaped more spectacular profits. Goodyear, for example, had invested $64 in a Gauguin, *J'attends ta reponse,* back in 1895 and sold it for $520,000 in 1959.[94]

Clearly, a museum trustee could do well by doing good. If the organizers of the MOMA had merely aggrandized their own portfolios of paintings, they would have been no different from those collectors of traditional works who sat as trustees of traditional museums. But for some ten years after its founding, they encouraged the MOMA to extend the definition of art so broadly and to disseminate its views so widely that a whole nation's visual sensibility was forever changed. By broadening the definition of art to include a mass of intrinsically valueless items—movies, photographs, advertisements, packages, furniture, articles of daily use—the museum diluted the overwhelming role of collectors, critics, and dealers in shaping taste and taught the public that it could exercise connoisseurship in a purchase as humble as a potato masher or a soup plate. The battle against *kitsch* was far from over, and the museum, weighed down by the great masterpieces of the early twentieth century, would itself become an institution rather than a movement. But the millions newly introduced to modern art during the Thirties, whether by MOMA circulating exhibitions, government-sponsored art centers, or artist-teachers exiled from Europe, formed an adventuresome nucleus for appreciating the next wave of artistic innovation, a wave which, uniquely and significantly, originated not in Europe but in America.

5

THE WORLD OF TOMORROW: FLUSHING MEADOWS, 1939

WHEN THE GREATEST world's fair ever held opened on April 30, 1939, Joseph F. Shadgen stayed home. His distinguished, elderly Packard, which had briefly carried him to the vortex of fair planning, was back in dead storage. Perhaps he listened on the radio to the echoing, amplified speeches, the brisk and brassy music, the announcers' breathless descriptions of the brilliant scene. The New York World's Fair at Flushing Meadows, not 10 miles from Mr. Shadgen's home, was an unparalleled project. Never before had such a huge fair been built. Never had so many nations taken part. Never had so much money been poured into a fair. Never had an international exposition been so ambitious, attempting to transport the visitor into "The World of Tomorrow." Alas, never had the world quailed, as the fair opened, in such despair—and overlaid its anxiety with such soaring hopes.

The nation's eyes, President Franklin Delano Roosevelt told the opening day crowd, "are fixed on the future. Our wagon is hitched to a star . . . a star of progress for mankind, a star of greater happiness and less hardship, a star of international good will, and above all, a star of peace."[1] The President's aristocratic diction mysteriously touched the heartstrings of ordinary men, people like Joseph F. Shadgen, "a man of modest means, a civil engineer without excessive forcefulness of personality and without wide acquaintanceship among the great or even near-great." Shadgen was the very model of the common man, the typical "American citizen" who could learn at the fair "how his life may be enriched if the resources of science, art, education, play and industry are utilized to the full in a spirit of enlightenment and cooperation."[2]

The rhetoric—and the reality that followed—had traveled many miles from the idea Shadgen had conceived one evening near the end of 1934. His daughter Jacqueline had learned in school that day that the United States was 158 years old, counting from the Declaration of Independence in 1776. Her father thought the count should begin with the inauguration of George Washington in 1789. As Mrs. Shadgen called them to supper, Joseph wondered if New York couldn't have a world's fair to celebrate the 150th anniversary of that event. In the next few weeks, Shadgen had managed to plant his idea where it would blossom.[3]

But Joseph F. Shadgen was not among the dignitaries on opening day, those who lunched on roast beef, turkey, cheese, salads, and biscuit tortoni and listened to Guy Lombardo's orchestra playing "Dawn of Tomorrow," a swing tune composed especially for the fair by George Gershwin.[4] Nor was he present when the newspaper cartoonist Denys Wortman, garbed as George Washington, galloped into the fairgrounds just in time for the unveiling of a 65-foot sculpture of the first President. In a bustle of ballyhoo typical of the time, the bogus Washington had traveled the 250 miles from Mt. Vernon, Virginia, by horse, stagecoach—and bus.[5] The ordinary Mr. Shadgen also missed Albert Einstein throwing the cosmic ray switch to turn on the fairyland lighting for the first time. Asked to explain cosmic rays in five minutes, the great scientist had first protested that it would take a full volume. Then, alert to the era's impatience with complexity, he offered just seven hundred words. "I am very sorry," he said, "but I can't cut it down any further."[6]

Instead of representing the much-extolled common man at spectacle and ceremonial, Shadgen had recently collected $45,000 ($17,000 net, after attorneys' fees) from a $2 million lawsuit against the fair corporation for theft of his idea. Having gained the ear of a remote Roosevelt relative, he was briefly swept into the milieu of New York's elite, who leaped at the idea of a fair as a way to revive New York's depressed tourist industry. But while the common man dominated the rhetoric, it didn't seem reasonable to admit him into the inner sanctums of power. Briefly, Shadgen had extracted his ancient Packard from dead storage and refurbished it for drives from his home in Jackson Heights to luncheon in the Oval Room of the Ritz. In September 1935, when Grover Whalen became Fair president at $100,000 a year, Shadgen was hired at $625 a month. For nine months, as blizzards of memos emblazoned with Whalen's slogan "Time Tears On!" swirled around him, he sat at his desk from 9 A.M. to 5 P.M. with nothing to do. The Packard went back into storage. Then he was fired. He sued.[7] As the World of Tomorrow was being dedicated to the Common Man, Shadgen was perhaps alone in being unimpressed.

Grover Whalen's opening pageantry was a masterpiece of media manipulation. In the Court of Peace, a vast space ringed by sixty international pavilions, some 50,000 troops from all "major nations" except Spain, China, and Germany massed for a "Salute to Peace." Elmer Davis thought "they had better keep some of those detachments pretty far apart."[8] Hundreds of reporters bustled through the well-dressed crowd. Newsreel crews searched out the notable and the photogenic, while radio commentators hoarsely filled the air time that yawned so voraciously before the broadcaster. Inside a truck parked near the speaker's platform, the NBC technical crew calmly performed what it had practiced previously only in a dry run: the first live television news report ever done.

Before the President spoke, the single television camera, a huge contraption clumsily planted on a static tripod, panned through the audience. It picked up Secretary of Labor Frances Perkins in a large white hat; Mrs. Roosevelt in a "luggage tan" silk dress printed with white emblems of the fair—the Trylon and Perisphere; the President's mother, Sara, regal in a full-length black coat over a black and white silk print frock; and the men in full morning dress—Vice President Henry Wallace, Speaker of the House William Bankhead, Secretary of War Harry Woodring, and Attorney General Frank Murphy.

The camera barely lingered on the impeccably tailored phalanx of New Yorkers who had seized so shamelessly on Mr. Shadgen's idea. Sleek and smug—but frightened—they had developed his modest proposal into the record-shattering exposition now unfolding. Edward F. Roosevelt, a second cousin of Eleanor and a sixth cousin of Franklin D., whom he had met at a cocktail party, had introduced Shadgen to his cousin, Nicholas Roosevelt, an editor at the *New York Herald-Tribune*, who passed them along to George McAneny, a banker and politician, early in 1935. "A number of us have been sitting around talking off and on for three years trying to figure out what to do about the commercial situation in New York," McAneny elatedly told them. "I think you gentleman have found the solution."[9]

McAneny, whose phlegmatic ways had earned him the nickname "Mañana Mac," acted swiftly for once. On June 15 Shadgen shared his idea with a small group summoned by McAneny, and by September 23 Mayor Fiorello LaGuardia and Governor Herbert H. Lehman joined sixty prominent New Yorkers for dinner at the Ritz (where McAneny conveniently was a director) and heard the timely proposal for a World's Fair in New York in 1939 to celebrate the 150th anniversary of George Washington's inauguration. Within a month, the New York World's Fair Corporation was formed. Its incorporators included a concentration of power and wealth seldom gathered on a single letterhead: Owen D. Young, chairman of General Electric; Alfred P. Sloan, president of General Motors; Walter C. Teagle, president of Standard Oil of New Jersey; Thomas J. Watson, president of IBM; Clarence J. Shearn, president of the New York Bar Association; Dr. Eugene H. Pool, president of the New York Academy of Medicine; Nelson Rockefeller and Cornelius Vanderbilt; John Erskine, president of the Juilliard School of Music; George Blumenthal, president of the Metropolitan Museum of Art; James H. Perkins, president of the National City Bank of New York; and, democratically, Joseph P. Ryan, president of the Central Trades and Labor Council of Greater New York and Vicinity.

Of the 121 incorporators, ninety-five were listed in *Who's Who in America*. The forty-six-man Board of Directors added William S. Paley, president of CBS, and David Sarnoff, presi-

dent of NBC; the department store magnates Bernard Gimbel
and Percy S. Straus, president of Macy's; the financier Joseph
P. Kennedy; Mayor LaGuardia; and the Democratic presidential candidate, Alfred E. Smith. The two lists comprised the
heads of twenty-three banking and trust companies, fifteen
Wall Street law firms, eight insurance and retail giants, and
eight business associations. Those were "balanced" by fifteen
politicians.[10] Conspicuously absent from the potent assem-
blage were Arthur Hays Sulzberger, publisher of the *New
York Times*, whose newspaper would sell hundreds of extra
pages of fair-related advertising, and, of course, the common
man with an idea, Joseph Shadgen, who had triggered the
whole ambitious enterprise.

Throughout the President's speech at the Fair opening, the
single television camera stayed with FDR, the picture "occasionally marred by white streaks," the *Times* noted, "believed
to have been caused by switching operations." A delegation
from the BBC, where television experiments had been conducted for some years, gave the broadcast a poor grade; at
least three or four cameras should have been on hand, they
said, in order to provide varying angles of view. Within a
50-mile radius, a tiny audience was watching the opening cere-
monies on some 200 flickering 9-inch screens, the first telecast
of an American President. In stores where television sets were
available (at $200 to $1,000) the next day's sales were brisk.[11]

The gala at Flushing Meadows had begun under brilliant
sunshine, but soon "the thin cumulus clouds grew into rolling
thunderheads and shadbelly grays." When the President was
announced, "the skies were gray and sullen," and by 3 P.M.
a rain squall, said the *Times*, left "the crowd's spirit . . .
broken."[12]

Not so the spirit of New York's mayor, the feisty Fiorello
LaGuardia, who had already been judged by NBC technicians
as the city's "most telegenic man." Before appearing at the
Plaza of Freedom, he had changed from formal regalia into
a short Oxford-gray morning coat and his customary wide-
brimmed black sombrero. Dedicating sculptures representing
the Four Freedoms, he confided to the crowd: "I just can't
get myself to talk about freedom in a cutaway coat and high

hat." He spoke mostly about World War I, pointing to the flag of Belgium as symbolizing a brave little country resisting invasion.[13] In the evening, the mayor paid tribute, perhaps, to the memory of his father, who had been an Army bandmaster in Arizona, as he bounced to the podium to lead the New York Philharmonic in a specially composed fanfare and "The Star Spangled Banner."

The inclement weather was a convenient symbol for the tempest that beset the times; the first day's attendance was an ominous reality. Grover Whalen had predicted 1 million, but the very prospect of such a crush had discouraged many visitors. By 7 P.M. the official attendance was 204,589. An hour later, it was posted as 501,012. The check on turnstiles had broken down, it was explained; the second figure came from the fair management, whose spokesman, Whalen, called it "marvelous," although eventually it would turn out that fewer than 198,000 had paid for admission.[14]

Excluded from the jubilation of the fair's opening day, world events cast their own turbulent clouds over the festivities. The best-seller list of that week bespoke the twin shadows of public concern. At the top for fiction was John Steinbeck's *The Grapes of Wrath*. Leading the nonfiction list was Adolf Hitler's *Mein Kampf* in an edition pirated to prevent the Nazi dictator from garnering royalties. A few days before the opening, Hitler had harangued the Reichstag for two and a half hours, pouring sarcasm on the American President and threatening an imminent showdown over the Danzig corridor. The British Parliament had approved conscription. At home, 11 million Americans remained unemployed, some 26 percent of the labor force. The only segments of the economy in which jobs had increased were management, by 300,000, and government service, by 700,000. In the deepest doldrums was construction, where jobs had declined by 1.3 million since 1929.[15]

The World of Tomorrow would never have been built, had the world of today not been so dismal. But no breath of that naked fact stirs the tons of publicity releases churned out for the fair. A reader of those sunny, fact-crammed epistles would have no idea that in October 1933, a year before Mr. Shadgen thought of a fair, some 1,250,000 New Yorkers were on relief and a million more were probably eligible. Theirs was "a vast pit of human misery," the journalist Lorena Hickock wrote; it had engulfed "the most intelligent, the most highly educated and the most helpless and . . . ignorant." Their rescue was "the biggest community relief job . . . ever undertaken by any city since the world began."[16]

In step with the problem it was designed to address, the fair was built on a colossal scale. The superlatives flowing into its description mingled trivia and substance, like a shimmering pile of diamonds and glass. Its site was the largest for any international exposition, 1267.5 acres. Its total paved area was equivalent to 60 miles of two-lane highway. It had cost more— $155 million—than any similar enterprise. It would attract more visitors—60 million, said some—than any other fair. They would consume 15 million hot dogs and 15 million hamburgers, which, if strung necklace-fashion, would reach from New York to London. The Perisphere was the "largest globe ever made by man." Among the exhibits were the world's largest locomotive and the world's smallest bonnet. Its site had been a dump, rife with "stagnant pools and muddy runlets, a source of evil odors that threatened asphyxiation to the distressed inhabitants for miles around." Its grading was the "largest single reclamation project in the eastern United States." An entire forest had been razed for the 758 miles of pilings on which the buildings rested. It was, the *New York Herald-Tribune* boasted, simply "the mightiest exposition ever conceived and built by man." Nor would it end with a whimper. After the fair was over, its site would become a park half again as big as Central Park.[17]

In its paradoxical mingling of past and future, with a minimal pause in the present, the fair reflected the peculiar Janus-vision of Thirties culture. Its impetus came from the past— Washington's inauguration—but its theme was the World of Tomorrow. Its ground plan, featuring streets radiating from several focal plazas, was reminiscent of Charles L'Enfant's early-nineteenth-century plan for Washington, D.C., and reflected the conservative Beaux Arts bent of the fair's Board of Design. Many of the buildings, by contrast, featured futuristic streamlining, sinuous curves, and seductive new shapes. They represented the synthesis of art and profit in a new profession, industrial design. Not architects, but men who had sprung into prominence by sleekening refrigerators and streamlining the telephone had designed not only the most interesting buildings but also the liveliest exhibits.

The fair's theme structures show the same ambivalence. The 700-foot needlelike pyramid and the perfect sphere, a trademark and thus the obvious bailiwick of an industrial designer, were devised by Wallace K. Harrison and J. Andre Fouilhoux, who had been among the principal architects of Rockefeller Center. While reaching into the future for its theme shapes, the fair management delved deep into the past to name them. But it delved with the spurious historicism of a Cecil B. de Mille. "Trylon" was a bastard spawned by the Greek prefix "tri" (three, referring to its three sides) and "pylon" (a gateway). "Perisphere" redundantly welded the Greek prefix "peri" (encircling) with "sphere" (ball).[18]

Publicity endlessly embroidered the profound meaning of those symbols. The Trylon, Whalen told *Time*, is "the pointer to Infinity," while the Perisphere symbolized the all-inclusive world of tomorrow.[19] But the flood of "information" poured out upon the media quickly eroded such lofty significance. Some months before the fair opened, the staff's resident intellectual, the Yale historian Frank Monaghan, admitted that sometimes he referred to the Trylon as representing "the infinite aspirations of man" and the Perisphere as "symbolizing the finite," while at other times he said the reverse.[20] Whalen loftily called the *kitsch* bearing the fair's trademark—the hat bands at $24 a gross, the 18-karat gold Cartier tieclasps, the fifteen-cent rabbit's foot keychains, not to mention all of the license plates of the state of New York—"the Merchandise of Tomorrow."[21]

Yet in their stark, geometric purity, the Trylon and Perisphere were unquestionably impressive. *Architectural Forum* called them "the first adequate trademark since Eiffel built his tower for the Paris fair of 1889."[22] The designers insisted that they had drawn "practical shapes for practical purposes."

While Fouilhoux referred to inspiration from the dome of Venice's St. Mark's, Harrison pointed out their functionalism: "Everybody knows that a ball encloses more space than . . . any other geometric form."[23] Certainly the severe geometrics of Bauhaus architecture were called to mind, while the pristine needle and sphere also echoed some of the ideal shapes posited by Paul Cézanne: the sphere, the cylinder, the cone, and the cube.

Though they faithfully printed reams of high-minded publicity rhetoric, New York newspapers also had their fun with the fair's ubiquitous trademark. The Perisphere was "a big apple," the *Post* said. The *Times* called the trademark "the egg and the tack." H. I. Phillips, in his *New York Sun* column, "The Sun Dial," printed a mythical dialogue between a reporter and the perisphere: "What is your role, would you mind telling?" "I'm a theme, sir, that is not jelling." New York Park Commissioner Robert Moses tartly remarked that "Barnum had his sacred white elephant and every fair is entitled to at least one theme tower."[24] But when the fair opened, not a snigger broke through the solemnity and grandiosity the press described. The *Times* forgot that it was a newspaper of record for the nation and gave the fair half of its front page and all of the next nine pages.

In its courtship of the common man, the fair management tried to clothe much of the traditional hucksterism of the big commercial exhibitors in the idealistic garments of the times. It provided seven "focal exhibits" around which the paying exhibitors could cluster. Winnowed down from many possibilities considered by the Executive Committee, those built hewed close to basic human concerns: food, shelter, health, transportation, communications, production and distribution, science, and education. But they were cleverly designed to intrigue—and then earnestly educate—the visitor.

In the food exhibit, for example, the designer Russell Wright had created a colorful surrealist lesson in nutrition. Based on his consultations with a nutritionist, C. C. Furnas, author of *Man, Bread and Destiny,* Wright designed a 60-foot egg in which, among other dream visions, an avocado flashing five jewels climbed a mountain while a flock of lobsters flew into the interior. An eye blinked from a cave, and a clock rushed backward inside a can. A narrator explained how the five jewels represented vitamins; the flying lobsters, the speedy distribution of foods; the eye, the defeat of night blindness through Vitamin A; and the clock in the can, the preservation of fresh foods.[25]

Nutrition was a frighteningly live issue during the Thirties. The one-third of the nation so dramatically described by Roosevelt in his second inaugural address as ill-housed, ill-clad, and ill-fed had little improved its lot by 1939. And many Americans had been hungry since long before the crash of 1929. In Bottineau, North Dakota, in 1933, Lorena Hickock found that no "decent crop" had been harvested for more than four years. The Red Cross there was afraid to distribute a supply of one-dollar blankets "lest it cause a riot."[26] The Brookings Institution discovered that during the prosperous part of 1929, 79.3 percent of American family incomes were at the "minimum comfort" level or below; 74 percent of all nonfarm families could not afford "an adequate diet at moderate cost."[27]

Another focal exhibit, Transportation, was supposed to show how new highways were erasing the gap between urban and rural America. However, its designer, Raymond Loewy, preferred to develop a huge map on which lights showed the distances man could travel by various modes of transportation. The capstone of the exhibit, considered "socially irrelevant" at the time, took visitors to a "rocketport" and then into a "spaceship." A magnet picked up the spaceship and loaded it into the breech of a "rocketgun." Then, after a countdown, sound effects, and the vibration of a blast-off, the passengers felt themselves "bound for Mars as casually as the man of today embarks via autos, trains and airplanes."[28]

But the American of the day hardly embarked "casually" for an automobile trip of any distance. While a few limited access highways had opened—parkways in Westchester County and Connecticut—the average motorist confronted quagmires and washouts in the country and steaming traffic jams in cities. The nation's road mileage had grown imperceptibly during the Twenties and Thirties: only 3 percent in each decade. While road improvement was a New Deal priority, more than half of all American highways in 1939 remained "unimproved." Those listed as "improved" or "surfaced" included thousands of miles surfaced with soil, sand, gravel, or stone. Furthermore, the states at first were forbidden to use Federal highway money in cities. Thus, improved arterials dumped traffic into seething bottlenecks at city centers.[29]

Still, throughout the Thirties the American love affair with the automobile remained passionate. Car registrations declined only 10 percent after 1929 and rebounded quickly. By 1934, James Agee in *Fortune* described the American roadside as "incomparably the most hugely extensive market the human race has ever set up to tease and tempt and take money from the human race." The restiveness of Americans was unique, mysterious. "Not to eat, not for love, nor even for money, nor for fear, nor really for adventure, nor truly out of any known necessity is this desire to move upon even the most docile of us." The depressed economy had touched car sales relatively lightly. After dropping almost two-thirds from 1929 to 1933, car production by 1935 had rebounded to 74 percent of 1929, and by 1937 it was 89 percent of 1929. Truly, as Agee wrote, the auto was "the opium of the American people."[30]

The fair pavilions constructed by automobile companies flamboyantly reflected the car's central role in American life. They dominated the fair's sector devoted to transportation. There, all the railroads shared one building and all shipping companies another. Aviation clustered in a modest hangar-shaped shed. But in the center of this large section, in the shadow of the Trylon and Perisphere, appropriately flanked on one side by a parking lot and on the other by the brand-new multilaned Grand Central Parkway, preened the spacious, sleek, expensive structures promoting Chrysler, Ford, and General Motors.

Visitors entered the Chrysler pavilion between streamlined twin towers, their shape foreshadowing the fins in the automobile's future. Inside, past the rotunda containing the transportation focal exhibit, past the chromed cruisers for 1939, they could view, through polarized glasses, the first 3-D film ever made. Major Bowes, a radio personality, narrated as the screen showed "In Tune with Tomorrow," a ten-minute time-lapse version of the birth of a Plymouth. One observer found the effect so realistic that, as the car parts swung down, he ducked his head.[31]

Raymond Loewy, who had devised the Chrysler exhibit, was "the only U.S. designer who could cross the country in a car, bus, plane and train of his own design."[32] Growing up in Paris, he had won the James Gordon Bennett Cup in 1908, at the age of fifteen, with a model airplane. He then mass produced a toy airplane, the *Ayrel,* which was so successful that he sold the manufacturing rights and went back to school. "I had discovered," he wrote later, "that design could be fun and profitable." After he had moved to the United States with his parents in the late Twenties, Loewy did graphics for *Vogue* and *Harper's Bazaar* and window displays for Macy's and Saks, all the while sending various manufacturers an attractively printed card reading: "Between two products equal in price, function and quality, the better looking will outsell the other." By 1930, he was able to open an industrial design office to serve clients like Hupmobile, the Pennsylvania Railroad, and Sears.[33]

In no small measure, industrial designers like Raymond Loewy were the midwives of the profound structural changes in the American economy that accompanied—and often deepened—the Great Depression. Good design, as his card had asserted, not only sold goods but frequently cut corners in manufacturing. Loewy made his reputation in 1935 with a redesign of Sears's Coldspot refrigerator. Following the Bauhaus dictum that form follows function, he stripped the machine of all resemblance to its parent, the ice box. He amputated its clumsy legs, sleekened and streamlined its silhouette, and integrated the hardware, cutting many expensive steps in the production process. Best of all, "good design" was also profitable; in a year, sales zoomed from 65,000 to 275,000.

By 1937, when the fair hired him to design the transportation focal exhibit, Loewy had streamlined trains and locomotives for the Pennsylvania Railroad; designed buses and terminals for Greyhound; developed a revolutionary car for

Studebaker; functionalized airplane interiors for TWA, Boeing, Douglas, and Fairchild; and redone trucks, tractors, offices, and showrooms for International Harvester. Unfortunately, he had also learned the spongy platitudes of corporate prose. His Chrysler exhibit at the fair was designed, he wrote, "as an expression of the corporation's long-range vision and technological leadership."[34]

The Ford exhibit next door was an even more ambitious effort. Planned by the dean of industrial designers, Walter Dorwin Teague, it was a masterpiece not only of functionalism, in handling crowds while impressing them with the utility and beauty of Ford automobiles, but also of pure design. Seen from the air, it suggested an elegant machine, with one wing resembling a giant gear wheel and the other curling into a corkscrew ramp. There, a visitor could glide over a half-mile of the highway of the future at the wheel of an actual Ford. Inside, among the Fords, Mercurys, and Lincoln Zephyrs, was one of the fair's most admired displays, the Ford Cycle of Production. On this 100-foot-wide turntable, revolving slowly on pontoons floating in a circular moat, eighty-seven animated groups showed every step in the manufacture of a car, beginning with the extraction of the necessary ores.

A lean, mustached, tweedy man with a penchant for working late into the night, Teague had shaped the fair from the beginning. As a member of the Board of Design, he played a principal role in developing the theme and the layout of the grounds. Furthermore, his imaginative pavilions and exhibits adorned every corner of the fair. For du Pont, he created a futuristic tower seemingly abubble with chemical miracles. For NCR, he devised a building shaped like a cash register; where the price would have popped up, a constant tally of fair attendance appeared. For US Steel, he invented a steel dome suspended from curved exterior girders, so that no supports would mar the inside. Eastman Kodak was an old client. He had designed its one-dollar Brownie Hawkeye, which by 1940 had outsold any other camera ever made.[35] At the fair the company was introducing Kodachrome, the first color film. Teague's design for Kodak's exhibit therefore featured giant color photographs, to show visitors what could be done with the new film, and a Photo-Garden with unusual settings, where they could try it for themselves. Teague also helped design the world's largest diorama for Consolidated Edison. The length of a city block and three stories high, this animated model of New York showed a full day in the electric life of the city, climaxed by a violent thunderstorm.

Born in 1884, the son of a circuit-riding minister in Decatur, Illinois, Teague was largely self-educated. He attended the Art Students League after migrating to New York in 1903, and by 1911 he had rented a hall-bedroom at 210 Madison Avenue as a graphics studio. His imaginative edgings on advertisements made him famous; they were called "Teague borders." By the time he joined the fair's board of design, he employed twenty-five and had taken over an entire floor at 210 Madison. The firm had designed railroad coaches for the New Haven Railroad and silk patterns for Marshall Field, turbines for Dresser Manufacturing Co. and art glass for Steuben, oil heaters, thermometers, pewter ware, tractors, shop fronts, and five kinds of gas stations for Texaco.[36]

Beyond smoothing and rationalizing objects of daily life, Teague had developed a philosophy that extended the principles of good design to society as a whole. "Better household equipment and better mechanical devices are of no real value," he wrote in 1940, "unless they are easy first essays in the fundamental redesign of our world. . . . The world is in too dire need of redesign . . . for us to be satisfied with better gadgets. We can cut our teeth on them, but we have stronger meat to chew and digest." His solution of political and economic problems was improved design, "creation of an environment in which men can live with health, interest, good will, urbanity and dignity." The prerequisites of such an environment would involve abolition of large cities, with their evil slums, traffic jams, and inevitable human frictions. Instead, people would work in small, decentralized factories, while "they live on the land and cultivate their gardens with Voltairean equanimity." The means were at hand "to build Utopia tomorrow," he argued, the only impediment was "the stupidity of men."[37]

On the fair's Design Board, Teague's vision of Utopia was

balanced by the contrasting views of his colleague, Robert D. Kohn. A former president of the American Institute of Architects, Kohn was an 1890 graduate of the prestigious Columbia School of Architecture. He had also studied at the Ecole des Beaux Arts and had worked at the Paris Exposition of 1900. Kohn had served as president of New York's Society for Ethical Culture and had designed such New York landmarks as Temple Emanu-El, the Fieldston School, and portions of Mt. Sinai Hospital. Early in the New Deal, he had headed the housing division of the Public Works Administration.[38]

The differences between Teague and Kohn highlight a debate that shook intellectuals throughout the Thirties. While citizens of Teague's Utopia pursued their individualistic paths to happiness, Kohn envisioned a collective paradise. Where Teague doubted that government could build his smooth-running world of tomorrow, Kohn wanted the fair to show specifically how government could improve life for "the man in the street." In the Health exhibit, for example, he suggested a government-sponsored display on socialized medicine beside those presented by private medical groups. In the Shelter focal exhibit, he wanted to promote public housing, because decent shelter, he wrote, "can only be attained by group action." Kohn also vainly suggested that the advisory committees for focal exhibits include "men on the street."[39] Where Teague believed that the designer should play philosopher-king, Kohn thought that the common man had some special wisdom to be tapped.

Both men, however, united in a successful effort to turn the fair's vision from the past to the future. About all that remained of George Washington, by the time the fair opened, was his Brobdignagian sculptural portrait, serenely gazing like a kindly giant over the playful antics of his children. The first President, so shapely of leg in his knee breeches, so aristocratic of bearing in his lace jabot, might have smiled at the fair's importunate courtship of the common man, orchestrated by a group of men who occupied the summit of the nation's wealth and power.

But then, the first President had not confronted a mass society in crisis. Nor were there abroad in his world shrill and militant and totalitarian suitors for the allegiance of the common man. The American ideals of liberty and justice for all looked pale, insubstantial, and old-fashioned beside the seemingly coherent, streamlined visions of the future painted by Hitler and Mussolini. Nor did the Americans' simple goal of the pursuit of happiness measure up in fervor and precision to the scientifically materialist society being built, it was said, in the Soviet Union. The Thirties nurtured a swarm of ideologies, and the most potent were secular religions whose heaven would be built by men, in the near future, on earth.

The fair's planners saw their exposition as America's ideological rebuttal to those alien belief systems. The task was not easy. New Yorkers were drawing $310 million in relief in 1936, while Grover Whalen was promising that the fair would "light the way to the advancement of human welfare and the betterment of mankind in every category of existence."[40] In 1938, as Whalen gushed that the fair's "layout for a richer life . . . will not only predict, but may even dictate, the shape of things to come,"[41] New York counted 89,000 cases of active or suspected tuberculosis, 102,000 cases of diphtheria, and an average of 17,000 homeless lodged nightly in common shelters.[42] Not only was the hungry, sick, homeless common man to be educated and uplifted by the fair's exhibits, he was to be pacified, if not seduced, by its specific models of the future.

Two exhibits in particular offered such models: General Motors' Futurama and the fair's theme exhibit, Democracity, housed inside the Perisphere. Though designed by others, they exemplified the contrast between Teague's individualistic Utopia and Kohn's collectivist ideal.

The Futurama's 7-acre site was the largest leased by any fair exhibitor and, at $7 million, cost more to build than any other. Its designer, Norman Bel Geddes, was himself a bundle of superlatives. Short, chunky, wild-haired, voluble, temperamental, and eccentric, Bel Geddes had scandalized Broadway during the Twenties by designing so grandiose a set for a play that the entire theater had to be rebuilt. A friend remarked that "his head is in the clouds, but his feet are certainly not on the ground."[43] At the beginning of 1938, Bel Geddes had stormed the General Motors headquarters in Detroit and, after three failed attempts, managed to place his visions of America in twenty-two years before William S. Knudsen, chairman of the board; Alfred P. Sloan, president; and Charles F. Kettering, president of General Motors Research Corporation. They had already decided to refurbish, for New York, the assembly line exhibit GM had used at the 1933 Century of Progress Exposition in Chicago. But in a four-hour harangue, capped by "Can GM afford to spend $2 million to admit it hasn't had a new idea in five years?" Bel Geddes sold the Futurama.[44]

The exhibit took visitors on a fifteen-minute journey to the year 1960. Seated in pairs on velvety upholstered armchairs, they experienced, as the individual loudspeaker in each chair said, "a magic Aladdin-like flight through time and space." Gliding along at 103 feet per minute, they crossed America, beginning with dawn breaking in the east and ending as night fell over the Pacific. They marveled at orchards fruiting under glass domes and a dirigible hangar resting in a pool of oil so that it could be turned in any direction. But the Futurama's main impact came from its depiction of the city and the road.

Bel Geddes built his idealized city on a map of St. Louis. But around the aging, congested center along the Mississippi River he ringed new skyscrapers and mid-rise buildings. Seven standardized sizes of buildings were spaced so that none could cast its shadow on any other. They formed into self-contained blocks, linked by pedestrian ways high above the street traffic, Le Corbusier's Radiant City come to life. Beyond the city, through a generous greenbelt, superhighways linked garden suburbs with the city, with each other, and with the world beyond the horizon.[45]

But while the city received Bel Geddes's careful attention, he lavished pure passion on the highways. Seductive fourteen-lane ribbons, they swooped and curved through the diorama's 35,000 square feet. Some 10,000 scale model cars moved nimbly at three prescribed speeds, using transition lanes to reach grass-bordered lanes dedicated to speeds of 75 or even 100 miles per hour. Radio beams at the front and back of each car regulated the spacing between them, and at dusk light strips embedded in the edge of the road winked on as each car approached and off after it passed, obviating the need for headlights. Within the city, traffic moved on several levels. On the lowest, cars could drive into the buildings to park or to pick up passengers. The next level was for local traffic, unimpeded by pedestrians. Every ten blocks, an elevated arterial roadway carried through-traffic at 50 miles per hour. Toward the end of their ride through the future, visitors experienced late afternoon and gradually saw more details of the new city's streets—people walking, gazing into shop windows, and lounging in roof gardens; children playing in parks; cars moving. Then, suddenly, the chair whipped around and the rider found himself in a full-size replica of the street he had just been looking down upon. He stood up and joined the crowd, "a pedestrian in the heart of the city he has just seen."[46]

The Futurama was a stunning success. One art critic rejoiced that "the impossible has happened. . . . Big business has backed an artist on a gigantic scale and won."[47] A Gallup poll proved what was obvious to those who saw the endless line of people snaking slowly up a curved ramp and into the enfolding arms of Bel Geddes's General Motors Building: The Futurama was the most popular building at the fair. Grover Whalen called it "the best advertising investment GM ever made."[48] And it was memorable. An informal poll taken almost fifty years later indicates that those who visited the fair invariably delight in recalling the Futurama—and little else.

But there were a few killjoys. Rexford Guy Tugwell, an economist and an original member of FDR's "brains trust," as well as chairman of the New York City Planning Commission, thought that the Futurama exemplified "the failure of our generation. . . . We can make a beautiful train, but our railroads are insufficient; we can build a light and airy factory, which half the time is idle. . . . So too with the famous American bathroom . . . which most farmers cannot have. . . . And as for our cities: the jewels there of design are set in dumps of an obsolescent hideousness." The exhibit failed, he wrote, because it reinforced "our embrace of laissez-faire." If Americans rejected "collectivism, planning, overhead direction,"

Tugwell warned, they were "not entitled to the beauty which the Futurama had."[49]

Tugwell was voicing the collectivist ideal, which enchanted so many intellectuals during the Thirties. That vision came to life at the fair in the theme exhibit inside the Perisphere. While Democracity was supposed to depict the city of the year 2039, Robert Kohn believed that it could be built "tomorrow morning, if we willed it so. The great crushing, all-absorbing city of today . . . would no longer be a jumble of slum and chimney, built only for gain, but an effective instrument for human activities, to be used for the building of a better world."[50] The inhabitants of that world were to be mercilessly educated and uplifted. The designer of Democracity, Henry Dreyfuss, said he strove to create an environment where leisure time would "not be dissipated in idleness or carousing, but . . employed in improving man physically and mentally . . . through organized athletics, lectures, concerts and . . . pursuit of his own hobbies."[51]

Like the creators of so many fair exhibits, Dreyfuss was an industrial designer, a maverick who was largely self-educated. A tall man with heavy glasses, he always wore brown, even when sleeping or swimming. When he traveled, he carried a supply of stamped, self-addressed manila envelopes in which he mailed his laundry home each day. Like Bel Geddes, Dreyfuss had been a stage designer. The Broadway slump brought on by the talkies had channeled his career into industrial design. By 1931, when he was twenty-seven, he had already created a legless piano for Steinway and a cork and formica airplane cabin for Curtiss Wright, as well the classic desk telephone for AT&T.[52] In 1933, he became the man who put the refrigerator motor at the bottom of the box, a competitive coup that cemented his relationship with his client, General Electric. In 1936, he redesigned the Grand Central's crack Twentieth Century Limited. At the time he received the Democracity commission, Dreyfuss was so successful that he was turning down all but the fifteen or so jobs a year that intrigued him.[53]

For its theme exhibit, the fair management gave him an empty ball 200 feet in diameter and a vague assignment to depict the world of tomorrow and human interdependence. Dreyfuss's first step was to visit the Christian Science Globe in Boston for "an impression of what the interior of a sphere is." His first idea, "after long day-dreaming," was "something abstract—a great light effect, brilliant colors moving over forms, a show of magnificent movement, color and excitement." Interestingly, when the project began to jell as the city of the future, Dreyfuss became obsessed with accuracy and verisimilitude. He consulted city planners, traffic experts, landscape designers, and specialists in lighting, acoustics, projection, and astronomy. He collected a large library dealing with urban design and made plane trips purely to view cities from the air. For the final show, he prepared a script detailing precisely what happened in sound and light during each of its 360 seconds.[54]

After riding up inside the Trylon on the two largest escalators ever built, visitors reached an arched bridge to the entrance of Democracity. Inside, they filed onto one of two platforms, one above the other, which circled the sphere's interior. The platforms revolved silently, as the audience gazed upon the changing panorama of the city below and the spectacle projected on the dome above. Precisely five and a half minutes later, the group was dismissed through automatic doors onto the Helicline, a gracefully curving (and pretentiously named) ramp. Dreyfuss' script allowed thirty seconds between cycles, repeated 120 times a day, so that 8,000 spectators passed through every hour.

The city Dreyfuss envisioned nestled in the bend of a river, with hills rolling toward the horizon. It would accommodate a million people, a working population of 250,000. But it had no inhabitants. Everyone lived in a rim of tall apartment houses, in suburban garden developments, or in satellite communities miles out in the country. The 30-mile green belts in between would be intensively farmed. Factories, too, would be scattered outside, among the satellite towns. As Grover Whalen described it in a book for children: "There is plenty of room for everybody. Houses have large friendly windows. . . . When Dad returns from his factory, store or office, he walks along avenues of trees and soon forgets the city street noises. . . . All the people who live in this world will sing songs of joy."[55]

Since the citizen did not live in it but depended on the central metropolis "only for direction in his business and in his cultural activities," Dreyfuss's city provided a lavish web of highways to move the transient population in and out, to shop in well-spaced stores surrounded by large lawns and parking areas; to work in the office buildings fanning out from the shopping center; to visit the amusement, cultural, and administrative centers. There were main express highways 500 feet wide and minor express highways 300 feet wide. Beneath them ran four-lane minor streets with grassy dividers. Circumambient boulevards eight lanes wide ringed the city core, and in the central plaza three levels of rotary traffic flowed smoothly in all directions. Dreyfuss envisioned no public transportation except buses.[56]

For the first two minutes of the show, visitors were permitted to contemplate this sunlit community—cars zipping along, flags waving, boats bustling around the harbor—able from Olympian heights "to pierce the fogs of ignorance, habit and prejudice" as, projected on the vast dome, great clouds drifted above and around them. "Ethereal symphonies" conducted by André Kostelanetz gave the audience "the sense of being raised above the earth and earthly affairs," as the news commentator H. V. Kaltenborn portentously narrated. Then a complicated system of twenty-four specially designed projectors flashed onto the vast dome marching legions of farmers, workers, school children, and other groups. They advanced through the clouds, growing larger and clearer until they loomed over the audience, a mass of militant humanity. They sang as they marched, at first softly and then, 1,000 voices strong, thundering:

> We're the rising tide come from far and wide,
> Marching side by side on our way,
> For a brave new world, Tomorrow's world,
> That we shall build today.

Dusk overtook the city as "the whole arch of heaven . . . filled with towering figures, arms upraised." As night fell, the music crescendoed, a rain of fire obliterated the inexorable throng, and the show was over.[57]

There could not have been a more graphic display of Thirties fascination with the masses. It was a time when poets, playwrights, and novelists crisscrossed the country scrutinizing the lives of ordinary men and women. Often in awe, they revealed the innate wisdom and simple, practical wit of coal miners, farm women, and sharecroppers. Musical folklorists like Woody Guthrie and Alan Lomax combed the Kentucky hills for down-to-earth traditional songs to popularize among sophisticated city audiences. Grant Wood affectionately painted *Stone City, Iowa,* (1930) and Charles Sheeler's *Classic Landscape* of 1931 depicted the Ford River Rouge plant. A Twenties person could get through a lifetime with but a vague sense of an underclass waiting on tables or shambling beside a shanty along the railroad tracks. But a Thirties person confronted a hollow-eyed woman and her ragged children in the pages of a picture magazine, right in his living room. As his radio brought him the hysterical pageantry of Hitler's rallies for the dispossessed, the magazine he was reading showed that great masses of Americans were as desperately poor and hopeless as those restless, volatile European crowds.

The Futurama and Democracity represented two contrasting schemes for buying off those menacing masses with largely materialistic promises.

The Futurama was a private idyll. Sponsored by America's largest corporation, it represented the nation's leading industry. In 1937, automobile manufacturers employed more than 5 percent of the work force and paid 7.5 percent of all wages.[58] A visitor to Futurama lounged on his private throne as it rolled magically through an orderly, magnificent landscape. He listened on a private speaker to a neighborly voice describing the wonders that passed before his eyes, wonders that featured the most precious of his possessions: his car. At the end, he could linger right in the midst of the fantasy world he had just seen.

Democracity, by contrast, emphasized a collective ideal. Audiences entered the exhibit in groups, and were dismissed, precisely five and a half minutes later, into the blinding heat of a typical New York summer day. The city they beheld could be built only through political action, by governmental regulation—planning and zoning—and public financing. And while the singing masses marching across the dome represented people from all walks of life, they strode so resolutely and loomed so large that the spectator's awe easily became terror.

The Futurama, furthermore, showed unspoiled countryside, the vastness of America, the variety of the land, the beauty of its terrain. It implied a perpetual frontier, a frontier that in the future would become more accessible than ever by automobile. Some people might have to—or even want to—live in cities, it suggested, but the American rural ideal was but a Sunday drive away. Democracity, by its very name, reminded the audience that America was, and had been since the Twenties, an urbanized nation. While it did away with city congestion, dirt, and noise, Democracity also banished the pulsating, tantalizing hurly-burly of city life. Americans had always been ambivalent, if not downright suspicious, about cities, but all through the twentieth century they had been briskly migrating into them. Was this bland, neat cosmopolis what they had been seeking?

Perhaps, but its image did not persist long in memory. Nor did it attract nearly as many visitors as the Futurama. During the fair's two-year run, almost 10 million visitors passed through the Futurama, many of them several times. Democracity, possibly hampered by a twenty-five-cent admission charge, attracted just over half as many. And of those who attended the fair, few today remember Democracity, while almost all recall the Futurama as virtually synonymous with the fair. A small sidelight also conveys the significant contrast between working for the government and for private industry: The fair management paid Dreyfuss $25,000 for his Democracity design, while Bel Geddes collected $200,000 for the Futurama.[59]

From a technical standpoint, both exhibits were marvels of the model-maker's art. The Futurama was constructed in the eye of the chaotic creative storm that Bel Geddes habitually generated. In March 1939, only two months before the fair opened, it was still "barely a sketch on paper." In an old movie studio at 126th Street and Second Avenue, some 3,000 workers feverishly milled among the more than four hundred 5-by-20-foot tables on which the Futurama came to life. Using aerial maps and photographs pasted onto the floor beneath each table, they built up contours by raising the table legs or gluing layers of celotex onto the table surface. For the Futurama's city, Bel Geddes and six staffers walked like Gullivers around a 40-by-60-foot map of St. Louis, their pockets bulging with "skyscrapers." Bel Geddes insisted that even clotheslines and splats of cow manure in pastures be precise miniatures. Eventually the model comprised 500,000 buildings, 10 million trees (of eighteen species), and 50,000 cars, of which 10,000 were in motion.[60]

Democracity was equally ambitious. Dreyfuss first projected a test film inside the perisphere to make sure that his concept worked. Eastman Kodak then built projectors, each of which could throw an image 20 feet high and 30 feet wide. They used lantern slides, advanced at a rate of twelve per second, almost the speed of movie film but with far better definition. For his nighttime effects, Dreyfuss consulted the Hayden Planetarium to learn the precise constellations visible on the fair's opening day. Then he wanted to add one extra star to Democracity's firmament. Brighter than all the rest, it was to be "the Star of Hope," but budget troubles extinguished it. Before constructing Democracity inside the perisphere, the Dreyfuss firm built a complete model of the model, on a scale of 200 feet to the inch. The final model, as built by the Diorama Corporation, varied in scale; structures at the center were as tall as 4 feet and became smaller toward the perimeter. The average building was about the size of a telephone book on end. Each one was made of ⅜-inch plywood and covered with cardboard, then painted with fluorescent touches to glow in the nighttime lighting. The entire display rested on a basin-shaped lath and plaster dish, 100 feet in diameter, supported from below on fireproof wooden stilts. Henry Dreyfuss spent the fair's opening day here, instead of marching in the parade, still fiddling with paint and plaster.[61]

In how they were created as well as in the information

they conveyed, both exhibits displayed the kind of technological pyrotechnics beloved of the Thirties. "To the modern man, his physical environment is merely new material, an opportunity for manipulation," Teague admiringly quoted Bertrand Russell. "It may be that God made the world, but that is no reason why we should not make it over." But the fair would be the last display of "technological frontiers that were intelligible to the average man." Soon, as Daniel Boorstin noted, the "heroic thrusts" would take place "in the laboratory, among cyclotrons and betatrons . . . on the edges of our comprehension . . . just beyond our understanding."[62]

> O engineering, open door
> To worlds unknown before,
> O chemistry, my final test!—
> Of all the sciences I love thee best![63]

So sang John Black, poet laureate of the fair. While all modern fairs since London's Crystal Palace Exhibition of 1851 stressed inventions, the New York fair's most striking exhibits showed a special kind of invention: a synthetic replica better, cheaper, or even more "real" than what it imitated. In its pavilion, du Pont unveiled nylon, a textile compounded of coal, water and air, stronger and cheaper than silk, and more versatile than any natural fiber. Visitors to the AT&T exhibit were astonished by Voder, a machine that imitated not only the human voice but sheep bleating, cattle lowing, pigs grunting, and woodpeckers rat-tat-tat-ing. True, Voder still required a complex box crammed with vacuum tubes and a trained operator for its complicated keyboard and pedals (and while it could sing, it had promised not to apply for an audition at the Met), but to the audience it was clearly only a matter of time before a machine replaced human speech.

The most treasured fair souvenir was another replica— H. J. Heinz's tiny green plastic pickle. At the Railroads building pageant, a diminutive lady played Kurt Weill tunes on a startling new instrument, the Hammond Novachord. Powered by 144 radio tubes, it could imitate the sounds of piano, harpsichord, trumpet, guitar, and violin—in stereo. The most popular attraction in the amusement area was a simulated parachute jump. It had been invented to provide safe training for military parachutists, but its synthetic experience proved so popular at the fair that it was later moved to Coney Island. And, of course, the televised live coverage of the fair's opening previewed a source of synthetic experience such as the world had never seen.[64]

The wonders of technology spilled over, too, into the fair's artistic side. The 105 gigantic murals and sixty sculptures commissioned by the fair enlivened its windowless buildings and also gave an artistic veneer to its educational message. On the exterior of the Food focal exhibit, for example, Witold Gordon combined cattle, poultry, fish, vegetables, and fruit with decorative representations of vitamins, carbohydrates, proteins, and fats. The best mural, in the opinion of *Life* magazine, was a three-dimensional creation by Henry Billings in the Ford building: 70 feet long and 40 feet high, it stood against a curved wall resembling the apse of a church. It suggested a gigantic altarpiece whose central figure was a V-8 engine.[65]

If not deifying technology, much of the fair's sculpture tried to bring a modern idiom to classical themes. Albert Stewart's *Mithrana,* spirit of the fair, dominated the entrance to the administration building. "What a heavy wench," the historian Monaghan wrote to Whalen, "what thick, muscular arms, what forbidding thighs, what deformed legs and bunioned feet! If only the medical building needed the statue and the administration building did not! A derrick will lift her into place and probably a derrick is the thing most fit to clasp her." Monaghan suggested that she be named after Mithras, the Persian god of sun and light, and Diana, goddess of the hunt, suggesting "a happy combination" of friendliness and light, questing, youth, and beauty. The name had a practical side as well, he reminded Whalen: Whenever a bizarre name was coined, the explanations created publicity for the fair.[66]

One of the fair's most admired sculptures gave off so many technological signals that it was massively misunderstood: Gertrude Vanderbilt Whitney's *To the Morrow,* a 30-foot rainbow arch supporting three 24-foot-wide wings on which was balanced a stylized couple 12 feet long. They gleamed with a coating of platinum foil, a technique in which Whitney specialized. Though Whitney insisted that the theme was youth, Mayor LaGuardia, who had been a flier in World War I, expatiated at the unveiling on its glorious tribute to aviation. Ogden Hammond, the U.S. Ambassador to Spain, was certain that it was a modern version of the *Winged Victory*. But the best explanation of its meaning came from a guide who was taking Whitney around the fair in a rickshaw. The metallic coating, he explained, was silver, and the sculpture's message was that "every cloud has a silver lining."[67]

The age seemed to demand that art, like every other manifestation of human activity, carry a social meaning. Most of the artists who worked at the fair complied. As Barbara Rose has noted, the Thirties were palpably a golden age for artists in America. For the first time in their careers, many could devote themselves fully to their art, supported by WPA commissions. The fair augmented that support, but it also demanded rigorous justifications for their art's usefulness. Stuart Davis, by far the most distinguished muralist at the fair, reflected with some resentment on those demands as he executed a colorful abstraction 136 feet long and 44 feet high for the American Art Today exhibition. "The social content of art is always simply art itself," he wrote. "The social meaning of art consists at all times of an affirmation of the joy felt in successful resolution of a problem. This expression has social meaning because it gives concrete proof of the possibility of establishing order in certain aspects of man's relation to Nature. Such expression is a moral force and provides courage for life to those who experience it."[68]

But so strong was the fair's pragmatic impetus that the original plans had included no art building at all. The omission raised a chorus of rage. It was conceivable, the art critic Edward Alden Jewell fumed, "that the world of tomorrow will cast into . . . active opprobrium all art that fails to submit a *raison d'être* rooted in pure utilitarian purpose." The "useless" plastic arts might "be accompanied into oblivion" by all music, literature, and drama lacking "pragmatic, sociological or propagandizing function."[69] Eventually New York's modern art establishment, which happened to include the fair directors Nelson Rockefeller and Winthrop Aldrich, persuaded the fair management to grapple with providing a fireproof building and insurance for an exhibition of American art. The outcome was an extraordinary show, but extraordinary more for its expression of Thirties preoccupation with democratic process than as a display of aesthetic excellence.

Those friendly to modern art dominated the show's five-person organizing committee. Chaired by the Museum of Modern Art's founding president, A. Conger Goodyear, it also included Juliana Force and Holger Cahill. Force was director of Gertrude Vanderbilt Whitney's burgeoning collection of contemporary American art. Cahill had been an adviser on primitive American art to Abby Aldrich Rockefeller, a MOMA founder, and had organized some of the museum's exhibitions of modern American art. He had also headed the WPA Fine Arts Project. Now he devised a uniquely populist system for selecting works for the fair's art show. He organized six regional selection committees (plus three in New York), each comprising nine members. Supposedly they represented the spectrum of artistic styles from rigid traditionalists to wild-eyed modernists. Those juries viewed every work submitted and balloted by electric voting machine, so that each individual's vote was secret. A work receiving seven or more votes was automatically admitted, while one receiving three or less was rejected. The juries reconsidered those in between as often as four times in an effort to muster the five votes required for inclusion. In a truly heroic exercise of aesthetic judgment, the groups eventually selected some 1,200 works to be shown from among the more than 25,000 pieces submitted.

Cahill rejoiced that the show was "the most extensive and the most thorough winnowing of American Art which has ever taken place, a winnowing based on competent professional opinion." Indeed, the show displayed the work of many unknown artists from remote corners of the country, while the system of judging works blind left out many who were established "names." But it also resulted in a mild, homogeneous exhibition, a survey of common themes and styles rather than a provocative gathering of the avant-garde. "To obtain a cross-section of average American art no better mode of selection . . . could be found," the critic James Johnson Sweeney wrote. "But if the ideal were a stimulus and a redirection of American art in general, perhaps a less 'fair' and more prejudiced approach might bring richer results. Art expression is based on emotional expression and emotions imply prejudices."[70]

Far less self-consciously democratic than the art show was the fair's most impressive aesthetic achievement: its spectacular use of illumination. Using masses of fluorescents and capillary mercury lights for the first time, it revolutionized "all our ideas of the use of light," one observer wrote. The scheme was not devised by an artist but by a lighting engineer, Julian E. Garnsey. Its glow shaded from brilliant white at the central Trylon and Perisphere to deepening blues down the Avenue of Pioneers, yellows to golds down the Avenue of Patriots and gradually intensifying reds down Constitution Mall. Along the arc of Rainbow Avenue, golds shaded into oranges, reds, violets, and blues, suggesting the fantasy realm in a movie that opened the same year as the fair, *The Wizard of Oz.* Drawing from a palette of 499 colors developed by Garnsey, light became part of the architectural design and, by means of thousands of bulbs illuminating individual trees from below, part of the landscaping as well. "Odd-shaped buildings that had stared blankly on the fair lawns" by day became "a Wellsian fantasy of color" after dark.[71]

Spectacular lighting had been a central part of world's fairs ever since the Paris Exhibition of 1900, but the New York Fair's ambitious electrical pyrotechnics surpassed any before or since. Every evening at nine, the Lagoon of Nations erupted in a "Ballet of Fountains," which dazzled observers. No one seemed to worry about the social significance of more than 1,400 water nozzles and 400 flaming gas jets, dancing in unison to original musical scores on such themes as "The Spirit of George Washington," "Fire Dance," "Isle of Dreams," and "Creation." No one asked for the precise meaning of the spectacle as 585 colored drum lamps and five giant spotlights played over the fires and the waters. No one worried publicly about the cost—more than $1,000 each night—of bedazzling visitors with rockets fired from 350 fireworks guns. Nor did a single public voice complain that Jean Labatut, professor of architecture at Princeton, who designed the show and its complex electronic infrastructure, had wasted his time on costly frivolity.

Abstract and innovative, lavish and joyful, the water ballet may well have represented the democratic answer to such awesome and frightening spectacles as the Nazis' Nuremberg rallies orchestrated by Alfred Speer. Devoid of ideological content and devoted purely to the senses, the show conveyed the creativity of a free society far more convincingly than any heavy rhetoric could. Not that contemporary observers noted such comparisons. They were too stunned by the display. It is "one of the most superlatively beautiful sights we shall ever see" was a typical comment. Few had such sophisticated perceptions of it as the fair's music consultant, Gretl Urban, who realized that it was "a new type of esthetic expression . . . a choreographic composition" in which "the dancer is not man but matter."[72]

The hyperbole that greeted so many of the fair's attractions paled by comparison with the puffery issued by the fair's management. From the beginning, the fair's publicity was orchestrated by a Machiavelli of media hype, Grover Whalen. When he became the fair's president in 1936, Whalen had had more experience than any other New Yorker in the cunning new art of the news conference, the planted story, the judicious leak, the media event, the calculated publicity campaign. Officially, he had served the City of New York as secretary to Mayor John F. Hylan from 1917 to 1919, as Commissioner of Plant and Structures from 1919 to 1924 and as police commissioner under Mayor Jimmy Walker from 1928 to 1930. But it was his work as the city's volunteer host that caused more New Yorkers to recognize Whalen's genial Irish face and elegant figure than anyone except Al Smith, Jack Dempsey, and Babe Ruth.

Beginning in the early Twenties, Whalen had refined the art of greeting visiting dignitaries into a glittering but seemly spectacle. While not the inventor of the ticker tape parade up Broadway, he magnified those rites from casual expressions of enthusiasm into precisely planned extravaganzas of civic ardor. From his white spats to his dazzling silk hat, his trousers razor-creased, his shoulders "a tailor's delight" inside the black cutaway, his carnation boutonniere perpetually fresh, Whalen himself had over the years become more newsworthy, often, than the celebrities he was greeting. Whether the dignitary was Queen Marie of Rumania or the Prince of Wales, Georges Clemenceau or Marshal Foche, the explorer Richard E. Byrd or the channel swimmer Gertrude Ederle, or even America's boy hero of 1927, Charles Lindbergh (whose reception cost the city $71,850.87), the entire nation's reputation for hospitality, Whalen was convinced, rested on his knowledge of the most trifling point of protocol. His guests, in turn, had showered on him such Ruritanian-sounding decorations as the Royal Victorian Order, the Order of Simon Bolivar, Chevalier (later upgraded to Commander) of the Legion of Honor, Officier d'Instruction Publique, and Commander in Chief of the Order of the (Rumanian) Crown.[73]

Whalen had also organized lesser, though always rousing, receptions for the Supreme Chancellor of the Knights of Pythias, the president of the Vienna Board of Health, Miss Brazil, the French Boy Scout singers, the University of Arizona polo team, and the three oldest traveling salesmen in America. But the crash of 1929 had cast a somber connotation on blizzards of ticker tape, and the Depression that followed had wiped out all city budget support for Whalen's greeting activities.

During his tenure as police commissioner, Whalen had had to slake his sartorial appetite by designing snappier uniforms for his "18,000 horse, foot, and motorcycle." He maintained his personal standard of elegance by continuing to receive his daily shave while ensconced in his private barber chair and kept physically fit with the aid of a personal trainer, Artie McGovern, who called daily at his Washington Mews townhouse. Traversing the city on Police Department business, Whalen favored an open chauffeured car. Frequently he would activate the siren by pressing a button close to hand. When he alighted, the chauffeur sat in Whalen's seat, keeping it warm in winter and cool in summer. A bystander once gave Whalen a Bronx cheer. Arrested, the man was released with a warning that "it would have gone hard with him had the Commissioner cared to prosecute."[74]

So richly encrusted was the Whalen image with sartorial and stylistic trivia that his genuine accomplishments came as a surprise. During all those years of dutifully breasting the swells of New York Harbor in a police launch to greet the crowned heads of Europe, he had also labored as a keen executive at Wanamaker's department store. While smiling benignly on the Sanitation Band's umpteenth rendition of the "Star Spangled Banner," he had earned the trust of New York's Establishment with quiet civic volunteer work. The press may have snickered over the statue of Napoleon adorning his desk and the black pajamas trimmed in red in which he posed for his portrait as police commissioner, but he had also, in his thirteen-month tenure, revamped the police academy, set up classes for drivers, and started a crime prevention bureau and a homicide squad.

In an experience that would prove useful for the fair, he had been in charge of New York's celebration of George Washington's bicentennial in 1932. As a Depression make-work project, he ordered construction of a replica of Mt. Vernon in Brooklyn's Prospect Park and one of Federal Hall, where Washington was inaugurated, in Manhattan's Bryant Park. Foreshadowing fair problems, "when the hat was passed to make up one of Whalen's deficits very little was dropped into it," and the bills for this patriotic exercise were still unpaid in 1938.[75]

In 1933 he organized the biggest parade yet seen in New York—250,000 marchers and 1.5 million spectators—on behalf of the National Recovery Administration, a short-lived New Deal agency charged with mitigating labor strife. As state NRA director, Whalen had also settled 130 labor disputes. With the end of Prohibition, late in 1933, he became chairman of Schenley Products at a reported salary of $100,000 a year. The son of an Irish immigrant who ran a modest trash removal business on the lower East Side, Grover had marched steadily, noisily, uptown. Unquestionably he had a virtuoso's talent for playing on the organs of publicity, but his accomplishments were impressive. Elmer Davis may have wondered whether any substance of character lay behind the baroque façade Whalen presented, "perhaps the front goes right through," but his expansive vision and elegant style seemed to be just what the fair needed.[76]

In tune with the times, Whalen dressed less formally after he became the fair's chairman of the board and chief executive officer in April 1936, playing down the title of best-dressed man in America that the Custom Tailors Guild of America had bestowed upon him in 1932. In fact, a financial adviser to a French cosmetics firm, Coty, thought Whalen downright inelegant because he wore a blue shirt. But the Frenchman's esteem rose when he called on Whalen at his fair office, found him in a private barber chair getting his daily shave, and was invited to occupy a second private chair for a shave and haircut. Coty ended up building an elegant fair pavilion shaped like a powder box.[77]

Within a few months after taking over the fair's management, Whalen began announcing the pathbreaking innovations that would make this exposition unique in the history of such events. No exhibitor could pick the location of his display; instead, the fair would be organized around focal exhibits, and space would be "allotted in an orderly, scientific manner." The fair's size would be double, or even triple that of any previous fair. Naturally, its cost would be greater too—some $65 million, Whalen estimated, twice the cost of the most recent American fair, the 1933 Century of Progress Exhibition in Chicago. In its theme the fair would go far beyond furnishing "gayety, festivity, novelty, beauty, drama, comfort and delight." Its chief purpose would be "the betterment of mankind," he announced. "We shall try to answer the question—'What kind of world have we built; what kind of world are we building? What kind of world should we build?' "[78]

All through the fair's development the silken thread of its noble, even grandiloquent theme ran parallel to the baser and perhaps more convincing thread of how many bucks it would bring into New York City. Whalen adroitly intertwined those themes, stressing ideals for the press and the brass-tacks bottom line for exhibitors and investors. In a bulletin issued to promote sales of more than $27 million fair bonds in November 1936, he wove a richly enticing tapestry from those two motifs. The fair's "enlightening influence will be engraved into the hard surface of our times," he promised. And of the $1 billion expected to be spent by fair visitors, "our statisticians estimate . . . that every dollar will change hands 10 times," implying that turnover would magically multiply the $1 billion tenfold.[79]

More than greed was involved. At the fair's groundbreaking on June 15, 1936, while photographers and newsreel cameramen jostled for a clear shot of Whalen digging the first bucketful of dirt with a steamshovel, hundreds of ragged men also jostled nearby, hoping for work. But it took only 325 men, masked like desperados in great swirling clouds of dust, to prepare the site. In nine months, they would move 7 million cubic yards of dirt, a volume that, were it concrete, would pave a four-lane highway from New York to Daytona Beach, Florida. The real measure of New Yorkers' desperation were the forty or more junk trucks that haunted the grading site, hauling off thousands of tons of metal for salvage—bedsteads, boilers, bathtubs. Even more pathetic were hundreds of children who swarmed through the filth in "salvage gangs: one band taking copper only, another brass, a third lead."[80]

Another kind of desperation haunted the elegant 2,000 who, on November 23, 1936, donned perhaps last year's formal gowns and tuxedoes to attend the bond sales kickoff banquet. The financial system they relied on had simply stopped functioning. Unlike previous recoveries from a slump, the economy had not righted itself for more than seven years. Furthermore, even conservative analysts like the Brookings Institution had blamed rising concentrations of wealth in a few hands and investment of that wealth in unproductive speculation for much of the economic disaster.[81] For most of the chic crowd that evening, FDR was not the savior of capitalism but the architect of bureaucratic totalitarianism in America.

Meanwhile, some of the managers of the moribund capitalist system would shortly be unmasked in headlines as common crooks. At the head table in the Hotel Astor's ballroom, under a blue canopy studded with stars, for example, sat Richard

Whitney. While serving five terms as president of the New York Stock Exchange and heatedly defending the exchange's system against Federal investigators, he had also been secretly stealing the securities entrusted to him by investors. He was named on that evening as chairman of the drive to sell fair bonds.

While successfully peddling all $27,829,500 worth of fair bonds, Whitney was steadily stonewalling clients who demanded their securities. By November 1937, only legal threats had persuaded him to return more than $1 million to New York Stock Exchange president E. H. H. Simmons. The money was a Gratuities Fund, to be used to pension widows of stock exchange members. Already insolvent, Whitney paid off the stock exchange with a loan arranged through his brother, George, a partner at J. P. Morgan. Since 1931 Whitney had borrowed some $15 million, paying almost $1 million in interest. In that year also, he had borrowed $300,000 without collateral from the Corn Exchange Bank, where he was also a director. When the conflict of interest was called to his attention, he borrowed from Morgan through his brother to repay Corn Exchange. Eventually, he would owe Morgan more than $3 million, all unsecured. For other loans, he used his clients' securities as collateral.

Most of his firm's fifty-odd clients were relatives or members of New York's upper crust; many were among the glittering guests at the fair bonds kickoff banquet. Whitney's dealings on their behalf amounted to more than 10 percent of all New York bond transactions. When Whitney's peculations were unmasked some fifteen months later, they were viewed in New York's society world as a particularly foul betrayal. No witness was more indignant than William A. W. Stewart, Commodore of the New York Yacht Club, as he described how Richard Whitney, who had been the club's treasurer since 1928, had used $100,000 of the club's bonds as collateral for a $450,000 loan.

Nor was Whitney's business judgment cause for confidence in the system. The man who had been called Wall Street's "strong man" after he bravely tried to stem the market's plunge on Black Tuesday, October 24, 1929, had come to grief in a series of foolish investments. "A steadfast faith in the future of New Jersey applejack," for example, had caused him to pour millions into Distilled Liquors Corporation. Whitney's firm had been insolvent from the day it opened its doors in 1931, District Attorney Thomas E. Dewey reported in April 1938, when Whitney came up for sentence on several counts of grand larceny. Furthermore, Dewey revealed, Whitney had covered the insolvency with false financial statements, part of "a deliberate course of criminal conduct covering . . . six years."[82]

In an informal measure of public idleness and consequent thirst for sensation, more than 6,000 people turned up at the old Tombs prison and at Grand Central Station for a glimpse of the handcuffed Whitney on his way to Sing Sing prison in the spring of 1938, in the company of two extortionists, a holdup man, and a rapist. One newspaper breathlessly reported that his first prison meal consisted of baked lima beans, boiled potatoes, tea, bread, and cornstarch pudding, surely more carbohydrates than many a hungry reader ate that night.[83]

Most of those who bought fair bonds were large businesses that hoped to profit from the fair and banks that were covering the $1.6 million in unsecured loans they had advanced to get the fair under way. The bonds seemed like a reasonable investment. Scientific-sounding attendance estimates ranged from 250,000 on "ordinary days," to 800,000 on "special days." As the notion grew that the fair would run for a second year, so grew the conviction that 90 million would attend during the two years. By February 1937, the *World's Fair News*, a monthly published on the fairgrounds, was saying that the "bankers' estimate" seemed "ridiculously low." By December 1, 1938, the fair management raised its earlier estimates. "Simple mathematical calculations," a news release said, indicated 60 million would attend during the first year alone. Three surveys done "in accordance with modern accepted methods . . . properly weighted" showed that there could even be 90 million admissions. "Admitting that they are but straws in the wind," the research director, Frank Monaghan, wrote "they would indicate that a cyclone is imminent."[84]

In January 1939 George Gallup's American Institute of Public Opinion found that 33 million American were "considering" attending the fair, while 12.4 million said they were definitely going, most of them living within a 200-mile radius of New York City. The *New York Times* headlined the report of that survey "33,000,000 in the Nation Hope to Visit" the fair, while the subhead indicated that attendance "May Set Record." On the following day, a *Times* editorial exulted over those figures, claiming that each of the 33 million would visit the fairgrounds three times, thus promising over 100 million admissions. "If anybody ever doubted the success of our world's fair," an editorial commented, "his apprehensions should be dispelled."[85] Such optimism was typical of the Thirties' naïve belief in public opinion polls. Quickly forgotten was the notorious failure of the *Literary Digest* poll in predicting the result of the 1936 presidential election (because only telephone subscribers were polled). Now the *Times* was ignoring the possibility that the common man to whom the fair was dedicated might be ashamed to admit that he could not afford to visit the fair; the fair's buoyant boosterism was crowding out the skepticism natural to a journalist.

Nor were the fair's expense reports devoid of wishful thinking. As the fair opened, *Time* reported that it had cost the city $26.7 million and the state $6.2 million. Congress had wanted to contribute $5 million, but FDR trimmed it to $3 million. Once the bondholders were repaid, the fair's publicity blared, its profits were to benefit the public: The first $2 million would be spent to develop the fair site as a park, a luxurious facility, which Whalen estimated would be worth $100 million, and the rest would go for city, state, charitable, and scientific purposes. In fact, New York City eventually spent more than $48 million and New York State $7.5 million. From the $65 million cost estimate, which itself was a record, the fair's cost eventually soared beyond $170 million.[86]

But those grim facts emerged long after the fair ended. Meanwhile, Whalen was demonstrating miracles of salesmanship. He waylaid Henry Ford at the private entrance to his plant and signed him up for a large building. All through 1936 and 1937, he recalled, "I was going back and forth between here and Europe like a ferryboat," eventually persuading a record number of countries—sixty—to participate. He wanted to visit Moscow to sell the Soviet Union a pavilion but was persistently denied a visa because, while police commissioner, he had dealt roughly with Communist demonstrators. Undaunted, he dragged Soviet Ambassador Constantine A. Oumanski to the fairgrounds and persuaded him to telephone Stalin right then. The result was a lavish $4 million Soviet pavilion. Through a former Italian consul in New York, he obtained an audience with Mussolini. He found the Italian dictator at the far end of 200 feet of slippery parquet, staring imperiously out the window, seemingly unaware of his visitor. From a desk elevated like a stage, the 5 foot, 3 inch Duce towered over Whalen, who had been warned that no chairs were provided for visitors. But there was a chair for Grover Whalen. Mussolini told him that fascism was like the New Deal. Whalen's reply is unrecorded, but he walked out with a commitment for a $5 million Italian pavilion.[87]

Ebullient, optimistic, confident, Whalen was the living practitioner of the homely advice dished up in the biggest bestseller of the Thirties: Dale Carnegie's *How to Win Friends and Influence People*. The book was published in 1936, and one can't help but assume that Whalen took its homilies to heart. Certainly he was the type of man whom Carnegie wanted to help: ambitious, gregarious, nervy. Carnegie had said: "Smile." A gallery of toothy publicity photos demonstrated how seriously Whalen took that advice. Carnegie had said, "Dramatize your ideas." When Whalen showed reporters the first scale model of the fair, complete even with the white wake of a tiny motorboat in the harbor, he spoke "as if the miniatures were the completed reality."[88] Carnegie's book is crammed with the names of the famous and successful. The prospectus Whalen drew up to sell the fair, a magnificent 10-pound volume measuring 19 by 24 inches, devoted three of its thirty-two card-stock pages to a roll-call of the luminaries who were the fair's incorporators and directors.[89] Carnegie had said, "Appeal to the nobler motives." The fair's idealistic theme and grand execution had been trumpeted abroad via

131 million pamphlets, handbills, flyers, folders, displays, and even grocery bags and utility bill inserts. Between April 30 and July 15, 1939, 731 radio programs on 19,171 stations had extolled the fair's wonders. The coverage of the opening had exceeded that given to the Coronation of King George VI in 1937. Some 236 newsreels devoted to the fair were shown in 16,585 theaters. Newspapers gave the fair more than 12 million inches of space, the equivalent of 76,275 pages. Magazines published 160 special editions for the fair. From the outset of planning, the fair's publicity department distributed 305,412 photos.[90]

If a publicity blitz could guarantee success, the fair should have been a smash hit. But not even an army of Dale Carnegies could have wrested success for that fair out of those times. Splendid rhetoric aside, the fair had been created, financed, and built with only one goal: to attract prosperity to New York City. But ironically, the grim happenings that would eventually bring prosperity to the city and nation doomed the fair to financial failure.

Germany was the most conspicuous absentee among the sixty nations whose pavilions ringed the Court of Peace. Violent public protest had dissuaded the fair management from even approaching the Nazis about an exhibit. In January 1939, four months before the fair's opening, a committee of prominent New Yorkers had attempted to plan an anti-Nazi pavilion. It would include a Viennese café and show the work of exiled architects, scientists, artists, and writers. The fair offered a free site, but the idea was abandoned three weeks later for lack of time.[91]

Amid the colorful flags waving atop the international pavilions on opening day was a tiny set of banners at half-mast, a sorrowful echo of the sudden showers that had drenched the opening day celebrations. The blood-red flag with its black Hapsburg double eagle over the modest Albanian exhibit had been lowered to mourn the obliteration of that small Adriatic nation by Mussolini's Fascist forces just three weeks earlier.[92]

The serene, traditional temple that served as the Japanese pavilion displayed a profusion of Japanese art products and silks; certainly there was no hint in that tasteful building of what headlines and radio bulletins were regularly reporting: that Japan also manufactured the bombs and airplanes used to annihilate millions of Chinese and that its troops had driven the Chinese government deep into the interior at Chungking. Rather, the display featured a "Flame of Friendship" from the "sacred fires of the Grand Shrine of Izumo, which have burned for 1,500 years in Nikko, birth place of the gods." Dedicated with impressive Shinto services in Tokyo, the flame had been brought to the fair, a brochure informed visitors, to "symbolize the hopes of the Japanese people that the spirit of amity will forever bind the United States and Japan."[93]

Nearby, the Czech pavilion was opened a month late by President Eduard Beneš. Its red, white, and blue flags flew at half-mast to mourn the occupation of Czechoslovakia by Hitler only ten weeks earlier. Having "worked incessantly for peace in Europe," the fair's official guide to national pavilions said, the Czechs had "made the greatest sacrifice ever asked of a sovereign and undefeated people . . . in vain." Bravely, the exiled Czechs insisted that "no people can permanently subjugate a people stronger in character and will to survive as a free country." And as bravely, they searched for an acceptable American substitute for imported Pilsner.[94]

One exhibition proposal studied in considerable detail as the fair was being planned was a building devoted to "Goodwill and Peace." In it, a series of films would "demonstrate the effectiveness of the pacific settlement of disputes as contrasted with the futility of force and war" and would "call attention to the forces for goodwill that are operative in the world today." The fair's executive committee also considered including a historical survey showing the futility of war, beginning with the War of 1812, examples of successful arbitration of commercial disputes, and the benefit of international sports and cultural exchanges.[95]

Nothing came of the idea, although the kind of naïve optimism it expressed persisted throughout the years of fair planning. The fair "will present a clear, unified and comprehensive picture of the epochal achievements of a century and a half of modern civilization in the fields of art and literature, of science and industry, of government and the social services,"

Grover Whalen had written in his oversize selling brochure. "By giving a clear and orderly interpretation of our own age, the fair will project the average man into the World of Tomorrow."[96] Whalen believed that the fair "attempted to tell of the immediate necessity of enlightened and harmonious cooperation to preserve . . . the best of modern civilization."[97] Visitors would surely see, Frank Monaghan maintained, that "harmonious cooperation among men . . . classes, communities and nations . . . can take place only with peace." He expected that the fair would make "an indirect, though forcible contribution to the cause of peace."[98] The fair's planners were convinced that its mirror reflecting the future would enchant the world and tame the aggressive forces prowling its perimeters.

As the World of Tomorrow neared completion, such innocence gave way to more urgent appeals for sanity. The Federal Commissioner for the fair, Theodore T. Hayes, was impressed with the Court of Peace, around which "the nations of the world grouped harmoniously in conference," as he put it, "with the United States at the head of the peace table." The ground plan showed "that different nations . . . can cooperate."[99] But the shape of international cooperation was as vague as its rhetoric, and the substance of international ties was surprisingly ephemeral. During the week the fair opened, for example, overseas phone calls from Washington averaged three a day. During the Munich crisis of the previous September, such calls had averaged just over two a day. True, government communications usually went by cable, but remarkably few individuals thought to reach out and touch someone overseas during those tense days.[100]

Much of America was isolated, as well as isolationist, the result of a decade of internal crisis and change. That isolation found its echo in the innocent optimism of many who were clearly internationalists. "The means are at hand for a new era in human relationships," RCA's president David Sarnoff wrote on the eve of the fair's opening. "The human will and ingenuity to utilize them for the lasting benefit of mankind must be forthcoming." More specifically, "Europe has died a hundred deaths in the course of history," Anne O'Hare

McCormick wrote. "It is continually breaking into fragments and being patched together again. But it did not die and it is not dying now." She noted that no country had pulled out of the fair during the Munich crisis, and even Czechoslovakia, "under the shock of amputation . . . gathered up its depleted forces and went ahead."[101]

But as the summer wore on, European events would cast a bleak shadow indeed over Flushing Meadows. On August 21, as Russia and Germany signed a nonaggression pact, the *Times* headlined the "outlook blackest since 1914." The fair's managers hurriedly decided against permitting radio news broadcasts on the fairgrounds, but it was difficult "to block out all thought of what might really be in store for the World of Tomorrow," one fair visitor recalled. A touring Member of Parliament summed up the wishful, murderous thoughts of many: "We shall not be able to enjoy ourselves again until Franco's widow tells Stalin on his deathbed that Hitler has been assassinated at Mussolini's funeral."[102]

Attention increasingly focused, as the humid dog days of August crept by, on the Polish pavilion. There, each day at noon, a trumpeter sounded the "heynal," re-creating the bugle call played 698 years earlier when Genghis Khan was at the gates of Cracow. Visitors to that pavilion, with its gleaming golden tower, were invited to write a 1,000-word essay on "What I Would Like to See in Poland." The best essay would win a free, all-expense trip to "Europe's new holiday-vacationland, the country off the beaten path . . . gay, colorful Poland."[103] When World War II broke out on September 3 with the Nazi invasion of Poland, the pavilion became "a scene of anguish," one observer wrote, as bewildered men and women, holding back their tears, filed through the exhibition."[104]

Always optimistic, a Candide artlessly facing the searching queries of the press, Grover Whalen had insisted that even if war broke out in Europe, the fair would be unaffected. He expected only a half million European visitors, he had told *Time* as the fair opened. Furthermore, the Panama Pacific Expositions of 1915 in San Francisco and San Diego had been successful despite the World War then raging in Europe. Besides, he had said, the unprecedented European participation in the fair indicated that there would be no war.[105]

As the summer progressed, Whalen was fighting titanic battles of his own. "The greatest impresario of our times," it turned out, was also a "spender par excellence." Early in his tenure as president, Whalen had furnished the directors' room in the fair's Empire State Building headquarters with "cream leather chairs . . . worthy of the World Directorate of which utopists dream." When the administration building on the fairgrounds was completed, at a cost of almost $1 million, it included a state dining room with walls sheathed in copper and great copper floral pieces on the tables. By midsummer, secretaries were still calling Whalen "Mr. President" as he bustled in and out of his sumptuous oval office, but several hundred "Grover boys," smartly uniformed young men who formed a ceremonial phalanx around the fair president and important visitors, were summarily fired.[106]

Receipts, it turned out, had fallen far short of expenditures; the fair had had to borrow several million dollars from banks simply to open. In midsummer, unpaid contractors threatened to close the whole show, and only a desperate appeal to bondholders raised $3.5 million more to keep it open. Even worse, attendance was sparse. The common man for whom the fair was ostensibly built could not afford vacation travel. Many New Yorkers, who could buy a whole meal at a cheap restaurant for fifteen cents, found the fair's seventy-five-cent admission and fifteen-cent hot dogs beyond reach. A typical day at the fair might have cost as much as five dollars, more than half a week's wage for those with jobs. Instead of the 50 million "conservatively" estimated, only 25.8 million would visit the fair through its entire 1939 season.[107]

The fair's board of directors had had an "ironclad rule" that all expenditures be approved by the Executive Committee. But many expenses apparently had bypassed that route. Whalen had tried to economize, "but he had put so much of himself into the birth of the fair, that he was psychologically incapable of strangling his own baby." When the contractors threatened a lawsuit, the directors called in the banker Harvey D. Gibson, chairman of the Finance Committee, to clean up

the mess. He agreed, on condition that Whalen be "out of
the picture." No minutes reveal what occurred in the next
few days between the dapper Whalen and Gibson, "a short,
stocky white-haired man, whose eyes, behind their silver-
rimmed spectacles were sharp as a mother-in-law's tongue."
But on August 31 Whalen introduced Gibson to the press as
the fair's new board chairman. He would work full time at
no pay. Gibson announced that Whalen would stay on as president and "smilingly denied that anything of an emergency
nature had brought about the change." The fair, he said, "is
a pretty big job. I want to do everything I can to help
Grover."[108]

The fair limped on through the summer of 1940, with just
over 19 million attending the second year. The bondholders
eventually received twenty cents on the dollar. As fairgoers
straggled out of the grounds for the last time, a radio enter-
tainer named Dave Driscoll addressed a small group in double-
talk: "In this vast amphitheater millions from all the Americas
and from all corners of the world have heard addresses by
statesmen, Whalen, gravisnas, McAneny, cabishon, Gibson,
forbine and nobility. Here was the pledge of peace which
might well have been the fiederness, bedistran and grodle
of this great exposition. Now that pledge is forgotten. Sleed-
ment, twaint and broint forbish the doldrum all over the
world. Alas!"[109]

With that absurd eulogy, the fair was interred. But the
World of Tomorrow, literally constructed on the garbage heap
of the past, was no empty metaphor; it echoed too often elsewhere. Whether the ideal was as far-reaching as egalitarian
Communist world revolution or as mundane as giving the
folks in Goodland, Kansas, a hand-painted mural for their post
office, the people of the Thirties were convinced that the future was bright. The last line of the decade's most successful
film, based on its best-selling novel, *Gone with the Wind,* was
"Tomorrow's another day." In a decade shadowed by tragic
poverty and by madmen at the levers of power, it strikes a
contemporary observer as utterly inconceivable that men
would believe so fervently in a better tomorrow. But they
did.

Feisty, resilient, and inventive, these doughty optimists clamor still in the tapestry of the imagination: Lorena Hickock driving through a blinding dust storm to report firsthand on the misery of North Dakota farm families; H. V. Kaltenborn napping on a cot in the studio between breathless radio reports on the European crisis; Grover Whalen grandly constructing his futuristic fantasy fair; Margaret Bourke-White coolly adjusting her bulky camera amid the stench and squeals of a slaughterhouse; Lillian Hellman and Samuel Goldwyn yelling abuse at each other like two guttersnipes; the anonymous market researcher who struggled up a rutted country lane only to ask a farm wife: "Do you eat yeast?" Nelson Rockefeller and Diego Rivera chatting the nights away on a scaffold in Rockefeller Center.

On the cusp of the Thirties, the fair had gathered the hopes of the decade as well as its ashes. It ended in disarray.

But after a six-year interlude of unparalleled carnage, The World of Tomorrow would begin to unfold.

Notes

INTRODUCTION

1. "Time Capsule," a scrapbook compiled by the New York Public Library in 1938, New York World's Fair Archive, New York Public Library (NYPL).
2. José Ortega y Gasset, *The Revolt of the Masses* (New York: Norton, 1932; first published, 1930), p. 51.
3. Malcolm M. Willey and Stuart A. Rice, "The Agencies of Communication," in *Recent Social Trends* (New York: McGraw-Hill, 1933), pp. 198–99.

1. WRITTEN ON THE WIND

1. Ben Gross, *I Looked and I Listened* (New York: Random House, 1954), pp. 2–3; Charles Henry Stamps, *The Concept of the Mass Audience in American Broadcasting: An Historical Descriptive Study* (New York: Arno, 1959), p. 40; Ralph Lewis Smith, *A Study of the Professional Criticism of Broadcasting in the United States, 1920–1955* (New York: Arno, 1979), pp. 5, 20.
2. Robert Wood, *A World in Your Ear the Broadcasting of an Era 1923–64* (London: Macmillan, 1979), p. 25; Red Barber, *The Broadcasters* (New York: Dial, 1970), pp. 13–14.
3. Jonathan Hill, *"The Cat's Whiskers": Fifty Years of Radio Design* (London: Oresko, 1978), pp. 38, 49; G. Howard Poteet, *Radio!* (Dayton, Ohio: Pflaum, 1975), pp. 5–6.
4. Dick Perry, *Not Just a Sound: The Story of WLW* (Englewood Cliffs, N.J.: Prentice-Hall, 1971), pp. 15–16; Stamps, *Concept of Mass Audience*, p. 33.

5. Judith Waller, *Radio: the Fifth Estate* (Boston: Houghton Mif-flin, 1946), pp. 31–32; Frank Edwards, *My First 10,000,000 Sponsors* (New York: Ballantine, 1956), p. 34.

6. Peter Black, *The Biggest Aspidistra in the World* (London: BBC, 1973), p. 34.

7. Martin Codel, ed., *Radio and Its Future* (New York: Arno, 1971), p. 92; Carroll Carroll, *None of Your Business* (New York: Cowles, 1970), p. 29; Elliott M. Sanger, *Rebel in Radio* (New York: Hastings House, 1973), p. 16.

8. James Thurber, "Soapland: Part IV. The Invisible People," *New Yorker,* July 3, 1948, p. 37; Joseph Julian, *This Was Radio* (New York; Viking, 1975), p. 213; Hadley Cantril and Gordon W. Allport, *The Psychology of Radio* (New York: Harper, 1935), pp. 70–71.

9. Smith, *Study of Professional Criticism,* p. 21.

10. Gleason L. Archer, "Conventions, Campaigns and Kilocycles in 1924: The First Political Broadcasts," *Journal of Broadcasting,* Spring 1960, p. 118; Frank J. Kahn, *Documents of American Broadcasting* (New York: Appleton-Century-Crofts), 1968, p. 182; John W. Spalding, "Radio Becomes a Mass Advertising Medium," *Journal of Broadcasting,* Winter 1963–64, p. 33.

11. Kahn, *Documents,* pp. 183–84; William S. Paley, *As It Happened* (New York: Doubleday, 1979), p. 84; Spalding, "Radio Becomes," pp. 39–40.

12. H. Le B. Berkovici, "Station B-U-N-K," *American Mercury,* February 1929, p. 235; Merlin H. Aylesworth, "Radio's Accomplishment," *Century,* June 1929, p. 220; Kahn, *Documents,* pp. 152, 185–86.

13. Spalding, "Radio Becomes," pp. 36–37; Stamps, *Concept of Mass Audience,* p. 117.

14. Stamps, *Concept of Mass Audience,* pp. 135–40; Aylesworth, "Radio's Accomplishment," p. 221; Henry Volkening, "Abuses of Radio Broadcasting," *Current History,* December 1930, pp. 396–400; Smith, *Study of Professional Criticism,* p. 22.

15. John Snagge and Michael Barsley, *Those Vintage Years of Radio* (London: Putman, 1972), pp. 1–4, 15, 6; Black, *Biggest Aspidistra,* pp. 41, 58–59.

16. Harman Grisewood, *One Thing at a Time* (London: Hutchinson, 1968), pp. 107–10; Asa Briggs, *The Golden Age of Wireless* (London: Oxford, 1965), p. 47; Snagge and Barsley, *Vintage Years,* p. 11.

17. Briggs, *Golden Age,* p. 40; Black, *Biggest Aspidistra,* pp. 63–

64; "A Listener," "The BBC and Music," *Political Quarterly,* October–December 1935, pp. 527–28.

18. Briggs, *Golden Age,* pp. 253, 352–63.
19. *Ibid.,* p. 45.
20. Stamps, *Concept of Mass Audience,* p. 163.
21. "An Appraisal of Radio Advertising Today," *Fortune,* September 1932, p. 37; Harry Bannister, *The Education of a Broadcaster* (New York: Simon & Schuster, 1965), pp. 51, 20.
22. Carroll, *None of Your Business,* p. ix; Fred Allen, *Treadmill to Oblivion* (Boston: Little, Brown, 1954), pp. 13–15.
23. *Fortune,* September 1932, p. 39; Irving Kolodin, "Propaganda on the Air," *American Mercury,* July 1935, p. 299; Smith, *Study of Professional Criticism,* p. 25.
24. Paul W. White, *News on the Air* (New York: Harcourt, Brace, 1947), pp. 35–37; Abel A. Schechter and Edward Anthony, *I Live on Air* (New York: Stokes, 1941), pp. 1–2; Mitchell V. Charnley, *News by Radio* (New York: Macmillan, 1948), pp. 18–19.
25. Charnley, *News by Radio,* pp. 16–22.
26. Frederick H. Lumley, *Measurement in Radio* (New York: Arno, 1971), p. 185; Herman S. Hettinger, ed., *New Horizons in Radio* (New York: Arno, 1971), pp. 6–7; William S. Paley, *Radio as a Cultural Force* (New York: CBS, 1934), p. 104; David R. Mackey, "The Development of the National Assn. of Broadcasters," *Journal of Broadcasting,* Fall 1957, p. 322.
27. Merrill Dennison, "Editorial Policies of Broadcasting Companies," *Public Opinion Quarterly,* January 1937, pp. 77–78.
28. Stamps, *Concept of Mass Audience,* pp. 211, 189–91.
29. Volkening, "Abuses" (note 14), p. 397; Lumley, *Measurement in Radio,* pp. 67, 167.
30. Lumley, *Measurement in Radio,* pp. 50–52.
31. "Fan Mail," *Literary Digest,* May 22, 1937, p. 21.
32. David G. Clark, "Radio in Presidential Campaigns: The Early Years, 1924–32," *Journal of Broadcasting,* Summer 1962, pp. 229–30, 233–36; Paley, *As It Happened* (note 11), p. 119; Codel, *Radio and Its Future* (note 7), p. 190.
33. Clark, "Radio in Presidential Campaigns," pp. 236–37.
34. Hettinger, *New Horizons,* p. 17; Cantril and Allport, *Psychology of Radio* (note 8), p. 40; Clark, "Radio in Presidential Campaigns," p. 237.
35. Gross, *I Looked* (note 1), pp. 226–27.
36. Stamps, *Concept of Mass Audience,* pp. 163–64; Gross, *I*

Looked, p. 226; Ray Poindexter, *Golden Throats and Silver Tongues: The Radio Announcers* (Conway, Ark.: River Road, 1978), pp. 110–11.

37. Alice Goldfarb Marquis, "Words as Weapons: Propaganda in Britain and Germany During the First World War," *Journal of Contemporary History,* July 1978, pp. 467–98; Charles Stuart, ed., *The Reith Diaries* (London: Collins, 1975), p. 91.

38. William A. Robson, "The BBC as an Institution," *Political Quarterly,* No. 4 (1935), p. 484; Stuart, *Reith Diaries,* pp. 213, 55–57.

39. Black, *Biggest Aspidistra* (note 6), p. 55; Snagge and Barsley, *Vintage Years* (note 15), pp. 107–8.

40. Black, *Biggest Aspidistra,* p. 45; Robson, "BBC as Institution," p. 473.

41. Wood, *World in Your Ear* (note 2), p. 99; Snagge and Barsley, *Vintage Years,* p. 90.

42. Wood, *World in Your Ear,* pp. 103–9; White, *News on the Air* (note 24), p. 44; Wynford Vaughan-Thomas, *Trust to Talk* (London: Hutchinson, 1980), p. 134.

43. Robert J. Landry, "Edward R. Murrow," *Scribner's,* December 1938, p. 10.

44. Alexander Kendrick, *Prime Time: The Life of Edward R. Murrow* (Boston: Little, Brown, 1969), pp. 144–47, 141–42.

45. Paley, *Radio as Cultural Force,* pp. 23–24; Hettinger, *New Horizons* pp. 16–17; Schechter and Anthony, *I Live on Air* (note 24), p. 339.

46. Gilbert Seldes, *The Great Audience* (New York: Viking, 1950), p. 127; Gross, *I Looked,* p. 150.

47. "Toscanini on the Air," *Fortune,* January 1938, pp. 62, 67–68; Philip Kerby, "Radio's Music," *North American Review,* June 1938, pp. 303–4.

48. Sanger, *Rebel in Radio* (note 7), pp. 21–26.

49. *Ibid.,* pp. 21–26, 38–42; Dickson Skinner, "Music Goes into Mass Production," *Harper's,* April 1939, p. 489.

50. "A Listener," (note 17) p. 519; Arno Huth, *Radio Today: The Present State of Broadcasting* (New York: Arno, 1971), p. 37; Snagge and Barsley, *Vintage Years,* p. 43.

51. Paul F. Lazarsfeld and Frank N. Stanton, eds., *Radio Research 1941* (New York: Arno, 1979), pp. 110–39.

52. *Ibid.,* pp. 78–81, 92–99; Hettinger, *New Horizons,* pp. 16–17.

53. George A. Willey, "End of an Era: The Daytime Radio Serial,"

Journal of Broadcasting Spring 1961, pp. 99–100; Whitfield Cook, "Be Sure to Listen In," *American Mercury,* March 1940, pp. 314–15.

54. Perry, *Not Just a Sound* (note 4), p. 91; Seldes, *Great Audience,* pp. 113–14; Willey, "End of an Era," pp. 111–12; Merrill Dennison, "Soap Opera," *Harper's,* April 1940, p. 499.

55. Cantril and Allport, *Psychology of Radio* (note 8), pp. 85–87; Hettinger, *New Horizons,* p. 105; Poteet, *Radio!* (note 3), p. 107.

56. Gross, *I Looked,* p. 160; H. V. Kaltenborn, *Fifty Fabulous Years* (New York: G. P. Putnam's Sons, 1950), pp. 20–21.

57. Poindexter, *Golden Throats* (note 36), p. 139; Kendrick, *Prime Time* (note 44) p. 147.

58. *Fortune,* May 1938, pp. 112–13.

59. William L. Shirer, *The Nightmare Years* (New York: Bantam, 1985), pp. 291–303.

60. White, *News on the Air* (note 24), p. 45–46; Poindexter, *Golden Throats,* p. 161; Kendrick, *Prime Time,* pp. 152–60; Shirer, "Berlin Speaking, *Atlantic Monthly,* September 1940, p. 309; *idem, Nightmare Years,* pp. 304–12.

61. Kendrick, *Prime Time,* pp. 162–63. The director of NBC news devoted two chapters of his memoirs to these signal events: Schechter and Anthony, *I Live on Air* (note 24), pp. 178–201.

62. Landry, "Murrow" (note 43), p. 10; Kendrick, *Prime Time,* p. 165; Stuart, *Reith Diaries* (note 37), pp. 218–19.

63. Shirer, "Berlin Speaking," pp. 308–9; *idem, The Nightmare Years,* pp. 329–50; Kendrick, *Prime Time,* pp. 167–68.

64. Poindexter, *Golden Throats,* p. 16; Kaltenborn, *Fifty Fabulous Years,* pp. 210–11; Kendrick, *Prime Time,* pp. 164–65; Landry, "Murrow'," pp. 7–8.

65. H. V. Kaltenborn, "Covering the Crisis," *Current History,* October 1939, p. 35; *idem, Fifty Fabulous Years,* pp. 208, 211.

66. Charnley, *News by Radio* (note 24), p. 51.

2. SOUND AND FURY

1. Kenneth Macgowan, *Behind the Screen: The History and Techniques of the Motion Picture* (New York: Delacorte, 1965), p. 292.

2. Bela Balazs, *Theory of the Film* (New York: Roy, 1953), p. 239.

3. Evan William Cameron, ed., *Sound and the Cinema: The Coming of Sound to American Film* (Pleasantville, N.Y.: Redgrave, 1980), p. xiv.
4. *Ibid.*, pp. 27–28.
5. Matthew J. Bruccoli, ed., *F. Scott Fitzgerald's Screenplay for "Three Comrades" by Erich Maria Remarque* (Carbondale: Southern Illinois University Press, 1978), p. ix.
6. Cameron, *Sound and Cinema*, p. 33.
7. Jesse L. Lasky, *I Blow My Own Horn* (London: Gollancz, 1957), p. 221.
8. Budd Schulberg, *Moving Pictures: Memories of a Hollywood Prince* (New York: Stein & Day, 1981), p. 443.
9. Tom Stempel, *Screenwriter: The Life and Times of Nunnally Johnson* (San Diego: A. S. Barnes, 1980), pp. 11–12.
10. John Schultheiss, "The Eastern Writer in Hollywood," *Cinema Journal,* Fall 1971, pp. 13–14.
11. William C. de Mille, *Hollywood Saga* (New York: Dutton, 1939), pp. 126–27.
12. Richard Meryman, *Mank: The Wit, World and Life of Herman Mankiewicz* (New York: Morrow, 1978), p. 131.
13. Joseph Von Sternberg, *Fun in a Chinese Laundry* (New York: Macmillan, 1965), p. 219.
14. Meryman, *Mank*, pp. 138–39.
15. *Ibid.*, pp. 128–30.
16. Cameron, *Sound and Cinema*, pp. 98–99.
17. Robert McLaughlin, *Broadway and Hollywood: A History of Economic Interaction* (New York: Arno, 1974), pp. 91–97.
18. Frank Capra, *The Name Above the Title* (New York: Macmillan, 1971), pp. 101–3.
19. Garth Jowett, *Film: The Democratic Art* (Boston: Little, Brown, 1976), pp. 195–96.
20. William Cole and George Plimpton, *Writers at Work: The Paris Review Interviews* (Second Series) (New York: Viking, 1963), pp. 252–53.
21. Meryman, *Mank*, pp. 133–34.
22. Samuel Marx, *Mayer and Thalberg: The Make-Believe Saints* (New York: Random House, 1975), pp. x–xi.
23. Edward Dale, *How to Appreciate Motion Pictures* (New York: Macmillan, 1937), p. 79.
24. Garson Kanin, *Hollywood* (New York: Viking, 1974), pp. 1–8.

25. Raymond Chandler, "Farewell My Hollywood," *Antaeus,* Spring–Summer 1976, p. 24.
26. Jay Martin, *Nathanael West: The Art of His Life* (New York: Farrar, Straus & Giroux, 1970), p. 212.
27. Harry M. Geduld, ed., *Authors on Film* (Bloomington: Indiana University Press, 1972), p. 223; Edward Murray, *The Cinematic Imagination: Writers and the Motion Pictures* (New York: Ungar, 1972), pp. 182–83.
28. Schultheiss, "Eastern Writer" (note 10), p. 40.
29. Geduld, *Authors on Film,* p. 224.
30. Bruccoli, *Fitzgerald's Screenplay* (note 5), p. 263.
31. Schultheiss, "Eastern Writer," pp. 40–41.
32. Bruccoli, *Fitzgerald's Screenplay,* pp. 263–66.
33. Murray, *Cinematic Imagination,* pp. 182–88; Marx, *Mayer and Thalberg* (note 22) pp. 222–23.
34. F. Scott Fitzgerald, *The Pat Hobby Stories* (New York: Scribner's, 1962), p. 149.
35. Walter Wells, *Tycoons and Locusts: A Regional Look at Hollywood Fiction of the 1930's* (Carbondale: Southern Illinois University Press, 1973), pp. 119–21.
36. Fitzgerald, *Pat Hobby Stories,* pp. ix–xxxiii.
37. Richard Corliss, *The Hollywood Screenwriters* (New York: Avon, 1972), p. 135.
38. Macgowan, *Behind the Screen* (note 1), p. 383.
39. Jesse L. Lasky, Jr., *Whatever Happened to Hollywood?* (New York: Funk & Wagnalls, 1975), pp. 195–96.
40. Fred Lawrence Guiles, *Hanging On in Paradise* (New York: McGraw-Hill, 1975), p. 35; James Curtis, *Between Flops* (New York: Harcourt Brace Jovanovich, 1982), p. 93.
41. Macgowan, *Behind the Screen,* pp. 334–35.
42. Stempel, *Screenwriter* (note 9), pp. 44–46.
43. Lasky, *Whatever Happened,* pp. 154–55.
44. Margaret Thorp, *America at the Movies,* (New Haven: Yale University Press, 1939), pp. 3–4, 9–10.
45. Macgowan, *Behind the Screen,* pp. 338–39.
46. *Ibid.,* p. 358.
47. Schulberg, *Moving Pictures,* pp. 301–2; Marx, *Mayer and Thalberg* (note 22), pp. 174–75.
48. Schulberg, *Moving Pictures,* pp. 480–81.
49. Salka Viertel, *The Kindness of Strangers* (New York: Holt, Rinehart & Winston, 1969), p. 169.

50. Moss Hart and George S. Kaufman, *Once in a Lifetime* (New York: Farrar & Rinehart, 1930), pp. 141–43.
51. Marx, *Mayer and Thalberg*, pp. 152–53; Leo Rosten, "Hollywood Revisited," *Look*, January 10, 1956, p. 18.
52. Budd Schulberg, "The Hollywood Novel," *Harper's*, October 1959, p. 134.
53. Margaret Brenman-Gibson, *Clifford Odets: American Playwright, the Years from 1906–1940* (New York: Atheneum, 1981), p. 395.
54. Curtis, *Between Flops* (note 40), p. 303.
55. Guiles, *Hanging On* (note 40), p. 30.
56. Bruce F. Kawin, *Faulkner on Film* (New York: Ungar, 1977), pp. 70–72.
57. W. R. Robinson, ed., *Man and the Movies* (Baton Rouge: Louisiana State University, 1967), pp. 269–76.
58. Jerry Wald, "Faulkner and Hollywood," *Films in Review*, March 1959, pp. 129–30.
59. Schultheiss, "Eastern Writer" (note 10), p. 43.
60. Robinson, *Man and Movies*, pp. 299–303.
61. *Ibid.*, pp. 261–64; Murray, *Cinematic Imagination* (note 27), pp. 154, 164–66.
62. Schultheiss, "Eastern Writer," pp. 18–19.
63. Stempel, *Screenwriter* (note 9), pp. 36–40.
64. Cole and Plimpton, *Writers at Work* (note 20), pp. 251–52.
65. Mervyn LeRoy, *It Takes More than Talent* (New York: Knopf, 1953), p. 175.
66. *Ibid.*, p. 192.
67. John Keats, *You Might as Well Live: The Life and Times of Dorothy Parker* (New York: Simon & Schuster, 1970), pp. 178, 182–83.
68. Matthew J. Bruccoli, ed., *Selected Letters of John O'Hara* (New York: Random House, 1978), p. 116.
69. Keats, *You Might as Well Live*, pp. 206–8, 261.
70. Babette Rosmond, *Robert Benchley: His Life and Good Times* (Garden City, N.Y.: Doubleday, 1970), pp. 6–7.
71. Robert Benchley, "A Possible Revolution in Hollywood," *Yale Review*, September 1931, pp. 101–2.
72. Meryman, *Mank* (note 12), pp. 316–17.
73. Donald Ogden Stewart, *By a Stroke of Luck* (New York: Paddington, 1975), pp. 146–49, 139, 182—83, 199–200.

74. In 1950 he was blacklisted and fled to London. He never wrote another Hollywood screenplay under his own name.
75. Keats, *You Might as Well Live,* 192–93.
76. Bruccoli, *O'Hara Letters,* pp. 116–17.
77. Schultheiss, "Eastern Writer" (note 10), pp. 33–34.
78. Morton Eustis, "Additional Dialogue," *Theatre Arts,* June 1937, 451–52.
79. Meryman, *Mank,* pp. 162, 173–74, 288–89, 315.
80. John Schultheiss, "George Jean Nathan and the Dramatist in Hollywood," *Literature/Film Quarterly,* No. 1, 1976, p. 14.
81. George Jean Nathan, "The Play Is Still the Thing," *Forum,* July 1931, pp. 36–37.
82. Schultheiss, "George Jean Nathan," p. 16.
83. Schultheiss, "Eastern Writer," p. 20.
84. Curtis, *Between Flops* (note 40), pp. 70–71, 51–54.
85. McLaughlin, *Broadway and Hollywood* (note 17), pp. 140–41, 115–17, 151–52.
86. Cameron, *Sound and Cinema* (note 3), p. 111.
87. *Ibid.,* pp. 165–69, 147–48, 144.
88. Allardyce Nicoll, *Film and Theater* (London: Harrap, 1936), pp. 162–63, 129.
89. "Great Ideas that Never Got Filmed," *Show,* August 1963, p. 59.
90. J. B. Priestley, *Midnight on the Desert* (New York: Harper, 1937), pp. 165–67.
91. De Mille, *Hollywood Saga* (note 11), pp. 159–60.
92. Robert E. Sherwood, "Hollywood: The Blessed and the Cursed," in Fred J. Ringel, Jr., ed., *America as Americans See It* (New York: Literary Guild, 1932), p. 72.
93. John Mason Brown, *The World of Robert E. Sherwood: Mirror to His Times, 1896–1939* (New York: Harper & Row, 1965), p. 267.
94. Frances Taylor Patterson, "The Author and Hollywood," *North American Review,* Autumn 1937, p. 79.
95. Cameron, *Sound and Cinema* (note 3), pp. 86–87.
96. Schultheiss, "George Jean Nathan," p. 20.
97. Dudley Nichols, "Film Writing," *Theatre Arts,* December 1942, pp. 770–74.
98. Dudley Nichols, "The Writer and the Film," *Theatre Arts,* October 1943, p. 599.

99. Valerie Delacorte, "GBS in Filmland," *Esquire,* December 1964, p. 153.
100. John Howard Lawson, *Film: The Creative Process* (New York: Hill & Wang, 1964), pp. 102–3.
101. William J. Perlman, ed., *The Movies on Trial* (New York: Macmillan, 1936), pp. 20–25.
102. Thorp, *America at the Movies* (note 44), pp. 10–14.
103. Schulberg, *Moving Pictures,* pp. 195–96.
104. Carol Easton, *The Search for Samuel Goldwyn* (New York: Morrow, 1976), pp. 129–31; Arthur Marx, *Goldwyn: A Biography of the Man Behind the Myth* (New York: Norton, 1976), pp. 210–15.
105. S. N. Behrman, *Tribulations and Laughter* (London: Hamish Hamilton, 1972), pp. 1, 131, 145–47.
106. S. N. Behrman, "In Defense of Hollywood," *New Yorker,* January 20, 1934, p. 30.
107. "Writer Defends Producers," *New York Times,* January 14, 1934, Sec. IX, p. 5.
108. Behrman, "In Defense of Hollywood," p. 35.
109. S. N. Behrman, *People in a Diary* (Boston: Little, Brown, 1972), pp. 315–16.
110. Leo Rosten, *Hollywood: The Movie Colony, The Movie Makers* (New York: Harcourt, Brace, 1941), p. 309.
111. Milton Metfessel, "Personal Factors in Motion Picture Writing," *Journal of Abnormal Psychology,* October 1935, p. 335.
112. Charles Davy, ed., *Footnotes to the Film* (New York: Oxford University Press, 1937).
113. Graham Greene, *The Pleasure Dome* (London: Secker & Warburg, 1972).
114. Chandler, "Farewell My Hollywood" (note 25), pp. 23–29.
115. Cameron, *Sound and Cinema* (note 3), pp. 106–7.
116. Raymond Chandler, "Writers in Hollywood," *Atlantic,* November 1945, pp. 52–53.
117. Edmund Wilson, *Classics and Commercials* (New York: Farrar, Straus), 1950, pp. 46–48.
118. Budd Schulberg, "The Hollywood Novel," *Films,* Spring 1940, pp. 77–78.
119. Cameron, *Sound and Cinema,* pp. 24–27.
120. Budd Schulberg, "The Writer and Hollywood," *Harper's,* October 1959, p. 132.
121. Stewart, *By a Stroke* (note 73), pp. 182–83.
122. Rosten, *Hollywood* (note 110), pp. 322–25.

123. Thorp, *America at the Movies* (note 44), p. 138.
124. Rosten, "Hollywood Revisited" (note 51), pp. 25–26.
125. Rosten, *Hollywood*, p. 316.
126. Wells, *Tycoons and Locusts* (note 35), p. 10.
127. Priestley, *Midnight* (note 90), p. 181.
128. Macgowan, *Behind the Screen* (note 1), p. 36.
129. Thorp, *America at the Movies*, pp. 85–86.
130. Behrman, *Tribulations and Laughter* (note 105), pp. 157–58.
131. Viertel, *Kindness of Strangers* (note 49), p. 197.
132. Meryman, *Mank* (note 12), pp. 160–61.
133. "Metro-Goldwyn-Mayer," *Fortune*, December 1932, p. 63.
134. Arthur Hopkins, "Hollywood Takes over the Theater," *Scribner's*, March 1937, pp. 19–20.
135. Robinson, *Man and Movies* (note 57), p. 323.
136. Schulberg, *Moving Pictures*, (note 8), p. 191.
137. Schultheiss, "Eastern Writer" (note 10), pp. 46–47.
138. *Ibid.*, p. 27.
139. Daniel Fuchs, "Writing for the Movies," *Commentary*, February 1962, pp. 114–15.

3. GIVE ME MEN TO MATCH MY MEDIA

1. Theodore Peterson, *Magazines of the Twentieth Century* (Urbana: University of Illinois Press, 1956), pp. 130–65; Frederick Lewis Allen, "The American Magazine Grows Up," *Atlantic*, November 1947, p. 81.
2. "Woman's World," *Tide*, November 1, 1940, p. 14.
3. Roland E. Wolseley, *The Magazine World* (New York: Prentice-Hall, 1951), p. 127; Peterson, *Magazines of Twentieth Century*, p. 55.
4. *The Saturday Evening Post*'s only relationship with Benjamin Franklin was its birth, in 1821, in the same building where Franklin, much earlier, had published the *Pennsylvania Gazette*. Wolseley, *Magazine World*, pp. 14–15.
5. Peterson, *Magazines of Twentieth Century*, pp. 171–75.
6. J. E. Drewry, "American Magazines Today," *Sewanee Review*, July 1928, p. 352.
7. Thomas L. Greer, letter to business schools, October 26, 1921, J. Walter Thompson Archive (hereafter JWT).
8. *J. Walter Thompson's Portfolio Comprising of Facts and Figures*, 1924, unpaged; "How Many Homes Does Magazine Ad-

vertising Reach?" *J. Walter Thompson Newsletter,* January 1925, pp. 17–21; "Sam Meek's Blue Book," unpaged (all JWT).

9. "Fingertip-touch with Every Changing Market Condition," part of a sales exhibit, prepared by the Research Department (JWT).

10. "Rural and Small Town Investigation, Randolph County Indiana," 1924, Research Department (JWT).

11. "Untrammeled Cherington," *Tide,* June 1931; Archibald M. Crossley, "Pioneers in Marketing: Paul Terry Cherington 1876–1943," *Journal of Marketing,* October 1956, pp. 29–31.

12. Drewry, "American Magazines," p. 342.

13. Daniel Pope, *The Making of Modern Advertising* (New York: Basic Books, 1983), p. 112.

14. Gordon B. Hancock, "Commercial Advertisements and Social Pathology," *Social Forces,* June 1926, pp. 813–15.

15. Wilson Follett, "The Tenth Muse," *Virginia Quarterly Review,* July 1929, p. 358.

16. José Ortega y Gasset, *The Revolt of the Masses* (New York: W. W. Norton, 1957; first published 1930), pp. 11–12, 54, 16, 187.

17. W. A. Swanberg, *Luce and His Empire* (New York: Scribner's, 1972), pp. 105–6.

18. Stephen Shadegg, *Clare Booth Luce* (New York: Simon & Schuster, 1970), p. 84; Robert T. Elson, *Time Inc.: The Intimate History of a Publishing Enterprise 1923–1941* (New York: Atheneum, 1968), p. 25; Swanberg, *Luce and His Empire,* p. 29.

19. Swanberg, *Luce and His Empire,* pp. 31–32; Noel F. Busch, *Britton Hadden: a Biography of the Co-founder of Time* (New York: Farrar, Straus, 1949), pp. 25–26; Elson, *Time, Inc.,* p. 27.

20. John Kobler, *Luce: His Time, Life and Fortune* (New York: Doubleday, 1968), p. 33; Busch, *Britton Hadden,* p. 26; Elson, *Time, Inc.,* p. 28; John K. Jessup, ed., *The Ideas of Henry Luce* (New York: Atheneum, 1969), pp. 222–23.

21. Shadegg, *Clare Boothe Luce,* p. 85; Busch, *Britton Hadden,* pp. 23–24.

22. Swanberg, *Luce and His Empire,* p. 37, 39.

23. Busch, *Britton Hadden,* pp. 34–35, 40–42.

24. Elson, *Time, Inc.,* p. 30; Busch, *Britton Hadden,* pp. 113–17; Joseph J. Firebaugh, "The Vocabulary of *Time* Magazine,"

American Speech, October 1940, pp. 240–41.

25. Elson, *Time, Inc.,* pp. 5–6, 87.
26. Swanberg, *Luce and His Empire,* p. 60.
27. Firebaugh, "Vocabulary of *Time,*" pp. 241–42.
28. Kobler, *Luce,* p. 53.
29. John Chamberlain, *A Life with the Printed Word* (Chicago: Regnery Gateway, 1982), p. 18.
30. Charles H. Judd, "Education," in *Recent Social Trends* (New York: McGraw-Hill, 1933), pp. 342–43, 350–51.
31. Judd, "Education," pp. 338–40.
32. Ralph G. Hurlin and Meredeith P. Givens, "Occupations," in *Recent Social Trends* pp. 281–82; *Newsletter,* May 1928, pp. 1–6 (JWT); Pope, *Making of Modern Advertising* (note 13), p. 178.
33. Alfred Harcourt, "Changing Markets" (condensed version of a speech to J. Walter Thompson staff), *Newsletter,* May 1930, pp. 3, 9–10 (JWT).
34. "The New Yorker," *Fortune,* August 1934, p. 97.
35. Busch, *Britton Hadden,* pp. 98–99.
36. "The New Yorker," *Fortune,* p. 85.
37. "The New Yorker," *Time,* August 6, 1934, p. 42.
38. Wolcott Gibbs, "Time . . Fortune . . . Life . . . Luce," in *More in Sorrow* (New York: Holt, 1958), p. 19.
39. Kobler, *Luce* (note 20), pp. 72–73.
40. Kenneth Stewart and John Tebbell, *Makers of Modern Journalism* (New York: Prentice-Hall, 1952), p. 444; John Bainbridge, *Little Wonder* (New York: Reynal & Hitchcock, 1946), p. 24.
41. Dwight Macdonald, "Time, Fortune, Life," *Nation,* May 1, 1937, p. 502.
42. James Thurber, *The Years with Ross* (New York: New American Library, 1962; (first published 1957), p. 34.
43. Shadegg, *Clare Booth Luce* (note 18), p. 95.
44. Thurber, *Years with Ross,* p. 33.
45. *Ibid.,* p. 207.
46. T. S. Matthews, *Name and Address* (New York: Simon & Schuster, 1960), p. 246; Theodore H. White, *In Search of History* (New York: Warner, 1981; first published 1978), pp. 273–74; Bainbridge, *Little Wonder,* p. 89; Thurber, *Years with Ross,* p. 81.
47. Whittaker Chambers, *Witness* (New York: Random House,

1952), p. 494; Elson, *Time Inc.* (note 18), p. 218, White, *In Search*, p. 170.

48. Bainbridge, *Little Wonder,* pp. 6–9.
49. Thurber, *Years with Ross,* 74, 76, 80.
50. Judd, "Education" (note 30), pp. 342–43.
51. "Attention New York Department Stores," *Time* promotion booklet, 1938, Time Inc. Archive (hereafter TIA); Allen, "American Magazine Grows Up" (note 1), p. 81.
52. Advertisement in *Advertising and Selling,* Mar. 12, 1936, p. 1.
53. Swanberg, *Luce and His Empire* (note 17), pp. 106–7.
54. Elson, *Time Inc.,* pp. 123–25.
55. Advertisement for *Time* in *Advertising and Selling Fortnightly,* February 25, 1925, inside front cover (TIA).
56. "One Hundred . . . ," *Time,* January 16, 1928, inside back cover.
57. *Newsletter,* December 31, 1928, Time Inc. promotion department, unpaged (TIA).
58. Busch, Britton Hadden (note 19), pp. 188–89; David Cort, *The Sin of Henry R. Luce* (Secaucus N.J.: Lyle Stuart, 1974), pp. 10–11.
59. Poyntz Tyler, *Advertising in America* (New York: H. W. Wilson, 1959), pp. 49–50.
60. Jessup, *Ideas of Henry Luce* (note 20), p. 33.
61. Busch, Britton Hadden, pp. 105, 194, 207–8.
62. Elson, *Time Inc.,* p. 128.
63. *Time,* February 4, 1929, p. 43.
64. Elson, *Time Inc.,* pp. 128–30; Stewart and Tebbell, *Makers of Modern Journalism* (note 40), p. 437.
65. W. A. Kittredge (an executive at R. H. Donnelley, Chicago printer), letter to Parker Lloyd-Smith, February 14, 1929 (TIA).
66. *Time,* April 1, 1929, p. 56.
67. Henry Luce, letter to seventy-nine business executives, April 20, 1929 (TIA).
68. Kobler, *Luce* (note 20), p. 225; Swanberg, *Luce and His Empire* (note 17), p. 16; Elson, *Time Inc.,* p. 23.
69. "List of possible stories," undated memo, 1929; "Prospectus for a Montly Magazine herein to be known as *Fortune,*" undated 1929 draft (both TIA).
70. Margaret Bourke-White, *Portrait of Myself* (New York: Simon & Schuster, 1963).
71. *Time,* May 27, 1929, p. 73.

72. Henry Luce, memo to Time Inc. directors, May 24, 1929 (TIA).
73. *Time,* July 29, 1929, p. 45.
74. "Straws," undated memo, summer 1929 (TIA).
75. *Time,* August 19, 1929, p. 55.
76. Henry Luce, letter to the *Time* free list, August 12, 1929 (TIA).
77. *Time,* September 30, 1929, p. 44; "Confidential Newsletter to *Fortune* representatives," September 26, 1929 (TIA).
78. Swanberg, *Luce and His Empire,* pp. 81–82.
79. Elson, *Time Inc.* (note 18), p. 141.
80. *Time,* November 4, 1929, p. 48.
81. *Time,* January 27, 1930, p. 53.
82. Eric Hodgins, *Trolley to the Moon* (New York: Simon & Schuster, 1973), pp. 361–62, 365.
83. "Fortune—Editorial Contents," undated memo, 1929 (TIA).
84. Bourke-White, *Portrait of Myself* (note 70), p. 88.
85. "List of possible writers," undated memo, 1929 (TIA).
86. Elson, *Time Inc.,* p. 137.
87. Swanberg, *Luce and His Empire,* p. 83; Elson, *Time Inc.,* p. 137; Robert Fitzgerald, ed., *The Collected Short Prose of James Agee* (Boston: Houghton-Mifflin, 1968), p. 16.
88. Elson, *Time Inc.,* p. 139, Hodgins, *Trolley to the Moon,* p. 455.
89. Elson, *Time Inc.,* p. 148–49; Wolcott Gibbs, "A Very Active Type Man—I," *New Yorker,* May 2, 1942, p. 23.
90. Louis Kronenberger, *No Whippings, No Gold Watches* (Boston: Little, Brown, 1965), pp. 58, 45; Elson, *Time Inc.,* p. 139.
91. "Viscose," *Fortune,* July 1937, p. 108; "And Who Will Weave It?" *Fortune,* July 1937, p. 114; "U.S. Rubber III: Lastex," *Fortune,* February 1934, p. 63.
92. "Plywood," *Fortune,* January 1940, pp. 52, 54.
93. Chamberlain, *Life with Printed Word* (note 29), p. 78.
94. "An Album of Recovery," *Scribner's,* February 1937, pp. 43–51.
95. Robert S. Lynd and Helen Merrell Lynd, *Middletown* (New York: Harcourt, Brace, 1929), p. 256.
96. Roland S. Vaile, *Research Memorandum on Social Aspects of Consumption in the Depression* (New York: Arno, 1972; first published 1937), p. 19.
97. Daniel J. Boorstin, "Welcome to the Consumption Community," *Fortune,* September 1967, p. 118.
98. Clair Wilcox, "Brand Names, Quality and Price," *Annals of*

the American Academy of Political Science, May 1934, pp. 80–81.

99. "The Largest Clinic of Advertising Experience in the World," J. Walter Thompson promotion booklet, 1942; "Now," *People,* March 1937, p. 22; "Making Advertising Pay During the Depression," J. Walter Thompson promotion booklet, 1932 (JWT).

100. R. D. McKenzie, "The Rise of Metropolitan Communities," in *Recent Social Trends* (note 30), pp. 492–93.

101. "Analysis of Retail Grocery Sales by Type of Outlet," J. Walter Thompson Research Report, 1936 (JWT); Donald Curtiss, "Supermarkets and Self-Service Stores," *Advertising and Marketing,* June 1940, map following p. 24; Vaile, *Research Memorandum,* p. 19.

102. George Hooper of Daniel Starch Advertising Service, speech to JWT creative staff, February 7, 1934 (JWT); H. C. Link, "A New Method for Testing Advertising," *Journal of Applied Psychology,* February 1934, p. 15.

103. Darrell Blaine Lucas and Steuart Henderson Britt, *Advertising Psychology and Research* (New York: McGraw-Hill, 1950), pp. 8–10.

104. C. H. Sandage, "The Role of Advertising in Modern Society," *Journalism Quarterly,* Winter 1951, p. 33; Tyler, *Advertising in America* (note 59), pp. 150–51.

105. David M. Potter, "Advertising: The Institution of Abundance," *Yale Review,* Autumn 1953, p. 51.

106. William Allen White, "Ethics in Advertising," *Atlantic,* November 1939, pp. 669, 671; Colston Estey Warne, "Present-Day Advertising, *Annals of the American Academy of Political Science,* May 1934, p. 76; Charles Magee Adams, "Who Bred These Utopias?" *North American Review,* June 1935, p. 15.

107. Peterson, *Magazines of Twentieth Century* (note 1), p. 42.

108. Henry F. Pringle, "Sex, Esq.," *Scribner's,* March 1938, pp. 33, 35; "Time Inc.: 25 Years a Publishing Empire," *Business Week,* March 6, 1948, p. 98.

109. House ad, *Fortune,* February 1934, pp. 4–5.

110. Hodgins, *Trolley to the Moon* (note 82), pp. 457, 459; Chamberlain, *Life with Printed Word,* p. 73.

111. Hodgins, *Trolley to the Moon,* p. 442.

112. Kronenberger, *No Whippings* (note 90), pp. 47–49; Hodgins, *Trolley to the Moon,* p. 348.

113. Dwight MacDonald, "Fortune Magazine," *Nation*, May 8, 1937, p. 528.

114. Ralph Ingersoll, letter to H. G. Weaver, General Motors customer research staff, June 4, 1935 (TIA); Hodgins, *Trolley to the Moon*, p. 407.

115. Elson, *Time Inc.* (note 18), pp. 221–24; "A New Technique in Journalism," *Fortune*, July 1935, pp. 65–66; "Survey Entomology," Lawrence Babcock, memo to Allen Grover, associate managing editor of *Fortune*, July 5, 1935 (TIA).

116. Elson, *Time Inc.*, p. 247.

117. "Internal Report on Questionnaire to *Time* Readers . . . ," February 16, 1937 (TIA).

118. "Attention New York Department Stores" (note 51).

119. Roy E. Larsen, letter accompanying a questionnaire, "If I were Editor of *Time*," April 12, 1937 (TIA).

120. Kobler, *Luce* (note 20), p. 56; Mott, *History of American Magazines* (note 21), pp. 308–9, Firebaugh, "Vocabulary of *Time*" (note 24), pp. 238–40.

121. Winthrop Sargeant, *In Spite of Myself* (Garden City, N.Y.: Doubleday, 1970), pp. 229–30.

122. John Brooks, *The Big Wheel* (New York: Harper, 1949), pp. 59–60; Charles Wertenbaker, *The Death of Kings* (New York: Random House, 1954), pp. 47–48; Ralph Ingersoll, *The Great Ones* (New York: Harcourt, Brace, 1948), pp. 133–34.

123. House ad in *Time*, January 5, 1925 (TIA); "Rum, Romanism . . . ," *Time* advertisement in *Tide*, September 17, 1928 (TIA); Elson, *Time Inc.*, p. 164.

124. Kronenberger, *No Whippings* (note 90), p. 112.

125. Elson, *Time Inc.*, 414–15.

126. *Background for War*, booklet of reprints from *Time*, September 1939 (TIA).

127. Otha C. Spencer, "Twenty Years of Life," unpublished doctoral dissertation, University of Missouri School of Journalism, 1958, p. 63; Swanberg, *Luce and His Empire* (note 17), p. 148; Kobler, *Luce*, p. 6.

128. Busch, *Britton Hadden* (note 19), p. 224.

129. Frank Luther Mott, *History of American Magazines*, vol. v (Cambridge, Mass.: Harvard University Press, 1968), pp. 322–23; *Four Hours a Year* (New York: Time Inc., 1936).

130. Jackson Edwards, "One Every Minute: The Picture Magazines," *Scribner's*, May 1938, p. 18; *Four Hours*, pp. 44–45.

131. Kobler, *Luce* (note 20), p. 100.

132. Peterson, *Magazines of Twentieth Century* (note 1), p. 316; Roy E. Larsen, letter to *Life* charter subscribers, November 18, 1936 (TIA).

133. A. J. Van Zuilen, *The Life Cycle of Magazines* (Uithoorn, Netherlands: Graduate Press, 1977), pp. 25–26; "Life Begins," *Flash*, March 24, 1937, p. 1 (JWT).

134. P. I. Prentice, circulation manager, "Strictly Confidential about *Life*," memo to staff, Spring 1937 (TIA).

135. Kobler, *Luce*, pp. 107–8

136. "The First $10,000,000," and "The Miracle of *Life*," *Life* promotion booklets, 1938 (TIA).

137. Elson, *Time Inc.* (note 18), pp. 447–48; Spencer, "Twenty Years of Life," p. 266.

138. "How *Life* Sells for You," Time Inc. promotion booklet, October 1940 (TIA); Elson, *Time Inc.*, p. 305.

139. Carl Mydans, *More than Meets the Eye* (New York: Harper, 1959), pp. 9–10.

140. William Brinkley, *The Fun House* (New York: Random House, 1961), p. 3.

141. "Special News Release from *Life*," October 11, 1940; *"Life* Merchandising," January 1941 (both TIA).

142. "Breakdown of *Life* Circulation by States, Counties and Cities," May 1937; Elmo Roper, *"Life* Magazine Survey, Part II," January 1938; "A General Presentation of *Life*, September 1939 (all TIA).

143. Elson, *Time inc.*, pp. 342–44; "Continuing Study of Magazine Audiences," October 16, 1940, and *"Life* Circulation," October 28, 1940 (both TIA).

144. Harry Shaw, "Pocket and Pictorial Journalism," *North American Review*, June 1937, pp. 297, 302; J. L. Brown, "Picture Magazines and Morons," *American Mercury*, December 1938, p. 404.

145. Peterson, *Magazines of Twentieth Century* (note 1), p. 25.

146. Allen, "American Magazine Grows Up" (note 1), p. 80.

147. Ortega y Gasset, *Revolt of Masses* (note 16), p. 116.

4. ". . . BUT IS IT ART?"

1. "Museum of Modern Art," *Art News*, November 16, 1929, p. 14.

2. Henry McBride, quoted in "New York Season," *Art Digest*, November 15, 1929, p. 17.

3. Milton W. Brown, *The Story of the Armory Show* (New York:

New York Graphic Society, 1956), pp. 131–32; "New York Season," p. 16.

4. Gerald Reitlinger, *The Economics of Taste: The Rise and Fall of the Picture Market 1760–1960* (New York: Holt, Rinehart & Winston, 1961); Margaret Breuning, quoted in *Art Digest,* November 15, 1929, p. 16.

5. Prices paid for art in the past are extremely difficult to translate into current values. These prices, along with all others in this chapter, have been converted into 1960 dollars according to an "exceedingly tentative" table worked out by Reitlinger, *Economics of Taste,* p. xvi.

6. *Ibid.,* pp. 324, 271; A. Conger Goodyear, *The Museum of Modern Art: The First Ten Years* (New York: A. Conger Goodyear, 1943), pp. 19–20; Henry McBride, "The Palette Knife," *Creative Art,* December 1929, supplement, pp. ix–xi.

7. Alfred H. Barr, "Museum of Modern Art," *Art News,* January 4, 1930, p. 13.

8. Russell Lynes, *Good Old Modern: An Intimate Portrait of the Museum of Modern Art* (New York: Atheneum, 1973), pp. 3–4.

9. "Artists Rise in Aid of Impressionists," *New York Times,* September 7, 1921, scrapbook in Museum of Modern Art Archive (hereafter MOMA); Lynes, *Good Old Modern,* pp. 7–8; Nathaniel Burt, *Palaces for the People: A Social History of the American Art Museum* (Boston: Little, Brown, 1977), pp. 335–36.

10. Dwight MacDonald, "Action on West 53rd Street—II," *New Yorker,* December 19, 1953, p. 35; Goodyear, *Museum of Modern Art,* pp. 13–14; Burt, *Palaces,* p. 336.

11. John Walker, *Self-Portrait with Donors* (Boston: Little, Brown, 1974), pp. 24–25; *The Genesis, Methods and Results of the Parke-Bernet Galleries* (New York: Parke-Bernet, 1944), p. 44.

12. Calvin Tomkins, *Merchants and Masterpieces: The Story of the Metropolitan Museum of Art* (New York: Dutton, 1970), pp. 254–55; Dwight Macdonald, "Action on West 53rd Street—I," *New Yorker,* December 12, 1953, p. 82.

13. Lynes, *Good Old Modern,* pp. 19–20, 47–49.

14. Wyndham Lewis, *America, I Presume* (New York: Howell, Soskin, 1940), p. 4; Emily Genauer, "The Fur-lined Museum," *Harper's,* July 1944, p. 137; Macdonald, "Action," p. 75.

15. "A New Art Museum," undated flyer (MOMA).

16. Walker, *Self-Portrait,* p. 24; Alfred H. Barr, "Boston Is . . . . ," *Harvard Crimson,* October 30, 1926, unpaged clipping (MOMA).

17. "Did Its Beauty Cause Toledo to Ban This?" *Art Digest*, September 1929, p. 5.

18. Brochure dated 1928 in the Archives of the *Societé Anonyme*, Yale University; Aline Saarinen, *The Proud Possessors* (New York: Vintage, 1968), ". 239–43; see also Alice Goldfarb Marquis, *Marcel Duchamp: Eros, c'est la vie* (Albany N.Y.: Whitston, 1980).

19. Lynes, *Good Old Modern*, pp. 6–7, 16–17.

20. William S. Lieberman, in Museum of Modern Art, *Twentieth Century Art from the Nelson Aldrich Rockefeller Collection* (New York: New York Graphic Society, 1969), pp. 11, 13, 20; Peter Collier and David Horowitz, *The Rockefellers: An American Dynasty* (New York: Holt, Rinehart & Winston, 1976), pp. 146–47; Lynes, *Good Old Modern*, pp. 5–6.

21. Reitlinger, *Economics of Taste: Picture Market 1760–1960*, (note 4), p. 52; Cyril Connolly, quoted in MOMA, *Twentieth Century Art from Rockefeller Collection*, p. 9.

22. Avis Berman, "Juliana Force: Pioneers in American Museums," *Museum News*, November/December 1976.

23. Burt, *Palaces* (note 9), pp. 337–38; Museum of Modern Art, *Paintings by Nineteen Living Americans* (New York: MOMA, 1932), p. 9; Lynes, *Good Old Modern*, p. 71.

24. Museum of Modern Art, *Painting in Paris from American Collections* (New York: MOMA, 1930), pp. 11–13.

25. Lynes, *Good Old Modern*, p. 72; Albert Sterner, "Art Inventors," *Art Digest*, October 15, 1929, pp. 15–16.

26. "Beautiful Doings," *Time*, May 22, 1939, p. 86; Lynes, *Good Old Modern*, p. 74.

27. William Ralph Inge, quoted in *Art Notes* (New York: The Macbeth Gallery, November 1930), p. 1609; Kenneth Clark, "Boredom Balmed," *Art Digest*, November 15, 1935, p. 13.

28. Alfred H. Barr, "Modern Art Makes History Too," *College Art Journal*, November 1941, pp. 3–4.

29. Francis V. O'Connor, ed., *The New Deal Arts Projects: An Anthology of Memoirs* (Washington D.C.: Smithsonian, 1972), p. 306.

30. A. Conger Goodyear, "Museum of Modern Art," *Creative Art*, December 1931, pp. 456–57; Museum of Modern Art, *The Public as Artist* (New York: MOMA, July 1932), unpaged; "Museum of Modern Art," *Fortune*, December 1938, p. 131.

31. Alfred H. Barr, *Painting and Sculpture in the Museum of Modern Art 1929–1967* (New York: Museum of Modern Art, 1977), p. xiii; *The Museum of Modern Art, New York: The History*

and the Collection (New York: Harry N. Abrams in assocation with MOMA, 1984), p. 13.

32. Forbes Watson, "The Innocent Bystander," *American Magazine of Art,* January 1935, pp. 62, 48; Barr, *Painting and Sculpture 1929–1967,* p. ix.

33. Iris Barry, in Museum of Modern Art, *Art in Progress* (New York: MOMA), 1944, pp. 172–73; Lynes, *Good Old Modern,* pp. 111–12; "Museum of Modern Art," *Fortune,* p. 134.

34. "Report on the Work and Progress of the Film Library," December 9, 1937, mimeographed pamphlet; News release, October 24, 1936 (both MOMA).

35. *Scrapbook of Travelling Exhibitions,* unpaged (MOMA).

36. Museum of Modern Art, *The Public as Artist* (New York: MOMA, July 1932), unpaged; "Accumulative List of Circulating Exhibitions," pp. 1–4, duplicated report (MOMA).

37. Goodyear, *Museum of Modern Art* (note 6), pp. 42–43; "Museum of Modern Art," *Fortune,* p. 131.

38. Lieberman, in MOMA, *Twentieth Century Art from Rockefeller Collection* (note 20), p. 13.

39. Richard Lemon, "The House that Art Built," *Saturday Evening Post,* January 30, 1965, p. 74.

40. Museum of Modern Art, *Modern Works of Art: Fifth Anniversary Exhibition* (New York: MOMA, 1934), pp. 9, 17–18.

41. *Alfred H. Barr, Jr., A Memorial Tribute* (New York: Museum of Modern Art, 1981), unpaged; Russell Lynes, "Museum Maker," *Vogue,* May 1973, p. 199.

42. Lynes, *Good Old Modern,* p. 300.

43. Winston Wiseman, "Who Designed Rockefeller Center?" *Society for Architectural History Journal,* March 1951, p. 12; *The Last Rivet* (New York: Columbia University Press, 1940), pp. 12–13, 17; Federal Writers' Project, *The WPA Guide to New York* (New York: Pantheon, 1982; first published 1939), p. 341.

44. Wiseman, "Who Designed Rockefeller Center?" pp. 11, 16; G. E. Kidder Smith, *The Architecture of the United States,* Vol. 1, (Garden City, N.Y.: Anchor, 1981), p. 536.

45. "Modern Teapot Tempest," *Pencil Points,* May 1931, p. 61.

46. *Last Rivet,* p. 24; Ferdinand Lundberg, *The Rockefeller Syndrome* (Secaucus N.J.: Lyle Stuart, 1975), p. 192.

47. Lieberman, in MOMA, *Twentieth Century Art from Rockfeller Collection,* p. 20.

48. Hartley Alexander, "Rockefeller City: Thematic Synopsis," undated typescript, probably 1931 (MOMA).

49. Edward Laning, in O'Connor, ed., *New Deal Art Projects* (note

29), p. 82; Alvin Moscow, *The Rockefeller Inheritance* (Garden City N.Y.: Doubleday, 1977), p. 121; Lieberman, in MOMA, *Twentieth Century Art from Rockefeller Collection,* p. 22.

50. Lieberman, in MOMA, *Twentieth Century Art from Rockefeller Collection,* p. 20; Collier and Horowitz, *Rockefellers* (note 20), pp. 205–6n; Lynes, *Good Old Modern,* pp. 121–22; Marchal E. Landgren, in O'Connor, ed., *New Deal Art Projects,* p. 269; Federal Writers' Project, *WPA Guide to New York,* pp. 336–37.

51. Lynes, *Good Old Modern,* pp. 95, 98–99.

52. "Too much 'Red," *Boston Evening Transcript,* May 11, 1933, clipping in a scrapbook, MOMA: Landgren, in O'Connor, ed. *New Deal Art Projects,* p. 269; untitled article from *Modern Monthly,* June 1933, clipping in a scrapbook (MOMA).

53. Mary Randolph, "Rivera's Monopoly, *Art Front,* November 1935, p. 1, and December 1935, pp. 12–13.

54. Gerald M. Monroe, "The 30's: Art, Ideology and the WPA," *Art in America,* November 1975, p. 64; Richard D. McKinzie, *The New Deal for Artists* (Princeton N.J.: Princeton University Press, 1973, p. 31; Thomas Craven, *Modern Art: The Men, the Movements, the Meaning* (New York: Simon & Schuster, 1940, revised; first published 1934), pp. 378–79, 376.

55. Francis V. O'Connor, *Art for the Millions* (Greenwich, Conn.: New York Graphic Society, 1973), p. 305; O'Connor, ed., *New Deal Art Projects,* pp. 12, 43–44.

56. Russell Lynes, *Confessions of a Dilettante* (New York: Harper & Row, 1966), p. 19; McKinzie, *New Deal for Artists,* p. 87.

57. McKinzie, *New Deal for Artists,* pp. 29–32.

58. "Letters from Our Friends," *Art Front,* November 1934, p. 1.

59. McKinzie, *New Deal for Artists,* pp. 53–55; O'Connor, ed., *New Deal Art Projects,* p. 24.

60. O'Connor, *Art for the Millions,* p. 60.

61. Karal Ann Marling, *Wall-to-Wall America: A Cultural History of Post-Office Murals in the Great Depression* (Minneapolis: University of Minnesota Press, 1982), pp. 62–71.

62. O'Connor, *Art for the Millions,* pp. 208–9, 221–23; McKinzie, *New Deal for Artists,* pp. 144–145.

63. T. R. Adam, *The Museum and Popular Culture* (New York: American Association for Popular Education, 1939), pp. 49–50; Frederick P. Keppel, "The Arts in Social Life," in *Recent Social Trends* (New York: McGraw-Hill, 1933), pp. 968–70, 967.

64. Keppel, "Arts in Social Life," pp. 994, 996.

65. Audrey McMahon, in O'Connor, ed., *New Deal Art Projects,* pp. 305–6; Keppel, "Arts in Social Life," p. 1004.
66. Holger Cahill and Alfred H. Barr, Jr., *Art in America* (New York: Reynal & Hitchcock, 1934); News release, February 1, 1935 (MOMA).
67. Cahill and Barr, *Art in America,* p. 101.
68. News release, July 2, 1935; News release No. 27, undated, 1935; News release, October 14, 1935 (all MOMA).
69. New releases, March 20, 1936 and September 21, 1936 (both MOMA); Lynes, *Good Old Modern* (note 8), pp. 132–36.
70. "Museum of Modern Art," *Fortune* (note 30), p. 128.
71. Museum of Modern Art, *Cubism and Abstract Art* (New York: MOMA, 1936), pp. 11, 19.
72. *Memorial Tribute* (note 41).
73. News release No. 6a, undated, 1936 (MOMA); "Solid Abstraction, *Time,* March 9, 1936, pp. 50–51; *1936–37, The Museum of Modern Art Circulating Exhibitions,* unpaged (MOMA).
74. Lynes, "Museum Maker" (note 41) pp. 196, 199; Calvin Tomkins, "The Art World: Alfred H. Barr," *New Yorker,* November 16, 1981, p. 184.
75. "Surrealist Revolution Counter-clockwise," *Art Front,* February 1935, p. 1; "Museum of Modern Art" (note 30), p. 131; "Giddy Museum Exhibit," *Newsweek,* December 19, 1936, p. 26; *Annual Report to Members,* 1938, unpaged (MOMA).
76. *Scrapbook of Travelling Exhibitions* (note 35); Lynes, "Museum Maker," p. 196.
77. Marchal E. Landgren, Rosalind Bengelsdorf Browne, and Joseph Solman in O'Connor, ed. *New Deal Art Projects* (note 29), pp. 308, 227–29, 237, 124–25.
78. *Ibid.,* pp. 125–26, 230.
79. Marling, *Wall-to-Wall America* (note 61), pp. 23–24; McKinzie, *New Deal for Artists* (note 54), pp. 111–12.
80. McKinzie, *New Deal for Artists,* p. 66.
81. Genauer, "Fur-lined Museum" (note 14), pp. 132–33.
82. Keppel, "Arts in Social Life" (note 63), pp. 978–79, 969, 981–83; Museum of Modern Art, *Useful Objects Under $10,* catalogue of an exhibition, December 7, 1939, to January 7, 1940, unpaged.
83. Artemas Packard, *A Report on the Development of the Museum of Modern Art,* mimeographed book, 1936, p. 129 (MOMA).
84. Alfred H. Barr, "Art in the Third Reich—Preview, 1933," *Magazine of Art,* October 1945, pp. 213–18.
85. Cynthia Jaffee McCabe, *The Golden Door: Artist-Immigrants*

of America, 1876–1976 (Washington D.C.: Smithsonian Institution, 1976), pp. 31, 21.

86. *Ibid.,* pp. 31–34, 275, 260.
87. *Ibid.,* pp. 33–34; Philip Johnson in *Memorial Tribute* (note 41).
88. *Architecture A-2,* scrapbook of traveling exhibitions (MOMA).
89. Macdonald, "Action II" (note 10), p. 42; Museum of Modern Art, *Art in Our Time* (New York: MOMA, 1939), pp. 8–9, 6.
90. Lynes, *Good Old Modern* (note 8), pp. 211–12.
91. Paul J. Sachs, "Why Is a Museum of Art?" *Architectural Forum,* September 1939, p. 198.
92. Barr, *Painting and Sculpture 1929–1967* (note 8), p. xiii; Goodyear, *Museum of Modern Art* (note 6), p. 88; MacDonald, "Action II," p. 60; *Annual Report,* July 1, 1940 to June 30, 1941, unpaged (MOMA).
93. Museum of Modern Art, *Art in Progress* (New York: MOMA, 1944), p. 9.
94. Genesis of Parke-Bernet Galleries (note 11), p. 19; Reitlinger, *Economics of Taste* (note 4), pp. 67–68, 168–69.

5. THE WORLD OF TOMORROW

1. "Roosevelt Voices," *New York Times,* May 1, 1939, p. 4.
2, "Report of the Committee on Theme of the Fair to the Board of Design," July 16, 1936, New York World's Fair Archive, New York Public Library (hereafter NYPL).
3. John Bainbridge, and St. Clair McKelway, "That Was the New York World's Fair," *The New Yorker,* April 19, 1941, p. 35.
4. "Luncheon Given," *New York Times,* May 1, 1939, p. 6.
5. "$156,000,000 Show," *Newsweek,* May 1, 1939, p. 46.
6. "Einstein in New Triumph," *New York Times,* May 1, 1939, p. 6.
7. Bainbridge and McKelway, "That Was World's Fair," p. 46.
8. Elmer Davis, "Barnum in Modern Dress," *Harper's,* October 1938, p. 462.
9. Bainbridge and McKelway, "That Was World's Fair," p. 36.
10. *Official Guidebook,* New York World's Fair, 1939, pp. 224–25.
11. Orrin E. Dunlap, Jr., "Many Feminine Touches," *New York Times,* May 1, 1939, pp. 8, 3.
12. "Vastness of Fair," *New York Times,* May 1, 1939, pp. 1–2.
13. "Mayor Dedicates," *New York Times,* May 1, 1939, p. 4.
14. "Vastness of Fair," pp. 1–2.

15. "For Work Relief," *New York Times*, April 30, 1939, Sec. 4, p. 1.
16. Richard Lowitt and Maureen Beasley, eds., *One Third of a Nation* (Urbana: Illinois University Press, 1981), pp. 44–45.
17. "The Fair—The City," special section of *The New York Times*, April 30, 1939, pp. 1–2; August Heckscher, *When LaGuardia Was Mayor* New York: Norton, 1978), p. 245; *New York World's Fair Official Guidebook* (New York: Exposition Press, 1939).
18. Draft of press release on theme exhibit, no date (NYPL).
19. "Ball and Spike," *Time*, May 9, 1938, p. 35.
20. Robert D. Kohn, memo to Frank Monaghan, February 9, 1939 (NYPL).
21. *New York World's Fair Licensed Merchandise* (New York: New York World's Fair Merchandising Dept., 1939), p. 9 (NYPL).
22. "The New York Fair," *Architectural Forum*, June 1939, p. 399.
23. Draft of press release on theme exhibit (NYPL).
24. Undated file of assorted clippings in NYPL archive.
25. *Food in the World of Tomorrow;* Clifford Maitland Sage, "My Daze at the Fair," mimeographed report for the American Automobile Assn., September 8, 1939, p. 16 (NYPL).
26. Lowitt and Beasley, *One Third of a Nation*, pp. 68–69.
27. Maurice Leven, Harold G. Moulton, and Clark Warburton, *America's Capacity to Consume* (New York: Review of Reviews, for Brookings Institution, 1934), pp. 87, 122–23.
28. Helen A. Harrison, guest curator, *Dawn of a New Day* (New York: NYU Press, 1980), p. 8; *Transportation in the World of Tomorrow*, (NYPL).
29. John B. Rae, *The Road and the Car in American Life* (Cambridge, Mass.: MIT Press, 1971), pp. 65, 72–74.
30. "The Great American Roadside," *Fortune*, September 1934, pp. 53–54; Rae, *Road and Car*, pp. 45–48.
31. Sage, "Daze at Fair," p. 5.
32. "Design Decade," *Architectural Forum*, October 1940, p. 317.
33. Donald J. Bush, *The Streamlined Decade* (New York: Braziller, 1975), p. 20; Raymond Loewy, *Industrial Design* (Woodstock, N.Y.: Overlook Press, 1979), p. 10.
34. Loewy, *Industrial Design*, pp. 98–101, 108; *Minutes of the Executive Committee, 1937*, New York World's Fair, p. 175 (NYPL).

35. Kenneth Reid, "Walter Dorwin Teague, Master of Design," *Pencil Points,* September 1937, p. 541.

36. "Walter D. Teague," *New York Times,* December 6, 1960, p. 41; Reid, "Teague," pp. 539–70; "Standardized Service Stations," *Architectural Record,* September 1937, pp. 69–72.

37. Walter Dorwin Teague, *Design This Day: The Technique of Order in the Machine Age* (New York: Harcourt, Brace, 1940), pp. 1–2, 248–49, 256–57, 234–35.

38. News release, World's Fair Board of Design (NYPL).

39. Robert D. Kohn, memo on theme, June 22, 1936 (NYPL).

40. News release, December 9, 1936 (NYPL).

41. Harland Manchester, "Grover Aloysius Whalen," *Scribner's,* June 1938, p. 8.

42. Federal Writers' Project, *New York Panorama* (New York: Random House, 1938), pp. 456–66.

43. Geoffrey T. Hellman, "Design for a Living—I," *The New Yorker,* Feburary 8, 1941, p. 24.

44. Geoffrey T. Hellman, "Design for Living—III," *The New Yorker,* February 22, 1941, p. 21.

45. Bush, *Streamlined Decade* (note 33), pp. 161–62; Robert Coombs, "Norman Bel Geddes: Highways and Horizons," *Perspecta,* 1971, pp. 16–17, 20–23.

46. Coombs, "Bel Geddes," pp. 18–19, 22–23, 25–26.

47. Ralph M. Pearson, "The Artist's Point of View: General Motors Commissions an Artist," *Forum,* October 1939, p. 191.

48. Geoffrey T. Hellman, "For City and for Coty—II," *The New Yorker,* July 21, 1951, p. 39.

49. Rexford G. Tugwell, "Parts of New Civilization," *Saturday Review of Literature,* April 13, 1949, pp. 3–4.

50. Harrison, *Dawn of a New Day* (note 28), p. 14.

51. Jeffrey L. Meikle, *Twentieth Century Limited: Industrial Design in America, 1925–1939* (Philadelphia: Temple University Press 1979), p. 192.

52. Gilbert Seldes, "Artist in a Factory," *The New Yorker,* August 29, 1931, pp. 22–24; Henry Dreyfuss, *Designing for People* (self-published, 1936), p. 135.

53. "Streamlined Steamship Highlights March of Progress in Industrial Design," *Newsweek,* December 19, 1938, p. 23.

54. News release No. 438 (NYPL).

55. Grover Whalen, as told to Elsie-Jean, *A Trip to the World's Fair with Bobby and Betty* (New York: Dodge, 1938).

56. "A Digest of Information About the Fair," mimeographed

press kit, pp. 1–3 (NYPL); Henry Dreyfuss, "Preliminary Appearance Specifications for Theme Exhibit" (NYPL); *New York Herald-Tribune*, July 27, 1938.

57. Dreyfuss, "Preliminary Appearance Specification;" Harrison, *Dawn of a New Day* (note 28), p. 62; News Release No. 438.

58. Rae, *Road and Car* (note 29), p. 48.

59. Hellman, "Design I" (note 43), p. 24; "Budget for Theme Exhibit," Drawer 241 (NYPL).

60. Coombs, "Bel Geddes" (note 45), pp. 20–21; Meikle, *Twentieth Century Limited,* pp. 208–9; Hellman, "Design III" (note 44), p. 30.

61. New York World's Fair Archive, Drawer 241 (NYPL); Henry Dreyfuss, letter to Richard Engelken (lighting consultant to the fair), June 17, 1938 (NYPL); *New York Herald Tribune,* July 27, 1938, unpaged clipping in NYPL; News release No. 438 (NYPL).

62. Teague, *Design This Day* (note 37), p. 246; Daniel J. Boorstin, *The Image* (New York: Atheneum, 1961), p. 54.

63. John Black, *Songs of the World's Fair* (Boston: Bruce Humphries, 1939), p. 15.

64. Lawrence E. Davies, "Machine that Talks and Sings Has Tryout . . . ," *New York Times,* January 6, 1939, pp. 1, 10; Harrison, *Dawn of a New Day* (note 28), pp. 108–9.

65. "World's Fair," *Life,* March 13, 1939, pp. 42–43.

66. Frank Monaghan, memo to Whalen, August 3, 1937 (NYPL).

67. "Wings on Statue," *New York Times,* May 26, 1939, p. 18.

68. Barbara Rose, *American Art Since 1900* (New York: Praeger, 1967), pp. 125–28; Harrison, *Dawn of a New Day* (note 28), p. 67.

69. Edward Alden Jewell, "Tommorrow, Inc.," *Parnassus,* October 1937, p. 4.

70. *American Art Today* (New York; National Art Society, 1939) (show catalogue), pp. 6–10, 15–16, 35–37, 19–20; Russell Lynes, *Good Old Modern* (New York: Atheneum, 1973), p. 196; James Johnson Sweeney, "Thoughts Before the World's Fair," *Parnassus,* March 1939, p. 7.

71. Francis Tying, *Making a World's Fair* (New York: Vantage, 1958), pp. 30–31; "Lights Turn ON," *New York Times,* Apr. 11, 1939, p. 1.

72. Gardner Harding, "World's Fair, New York," *Harper's,* July 1939, p. 199; Harrison, *Dawn of a New Day* (note 28), p. 47.

73. Manchester, "Whalen" p. 10; Davis, "Barnum in Modern Dress" (note 8), p. 454.
74. Geoffrey T. Hellman, "For City and for Coty—I," *The New Yorker,* July 14, 1951, pp. 33–34; Davis, "Barnum in Modern Dress," pp. 456–57; Manchester, "Whalen," p. 61.
75. Davis, "Barnum in Modern Dress," p. 458.
76. Manchester, "Whalen," pp. 8–9, 60; Davis, "Barnum in Modern Dress," pp. 458, 462–63.
77. Hellman, "For City and for Coty—II" (note 48), p. 28.
78. Undated notes for press releases on theme and press release on theme, October 9, 1936 (NYPL).
79. *New York World's Fair Bulletin,* Debenture Edition, December 1936, pp. 7, 16 (NYPL).
80. *New York World's Fair Bulletin,* August 1936, pp. 7, 13, (NYPL); Victor H. Bernstein, *New York Times,* August 16, 1936, Sec. IV, p. 7; Heckscher, *When LaGuardia Was Mayor* (note 17), p. 134; Federal Writers Project, pp. 497–98.
81. Harold G. Moulton, *Income and Economic Progress* (Washington, D.C.: The Brookings Institution, 1935), pp. 31–47.
82. The account of Richard Whitney's bankruptcy and trial is drawn from the files of the *New York Times.* Pertinent articles are: "Whitney & Co. Fails," March 9, 1938, pp. 1, 5; "Whitney Assumes Blame," March 10, 1938, pp. 1, 2; "Exchange Funds," and "Applejack Stock," March 12, 1938, p. 18; "Whitney's Brother," March 26, 1938, pp. 1, 3; "Text of Dewey's Report," April 10, 1938, p. 37.
83. *New York World's Fair Bulletin,* Debenture Edition, December 1936, p. 1; Robert Bendiner, *Just Around the Corner,* New York: Harper & Row, 1967, pp. 56–57.
84. *World's Fair Bulletin,* Nov. 1936, p. 11 (NYPL); *World's Fair News,* February 1937, p. 3 (NYPL); News Release, December 1, 1938 (NYPL).
85. "33,000,000 in the Nation," *New York Times,* January 16, 1939, p. 2; "Crowds for the Fair," *New York Times,* January 17, 1939, p. 20.
86. *Information Manual,* unpaged, 1939 (NYPL); Bainbridge and McKelway, pp. 35, 38–39; "In Mr. Whalen's Image," *Time,* May 1, 1939, pp. 72–74.
87. Hellman, "For City and for Coty—II," p. 38; Tyng, pp. 36–37, 40–42.
88. News release, December 9, 1936 (NYPL).
89. *New York World's Fair, 1939,* 1936 (NYPL).

90. Dale Carnegie, *How to Win Friends and Influence People*, New York: Pocket Books, 1975 (102nd printing); Tyng, 84–85.

91. "Freedom Pavilion," *New York Times*, January 13, 1939, pp. 1, 16; "Pre-Nazi Exhibit," *New York Times*, Feburary 2, 1939, p. 5.

92. Sage, "Daze at Fair," p. 32.

93. Frank Monaghan, *Going to the Fair* (New York: Sun Dial Press, 1939), p. 31; brochure in publicity archive for the New York World's Fair, Performing Arts Branch (NYPL).

94. William Bernbach and Herman Jaffe, *Book of Nations* (New York: Winkler and Kelmans, 1939), pp. 47–48; Russell B. Porter, *New York Times*, June 1, 1939, p. 1; Russell Maloney and Eugene Kinkead, "Trylon, Trylon Again," *New Yorker*, May 11, 1940, p. 41.

95. *New York World's Fair 1939, Inc., Minutes of Executive Committee*, June 21, 1937, pp. 260–65.

96. *Building the World of Tomorrow* (NYPL).

97. Tyng, *Making a World's Fair*, p. 6.

98. Frank Monaghan, "The World of Yesterday and the World of Tomorrow," October 12, 1938, speech before the Robert E. Lee Memorial Foundation, Stratford Hall, Virginia (NYPL).

99. Monaghan, *Going to the Fair*, p. 40.

100. "Overseas Phone Calls of Capital," *New York Times*, April 30. 1939, Sec. 4, p. 6.

101. David Sarnoff, Anne O'Hare McCormick, *New York Times*, March 5, 1939, Sec 8, pp. 15, 16.

102. Bendiner, p. 221.

103. Brochure in publicity archive at Performing Arts Branch, NYPL.

104. Heckscher, 248.

105. "In Mr. Whalen's Image," *Time*, May 1, 1939, p. 78.

106. Manchester, p. 8; Davis, p. 460; "In Mr. Whalen's Image," *Time*, p. 78; Sidney M. Shalett, "Epitaph for the World's Fair," *Harper's*, December 1940, pp. 26–27.

107. Bainbridge and McKelway, p. 41.

108. Shalett, pp. 22, 27–28.

109. Bainbridge and McKelway, p. 45; Shalett, p. 23.

INDEX